Belle of
the Brawl

Belle of the Brawl

Letters Home from a B-17 Bombardier

Gary A. Best

I judge when the tale is all in, the bombardier, as a class, in working under the intense pressure that he does, will be found the glamour man of the air war. I have made analysis [*sic*] of hundreds of targets of every description and can testify without reservation to the genius of the boy in the glass cage in the nose.

– Gill Robb Wilson

Cover illustrations: front, top: a group of B-17s in formation. (Wikimedia Commons); bottom: Fred's letters. (Gary Hammerstrom). Back: 'At 22,000 feet you will leave dense and persistent contrails.' (Wilbur Richardson)

First published in the US by Inkwater Press, 2010

First published in the UK 2011
by Spellmount, an imprint of The History Press
The Mill, Brimscombe Port
Stroud, Gloucestershire, GL5 2QG
www.thehistorypress.co.uk

© Gary A. Best, 2010, 2011

British Library Cataloguing in Publication Data.
A catalogue record for this book is available from the British Library.

ISBN 978 0 7524 6468 8

Typesetting and origination by The History Press
Printed in Great Britain
Manufacturing managed by Jellyfish Print Solutions Ltd

Contents

Foreword

Gary Best thoughtfully weaves together the Second World War letters of his close friend, Fred Lull, who died many years ago. Best has also added pertinent historical war information to create this wonderful book, *Belle of the Brawl*. This combination illustrates behind-the-scenes glimpses of a young man's life training for the war and his aerial combat in the skies over Europe.

When Gary Best first read the personal letters Lull sent to his mother, Louise, they answered many lingering questions Best had about his friend's experiences of flying as a bombardier in a Boeing B-17 'Flying Fortress' and the realities of his war story. The long-hidden correspondence helped Best capture in words the human side of war and the mixed emotions his close friend experienced in battle, coupled with the anxiety of a mother waiting for his safe return.

I flew combat missions in Vietnam for a year, and I also wrote many, many letters to my wife and two young sons. Hoping to keep my wife from worrying about my welfare, I told her about the great group of guys I served with. I told her of the many air force and navy aviators who were shot down and we rescued. But if you read between the lines, you realised it was a daily struggle to stay alive and be ready for the next combat sortie, just as it was for Fred Lull.

This book is an absolutely first-rate read about one of the Second World War veterans NBC anchor Tom Brokaw called 'the greatest generation'. These veterans are dying at the rate of 1,000 per day and, fortunately for us, Gary Best and PBS producer Ken Burns' documentary, *The War*, permanently record the courage and sacrifice these young men exhibited in the cause of freedom.

George J. Marrett
Author of *Cheating Death: Combat Air Rescues in Vietnam and Laos*

Prologue

Fred was 36 years old when we first met. I was 19. During a friendship that lasted until his death in 1990, he, like many of those that Tom Brokaw has proclaimed as 'the Greatest Generation', rarely spoke of his part in the Second World War.[1] For the most part, I was unaware of his role in the war except for the four framed pictures that hung over his desk at home – a picture of a B-17, one of his bomber crew, one of him just after he returned from his last mission and one that announced his admission to the 'Lucky Bastard' club.

> These men do not proclaim the glory of war; but since it had to be, they are proud of their service. There is an ever-present respect for those who were lost and sincere gratefulness among those who survived.[2]

We met at a summer resident camp for children with physical disabilities; he was the camp director and I was one of his counsellors. When I completed college with a teaching credential in special education, I became a teacher in a special school for children with physical disabilities where Fred was the principal. He was influential in encouraging me to marry a young woman who was an occupational therapist at the same school, which I did, and he later supported my decision to leave teaching to go to graduate school.

As our relationship grew and matured and we spent considerable time together socialising in his home or ours, he never voluntarily spoke about his earlier life as a Second World War combat veteran, a bombardier in a B-17. Only once in our many years as friends did the war and his role in it ever come up, and then only when he and I were alone and each had had several martinis and were very relaxed.

It was almost as though the pictures on the wall above his desk played a dual role – a reminder of what had been and a warning sign of 'No Admittance' or, at least, 'Private Property, Trespassers Beware!' But, armed with a couple of martinis on my part and disarmed by a couple on his, I asked Fred about one of the pictures – the one of him at the side of a plane turning to look at something in the distance.

'That was taken after I had returned from my last mission. I flew it with another crew, because I hadn't completed my 30 with my own crew. I had been laid up with infected sinuses, so my crew flew its last one without me. Although they had finished their 30 missions and were eligible to return home, they wouldn't go without me. "We came over together, and we'll go home together!"'

Encouraged by this revelation, I asked what had been his worst or scariest mission. He looked at me and, without much hesitation, said, 'The last one. We flew a mission into France to drop supplies to the French Resistance. We carried no bombs because of the weight. We went in without fighter escort, dropped the supplies, turned and headed back to England. We were sitting ducks.'

There ended the conversation; a change of subject, another martini and never again did Fred talk about the war or his part in it. Somehow I knew that I shouldn't ask about or pursue further this part of his life. In later years, a small break in this abstinence would occur when he would occasionally and casually announce that he had returned from a reunion of his unit and would share photos from the reunion of surviving crewmembers and their wives.

Apparently some things warriors can only talk about to those who experienced them, also.[3]

When Fred died, a mutual friend – a former camp counsellor and teacher colleague – acquired the letters, scrapbooks and other personal memorabilia that form the core for *Belle of the Brawl*. This mutual friend's widow later gave them to me, and the entire collection lay hidden from view in a garage storage box for sixteen years.

Upon retirement, I discovered that I now had the time to get involved in those tasks around the house that are often put off until later – which translates into 'getting to them some time', some time way in the future. So, after sitting around for several weeks enjoying the freedom from my once work-a-day world, I attacked one of those long-forgotten tasks and settled into 'cleaning the garage'. It was somewhere in the middle of this six-week endurance challenge that I rediscovered 'Fred's box'. Opening the lid, I found the treasure that had been hidden for so many years. The rest of the day was shot.

There, jumbled together in Fred's box, were photo albums, scrapbooks, passports and the mother lode of the collection, Fred's leather writing case. Inside the case were 150 letters that Fred had written to his mother, from the time he was sent to the Army Air Forces Classification Center in the winter of 1943 until the end of the war in 1945. Also in the writing case were several telegrams, V-mail letters, his mission log, military orders, newspaper clippings and two copies of *Stars and Stripes* – a jigsaw puzzle of a personal era forever embedded in an historical context known only to Fred.

After spending several hours reading and rereading the letters, looking at the albums and scrapbooks and recalling memories of Fred and what he had meant to me throughout my adult life, I was in a dilemma about what to do next. So, I made the somewhat easy decision to do nothing. I repacked the box, carefully and to some degree painfully, and put it back to rest in the garage – but in a place where it was easily accessible. I had to think about what I was going to do with these highly personal pieces of history.

During the next couple of weeks, *Belle of the Brawl* began to take some ethereal shape, some form in my mind that could tell a story. What evolved was not a testament about the causes of war, its justification or its end results. It was not to become a treatise of the combat record of the Eighth Air Force, its bomb groups and bomb squadrons, or, for that matter, a memoir of the exploits of Fred and his fellow crewmembers. Accounts such as these had already been written, *The Man Who Flew the Memphis Belle*, a familiar example.[4]

So, what is *Belle of the Brawl*? It is part adventure story and part a coming-of-age saga. It is a story of a common man among common men who became engaged in uncommon acts of wartime heroics and struggles of survival. It is the unveiling of a relationship between a mother and her 'little boy' who becomes a combat veteran. It is part war story, part history lesson, part travelogue and cultural exploration. It is a recording of an expansion of the mind, the growth of the man, the development of the soul and the baptism by full immersion into the conflict of life.

Belle of the Brawl is a description of the warp and woof of the fabric of human existence, at times straightforward and clear-cut and at others veiled in contradictions, contrasts, and confusion. It tells of a mix of life experiences, both shared and in some cases only guessed at by those far and near, more stressful than many, less so than others.

It is always, always a tale of forging, pushing, blending, pulling, manipulating, grinding, kicking, screaming, hollering and complaining through change in general and in a single character specifically. It is the story of an eager teenager, opinionated and cocooned in a protected middle-class existence, who becomes world-weary, war-weary and old at 23. It is a story of lifestyle, loneliness, camaraderie and, sometimes, boredom.

Fred's letters reveal precious little about the war or his part in it. Throughout the letters there are expressions of concern about his mother's health, how she is getting along managing her life, their mutual finances and rationing. He asks questions regarding family members, mutual friends and his high school buddies, who were also serving in the war.

There is always an undercurrent in the letters of 'don't worry Mom'. Fred's letters seem to steer far away from any mention of the war that would cause Louise (Mom) to worry about her son. Kate Smith, a song stylist of the era with a zaftig presence that radiated warmth and engendered a Lady Liberty-like trust and patriotism, especially when she sang, *God Bless America*, introduced a song during the war that fits like a jigsaw puzzle piece into the intentions of Fred's letters: *Don't Worry Mom (A Morale Song for Mother)*:

Don't worry mom, there's little time to write. Don't worry mom, everything's all right.[5]

The letters provide a classic example of life's juxtaposition – what Fred writes to his mother lacks the bite of reality he experiences in combat as a bombardier. The exception is probably the one letter that caused her to worry more than any other – the one dated 20 February 1944. It explained, in part, what she should consider if she were ever to receive a telegram that told her that Fred's plane had been shot down. Indeed, 'Don't worry Mom'.

Taken together, the letters form a personal and porous picket fence that separates two worlds – Mom and Fred's – and that of everyone and everything else. Although there are many spaces in the picket fence that allow for glimpses into their relationship, a gateway through which entrance is invited and one can enter and pass through is not provided.

Fred's scrapbook, like many other such collections, is an autobiographical record enhanced with pictures, clippings of newspaper stories, and programmes and souvenirs of a life led: a dance card filled with persons, places and events at once personal and brimming with meaningful relationships. But across and in time, these relationships have become lost, are somehow out of context and reveal piecemeal insights into what was once important and real.

Like any family album of photos of an era, a scrapbook provides bits of evidence of a life that may provoke a sense of curiosity and a glance into the past. But links to the present are made only with effort, and to some the journey may not be worth it.

Is it possible to gain any insight into a person's character through faded pictures in a high school newspaper clipping? What do the pictures of Fred as an actor in a school play or participating in an athletic event or political debate reveal? Are these windows into the Dickensian precursors of what will be or are these framed events simply strung together in a time-related sequence?

Does one generation care about how previous ones looked, what clothes they wore, how they thought or acted or what they experienced one or more lifetimes ago? The success of *The Greatest Generation* would seem to suggest that this intergenerational connection is, indeed, important, valuable and sought after.

A scrapbook or family photo album easily falls into the genre, perhaps the chasm, of a history book – or worse yet into the league of a history textbook, especially when the viewer is given a spot quiz of its contents: 'Do you know who that is? Do you remember when that happened?'

How do you take bits and pieces from the past and discover if they somehow fit somewhere? Do autobiographical shards ever come together to form a whole? And even if they do, is there any meaning to the cracks and crazing of this life-like vessel? Are the reconstructed pictures of any particular importance? To whom? Why?

If there is a connectedness by which individuals from the past are linked with those of the present, then family albums, scrapbooks, home movies, box camera snapshots, 35mm slides, the ubiquitous matchbook covers and postcards of places visited and, finally, the letters stored away are of fundamental importance to the weave of a personal and generational fabric. So, here is *Belle of the Brawl*, a collection of memories, facts and to some extent conjecture. Fred was not a hero; he was one of a million heroes. He did what others did – he put his life on the line for what his country had committed itself to and communicated virtually none of this to his mother.

Very few of Fred's letters are reproduced in their entirety. Requests to be remembered to one or more relatives and friends are most often omitted in these pages, although they appear in almost every letter sent home. Fred's answers to Louise's questions that have no context within any other letter also have been omitted.

Military orders and correspondence often seem to have a code all their own, with abbreviations of words that appear to be mistakes or typewritten errors. These have been left intact and are reproduced here as they appeared in the original documents.

The letters reveal Fred's likes and dislikes for any number of things. He had no taste for Texas, or most Texans, and didn't much like train rides, although he took pride in what becomes a personal travelogue and the sense of discovery of the occasional tourist. Fred had somewhat of a passion for his Parker '51' fountain pen and seemed almost lost without his radio. His letters provide a virtual catalogue of radio broadcasts and films (shows) from the past with names of performers few today will recognise: the Great Gildersleeve, Gabriel Heatter, Arleen Whelan and many others.

Throughout *Belle of the Brawl*, there are inserts from a variety of sources that put into context what Fred writes to Louise about – official military orders, accounts of historical events, a few statistics and explanations about the planes of war and the men who flew them, and personal remembrances of others about the war, including interviews with former B-17 crewmembers. Wartime censorship prohibited Fred and others from writing about the details of base locations, combat missions and other sensitive war-related information. It was only later that this became known to others.

Even without the presence of correspondence censorship, it seems very unlikely that Fred would have sent home details about what was happening to him and around him. He simply would not have wanted his mother to worry. What he witnessed and experienced through the Plexiglas nose of a B-17 was not pretty. You do not write home to your mom and tell her about a friend's airplane, flying in close formation next to yours, disintegrate, as you watch, as a result of a direct hit from enemy anti-aircraft artillery.

I noticed some movement and a flash of light out of the corner of my right eye through the right side of the cockpit window. The plane that had been flying right next to us had exploded and simply disappeared.[6]

Don't worry Mom. Don't worry Mom.

'The letters reveal Fred's likes and dislikes for any number of things.' (Courtesy of Gary Hammerstrom)

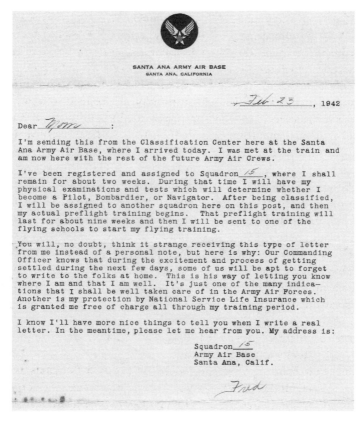

Note the incorrect year on the form above.

Chapter One

The Beginning

Fred was 19 on that day in 1941 when the USA joined the Second World War. He had been out of high school a year, lived with his mom in Los Angeles, and was employed as a bank teller.

He grew up in circumstances that were difficult both financially and socially. His dad had left home when Fred was a young boy and he and his mother had to fend for themselves. They moved frequently, and he learned to hang wallpaper to make their homes more attractive. During his high school years and while he was in the war, home for them was a small house in Los Angeles.

While he was in high school, Fred was a son a mother could be proud of: he was class president in his senior year, as well as student body president; received a high school athletic 'letter' as a gymnast with a specialty in side horse; was in the school's senior play; and was selected by faculty to receive the 'highest honor attainable by the high school graduate – membership in the Ephebian Society. To receive this distinction, a student must rank in the top ten per cent in scholarship or (be) nominated by the faculty or class.'[1] According to an article in the high school newspaper that listed the honourees and their feelings about the award, Fred '… seemed unable to find words to express his feelings on receipt of the Ephebianship, but has many ideas for the future. On graduating, he hopes to land a job, then in September, go to SC [University of Southern California]. He plans to become a social studies teacher.'[2]

As his class prepared for commencement, Fred, voted by his classmates as the most handsome boy and most popular senior, stated, 'A new order is coming into effect … it is up to each and every one of you to keep up Poly's many fine and noble traditions, traditions which the present group has admired and respected. To serve Poly in the capacity of ASBO [associated student body] president has meant more to me than mere words can tell; especially do I appreciate the fine cooperative spirit of the faculty and student body.'[3]

He graduated in February 1940 and, indeed, landed a job. But attendance at USC would have to wait, his dream of becoming a social studies teacher put on hold. The nation was soon at war. In the 110 minutes that turned Pearl Harbor into America's twentieth century Alamo, all thoughts of an immediate normal future dissolved.

From Fred's wartime scrapbook – he is
standing second from the right in the line.

(Author's collection)

Along with other 18–20-year-olds, Fred signed up in the nation's fifth draft call.
He is pictured in line with others in an article in a Los Angeles newspaper: 'All
eager to serve, these boys are shown signing up at Draft Board 231 at 910 South
Western Avenue. The 18 and 19-year-olds are not immediately eligible for the
draft, but can be called up as they reach 20.'[4]

The war was fought by civilians. We grew up during the Great Depression and
then the war started. We could enlist or wait to be drafted. For a lot of us, it
meant a job, food, clothes, etc., security we hadn't known in a long time.[5]

It was $21.00 a month to start off.[6]

Fred was called to duty nine days before his twentieth birthday in March 1942 and it is likely that he soon began his first encounter with the army by taking exams to establish his qualifications to become an aviation cadet and then sent home to await the results. In less than a year he was on his way to the Army Air Force Classification Center in Santa Ana, California, to begin cadet training.

We all sweated out the classification tests and nearly all wanted to be pilots.[7]

Not satisfied that the 'form' letter would be enough, another in his hand soon followed.

2/23/43
Tuesday
Santa Ana

Dear Mom,
Please excuse this writing as I've drawn an upper bunk. Some fun.
Boy what a day this has been!! We left downtown at exactly 10:00 am. Got to Santa Ana about 11:30 with stops and all.
You've never seen such mud as there is here.
We drove out to here in Army trucks and started right in filling out forms and stuff. They have really fed us today. It is almost 10:00. We're supposed to get up tomorrow morning at 5:30. Oh boy!
They're going to give us some clothes tomorrow. They call them 'Zoot suits.' This is all that has happened today.

Love,
Fred

★★★

2/24/43
Wednesday
Santa Ana

Dear Mom,
It has really been a busy day. Rained all night and boy has it been muddy all day. The time right now is 1530 or to you civilians 3:30 in the afternoon.
They really feed you plenty, but only firsts on butter and milk.
We got all of our clothes today.
Monday we take our first mental tests.
We are in a quarantined area now for two weeks, or until we are classified as pilots, bombardiers, or navigators. Then we can have visitors on Sunday from 9:00 until 3:00. You guys can't come out until I give the word, which will probably be in two weeks.
Then after that we can't leave here for a weekend until 42 days have passed since we first came here, which means if I'm classified as either pilot or so forth I can come home on a weekend about April 10th.

We had several lectures today.
Please make a small neat package and send my glasses to me.
Well that's all that has happened so far today so I'll write more news and details later. Take care of yourself and please don't worry because I'm o.k. and I want you to be that way!!

Your boy,
Fred

It's hard to believe, either from the form letter all new arrivals at the Classification Center sent home or from Fred's pencil scribbled notes that followed, that this 20-year-old inductee has gone someplace other than to summer camp. The messages are almost childlike in form and substance, and yet are written with a sense of assurance that all is well and that they certainly are being amply fed, except maybe for the apparent limited supply of milk and butter. And, boy, is this place really 'muddy', and don't forget to send my glasses!

However, the signs of change are also there: the regimentation of uniforms, limits on sleep, visits by family and friends and leave time, and the limitless supply of rumours. A further transformation begins as Fred and his companions, sometime, somehow, perhaps through 'mental tests', go through the process of being selected to be trained as pilots, bombardiers or navigators.

Pilot training must have been uppermost in the minds and desires of each of the cadets. Why would you want to be something other than the leader of your crew, captain of your ship?

Others had a more cynical view of the selection process:

Who would be dumb enough to get in the cockpit of a heavy bomber … loaded with 2,800 gallons of gasoline, ten 500-pound bombs, 7,000 rounds of 50-calibre ammunition, with an aluminum skin that burns with searing hot flames at the drop of a kitchen match … and fly straight and level for ten minutes … while everybody shot at them with every conceivable type of weapon intending to kill or maim him?[8]

All is well. Don't worry Mom. Don't worry Mom.

Chapter Two

Classification Center

What's this Classification Center, anyway? Just a big sorting machine. They'll give you fellows all sorts of examinations and aptitude tests. Inside of a week some of you will come out the pilot spout, some out the bombardier spout, while others will be classified as navigators. A few will be listed for G.D.O. What's G.D.O.? Ground duty only.[1]

3/1/43
8:15 in the evening
Santa Ana

Dear Mom,
The mail just came. The guys really stormed the fellow that brought it.
Almost everybody is in bed by now.
Boy did we have some day today! Starting at 8:00 this morning we took 8 hours of mental tests. Tomorrow we take manual dexterity and coordination tests.
Can't tell whether we pass or not for another week or so. Then if we pass certain tests and the physical we'll be classified.
No, there is no way to send a cake dear. Just your love is enough.
I'm glad Dan and Dorothy are having you out. You'll enjoy that.
How does it feel to be on the point system now for food?

Food rationing. Points. Ration stamps and books. Red tokens. Blue tokens. Limits on meat, sugar, cheese, butter. Rationing of gas, tyres and shoes. The Office of Price Administration issued ration books through local ration boards, and purchases of goods were fixed using a combination of cash and ration stamps or tokens. America was at war, and its citizens at home became participants, although not without some complaint:

The rationing point system, with its tiny color-coded stamps and red and blue cardboard tokens, created anxiety for housewives and drove grocers to distraction.[2]

'How does it feel to be on the point system now for food?' (Courtesy of Gary Hammerstrom)

Reflecting back on the war, Bob Brown, a B-17 pilot, remembered, 'It was a sacrifice for those who weren't in the military too, those at home who had to go without because of food and gas rationing.'[3]

When you get time please send my slippers, shorts, and a couple of coat hangers. The hangers that are wood and are shaped like this: ⌒ 2 or 3 are enough. Also that wire tie pin (the one that is hidden under the collar).

That's all the latest from here dear so until next time, Dear John.

Your son,

Fred

★★★

3/4/43
2:30 P.M.
Santa Ana

Dear Mom,

Yesterday at mail call I received 12 letters. The guys were really wondering what they all were. Most of them were birthday cards.

Well the mud is really deep here again. As the drill Sergeant put it, 'The mud is deep enough to be ass high to a nine foot Indian.'

Today we had a blood test, chest x-ray, and an interview with a mental doctor. Yesterday we had some tests that were fun, manual dexterity and muscular control.

Tomorrow the main thing comes up, the big physical. After the physical it will be about the 10th before we know what we are, if anything.

I'm really in with a swell bunch of fellows. There are 240 in our squadron. The squadron is divided into 4 flights and in each flight there are 60 fellows, thirty upstairs and 30 downstairs. They are called Flight A, B, C, D.

In Flight A all the fellows are 6 feet and over. The other flights have shorter boys. A lot of the fellows are from L.A. and the rest are from around San Francisco.

Also tell anybody that asks I can't write everybody because I don't know anything yet, so you explain to them.

Did anybody notify you of if my check came to Western-Olympic yet? If not, you call up and find out from Louise!

Well that's all for now.

> Love,
> Fred

P.S. Today I'm 21.

Two years before Fred was born, the United States of America War Office issued these 'Regulations for Operation of Aircraft'; a generation later, regulations and circumstances had changed, as he was finding out:

Commencing January 1920

1. Don't take the machine into the air unless you are satisfied it will fly.
2. Never leave the ground with motor leaking.
3. Don't turn sharply when taxiing. Instead of turning sharp, have someone lift the tail around.
4. In taking off, look at the ground and the air.
5. Never get out of a machine with motor running until the pilot relieving you can reach the engine controls.
6. Pilots should carry hankies in a handy position to wipe off goggles.
7. Riding on the steps, wings, or tail of a machine is prohibited.
8. In case the engine fails on takeoff, land straight ahead regardless of obstacles.
9. No machine must taxi faster than a man can walk.
10. Never run motor so that blast will blow on other machines.
11. Learn to gauge altitude, especially on landing.
12. If you see another machine near you, get out of the way.
13. No two cadets should ever ride together in the same machine.
14. Do not trust altitude instruments.
15. Before you begin a landing glide, see that no machines are under you.
16. Hedge-hopping will not be tolerated.
17. No spins on back or tail slides will be indulged in as they unnecessarily strain the machines.
18. If flying against the wind and you wish to fly with the wind, don't make a sharp turn near the ground. You may crash.

19. Motors have been known to stop during a long glide. If pilot wishes to use motor for landing, he should open throttle.

20. Don't attempt to force machine onto ground with more than flying speed. The result is bouncing and ricocheting.

21. Pilots will not wear spurs while flying.

22. Do not use aeronautical gasoline in cars or motorcycles.

23. You must not take off or land closer than 50 feet to the hangar.

24. Never take a machine into the air until you are familiar with its controls and instruments.

25. If an emergency occurs while flying, land as soon as possible.[4]

3/7/43
Santa Ana

Dear Mom,
Hi dear, how's everything going?

Here it is Sunday morning. We got to sleep until 7:15 this morning. I can't believe it. Every morning it's 5:30 and man is it dark and cold!!

Yesterday they told us we were going to march in the parade today. So we drilled for 5½ hours and now before the parade we have to drill for 2 or 3 more hours.

Our squadron marches second in line right behind the squadron that won the 'E' flag last week. The 'E' Flag is for the best marching squadron. Boy are they going to make us look rank.

Last night they told us we would probably be Classified by next Friday or Saturday. If so, that means that we can have visitors next Sunday. I sure hope so. I'll let you know as soon as I know!!

This morning the C.Q. (Charge of Quarters) came in and put ten boys on M.M. (Mess Management) for not turning out their lights at 10:00 last night. Most of us were so tired last night we were asleep before 9:30 so we didn't know anything about it.

Last night we really had a swell dinner. Steaks and stuff. How's the food problem at home now?

Apparently there was no 'food problem' at the AAF training centres. Besides 'steak and stuff', dinners might also include tomatoes and lettuce with dressing, fish, pork chops, potatoes and gravy, vegetables, rolls and butter and jams, dessert and coffee.

I'll finish this letter after the parade and let you know how we came out.
One of the fellows has a radio downstairs now.
I really feel swell and my face is getting tan, believe it or not with all this rain and clouds.
Here you don't have a worry such as you had in the Bank. They even think for you.
The airplanes really fly low around here and are they thick.
If we get classified by next Friday or Saturday we start school on Monday, March 15th.
I've still got $15.00 and I haven't touched any of the other yet. No use for money here. So don't worry about me. No idea when we get paid yet.
I wake up at 5:30 without being told and then I wake some of the others up. Wrote about 8 letters this morning and got caught up for awhile.

Next week while we're waiting to be classified we do M.M. (Mess Management) and guard duty.

This is the army, Mister Jones –
No private rooms or telephones.[5]

We're going to be getting some shots for lock jaw and stuff. Some of the boys fainted when they took their blood tests. If you fainted they washed you out, because they call it 'fainting without cause.'

You know me after I got out of the room I felt a little white so I put my head down between my knees and I was all right then. Shots don't bother me, but the other does. Dr. Randel will get a kick out of that. I was really pretty calm for me. My pulse and blood pressure tests were o.k. Tell Dr. Randel my Schneider was +11 and ask him what it means. It could have gone up to +18 and would have been perfect.

At the start of the (Schneider) I was ordered to lie down on a cot and relax for five minutes. At the end of that period a medical officer took my pulse and blood pressure. Then he told me to get up. Once again my pulse and blood pressure were recorded … 'Step up and down from that chair,' the medical officer ordered. 'Make it about five times in fifteen seconds.' I got up and down off the chair the required number of times. Once again my pulse and blood pressure were taken.

I learned that a pilot who had vasomotor stability (as measured by the Schneider) stood less chance of blacking out in a dive or fast turn than one who hadn't.[6]

The whistle just blew, so we have to go drill now for the parade.

(Pause from 10:30 until 6:00)
Just got back from the parade and dinner. I've never seen so many Air Cadets in my life!! Haven't found out who won yet.
Nothing more to add tonight.

(3/8/43 Monday morning)
The time is 7:00 right now. Just had breakfast at 6:00. Still don't know who won the parade yesterday.
We have to go to a lecture on gas today.
That's all for this morning dear.

With love,
Fred

The transformation from civilian life to that of the military is apparent in these letters home. Marching drill, parades and the ever-present Mess Management are the common denominators that provide the beginning basis for discipline, rule and authority that are an essential part of developing military personnel.

While Fred is learning the basic meaning of soldiering, there is an ongoing concern mentioned here and again in future letters about the family finances and the need for assurances that his mother has the money she needs. And, although the transformation into the rigors of military life form the substance of his letters, Fred still wants to bring a part of his former life to the barracks – slippers, coat hangers.

3/11/43
Santa Ana

Dear Mom,
Just a quick line as we have no time at all.
No visitors this Sunday as we won't be classified until Monday. Isn't that the nuts!! I'm so disappointed!
Tomorrow morning at 3:45 we do Mess Management.
I'll phone or write more as soon as possible.
You can't tell what they're going to do in this army.

Love,
Fred

This is the army Mister Green –
We like the barracks nice and clean;
You had a housemaid to clean your floor
But she won't help you out anymore.[7]

3/13/43
Santa Ana

Dear Mom,
It is now 9:45 Saturday night. We just got back from Santa Ana. We went to a radio show. Boy was it good. Guess who was on it? You guessed it, Ginny Sims. I've never seen or heard such beautiful music. The show started at 7:15 and was over at 7:45. Then until 8:30 they gave us more show. Virginia Bruce and Richard Dix were also on the program. Nobody can compare with Ginny Sims. I'm not the only one that said so either. I guess she really gives all her time for the Army and Navy.
We left here in an Army truck convoy. They stopped traffic all the way into town. They blocked all corners and all the people in town stood on the corners and watched. There was nothing to watch. About 240 of us went, but over the radio you'd swear it was over 3,000 Air Cadets.
I received your letter yesterday and also a slip from the post office to pick up a package so I went over there this morning and got it. Boy it's a beautiful pen! How did you like it? The point is just right! I sent my other pen right back to you while I was at the post office.
It's almost 10:00 now so I'll write more tomorrow (Sunday).

Sunday morning:
Didn't have to get up until 7:15 this morning. We had breakfast at 8:00. It is now 9:00. We have nothing to do this morning until 12:00 (lunch). Then I guess we'll drill for the parade.

'The point is just right!'

As far as we know tomorrow morning (Monday) at 8:00 we'll know what we'll be. Then we'll be out of quarantine and can go anywhere on the post, to the shows and etc. That also means we can have visitors next Sunday!!!!! (That is the best news of all!)

It also means we won't be in this squadron much longer. Then I'll have a new squadron and Flight number here at Santa Ana.

Now comes the best news of all for you. It's what we've been told, it could be changed, but I hardly think so. Because of the delay in classifying us we will miss pre-flight school if we're classified as pilots. If we miss pre-flight school we'll have to go to pre-pre-flight for a month or so until another pre-flight school starts. That means we'll be here about 3 or 4 months before ever seeing an airplane.

Although this might have been good news for Louise, having her son nearby for several more weeks, it could hardly have been welcome news for Fred. 'Let's get on with it. Let me see an airplane. Let me fly one.'

Well I haven't much more to write about so I'll phone you when we find out what we'll be if anything.

I'm hoping to be a pilot, because if you're classified as a bombardier or navigator there's a good chance to be shipped out of here to Texas. We have two Texans in our Flight and the more I see of Texans the more I hate Texas. Of course there are some exceptions.

It was their attitude, their Texan attitude:

> Texans thought that they were bigger and better than most and smarter than the average bear. You can always tell a Texan but you can't tell him much.[8]

That's all for now folks until I see you Sunday.

Love,
Fred

★★★

3/18/43
Santa Ana

Dear Mom,
Nothing to write except to tell you to bring my shoe trees and that little mirror from my kit.
Today it's cloudy and lousy, but the sun does manage to peek through now and then.
It surely is good to hear your voice over the phone. It seems as if I'm home.
Please tell Mrs. Paddock what I'm classified as because it's going to be more difficult from now on to write all these people. Explain to her why I'm not writing.
School starts Monday and there will be very little spare time.
There's nothing more to write as I talked to you yesterday.

Your loving son,
Fred

'What did you get?' I asked. 'Bombardier,' he grinned. 'Just what I wanted.' 'You mean you enlisted with the idea of being a bombardier?' I demanded. 'Do they give you your choice?' 'Sure,' he said. 'I want to be up there in the nose, the guy with the "now". You know, "now" is the second to push the button.'[9]

Fred was selected for bombardier training, for pushing the button.

> There are ten men in the ship – but you're the one who gets to press the little button … There's a terrific kick in your job – and a terrific responsibility. The entire reason for the existence and training of a combat crew is to put you where you push that button with the maximum results.[10]

HEADQUARTERS
SANTA ANA ARMY AIR BASE
OFFICE OF THE COMMANDING OFFICER
SANTA ANA, CALIFORNIA

23 March 1943

Mrs. Louise Alberta Lull,
1125 So. Catalina Street
Los Angeles, California

Dear Mrs. Lull,

The Classification Board has informed me that your son, Fred S. Lull, is qualified and has been selected for training as a Bombardier in the Army Air Forces. I congratulate both you and him upon this achievement.

In order to be selected for this most important training, it is imperative that an individual possess very definite qualifications. His character, integrity and trustworthiness must be unimpeachable, as he is one of the few entrusted with the carefully guarded secrets of the famous U. S. bombsight. The work of a Bombardier requires the highest degree of coordination between a keenly alert mind and a sound body. The success of every mission is dependent upon his precision and skill.

Your son will soon be assigned to an Army Air Forces West Coast Training Center bombardier school for a very intensive course of instruction. Upon the successful completion of this course, he will be awarded his Wings and rating as a qualified Bombardier.

It is my hope that you will derive great satisfaction from the selection of your son for training in this important duty and that his future career in the Army Air Forces will be one of continuing success and service.

Sincerely yours,

W. A. ROBERTSON,
Colonel, Army Air Forces,
Commanding

Chapter Three

Bombardier Training

5/4/43
Monday Eve.
Santa Ana

Dear Mom,

Just a few lines. I got this letter and check today in the mail. The green card is the check, just keep the other one and the letter for my scrap book.

Well here it is raining again.

How did you like the parade? Boy they really kept us standing for a long time!! Don't know why they had it on the grass.

We just got a rumor today. We might get 2 days off for Easter. That would not be so bad, eh?

I bought my bus ticket for next Sat. today. Can hardly wait!!

We went down to Newport Beach this morning at 7:30 and spent a half day down there shooting 30 caliber Browning Machine Guns, Thompson Sub-machine guns, and rifles. It surely looked good to see the ocean again!!

That's all for now.

I'll call up in a day or so!

Love,
Fred

P.S. All you have to do is to endorse the check to cash it or to deposit it.

★★★

4/15/43
Santa Ana

Dear Mom,

It's 9:45 in the evening now. We just got off M.M. We started at 4:00 this morning. Boy what a day!!

I've tried for the last 3 days to call you up, but you haven't answered. I called about 1:30 or 2:00.

The reason for this brief note is to tell you the very sad news. 3 or 4 fellows have broken out with Scarlet Fever and the whole Bombardier-Navigator school is quarantined this *weekend. That means I won't be home Sat. night. We don't know how long it will last. If it isn't one thing it's another.*

They're not taking any chances so we all have to stay here at dear old Santa Ana.

It's time for the lights to go out so I'll write more later or call you up.

Love,

Fred

P.S. I wanted to wish you a Happy Birthday over the phone, but you know.

★★★

5/4/43

Santa Ana

Dear Mom,

It's just six o'clock in the morning as I'm writing this letter. As I told you Sunday we started our new schedule yesterday. It's the nuts. We don't have a minute of free time. That's no kidding!! We still get up at 5:15, but don't go to breakfast until 7:00 so in the mean time we clean up around the barracks. After breakfast we have until 9:00 free, but nothing is open so that takes care of that.

At 9:00 we have athletics then start to school. Our last class in the afternoon starts at 5:20 and ends at 6:10. We have dinner at 7:00. So by this time you can see that we don't have any time at all. We can't even get to the P.X. (Post Exchange), cleaners, or hardly to the show. We have this schedule until we finish here. Won't that be fun! As far as I can figure out if and when I phone it will be about 8:15 or so in the mornings.

Found out our math grades yesterday. Well I passed, thank the Lord. We'll know today what our physics grades are if we pass.

Our first class is still meteorology, then first aid, military hygiene, next maps and charts, ground forces and last is code. Oh by the way, we have our final test in code Wednesday. Gosh here it is May 4th so soon. How time does fly.

Did you get my pants fixed yet? Have any trouble doing it?

They just blew the whistle for breakfast so I'll add to this letter as soon as we find out about our physics grades.

Later: (Much later, in fact 8:00 in the evening)

Well I also passed physics. Boy what a relief!! About 40 guys in our squadron failed in either math or physics.

Got the proof of my pictures today. One is pretty good, so everyone says. It will be about 15 days before I can get them.

Well hold onto your hat. We have to be on M. M. Sunday. Wouldn't that knock your teeth out!! There's nothing we can do about it though.

Oh by the way, you might as well send my pants to me.

Well, I've got to get cleaned up and study meteorology for a test tomorrow.

Good night dear,

Fred

★★★

5/16/43
Wed. afternoon
Santa Ana

Dear Mom,
Just a few lines as we've a few minutes between classes. Boy has it been hot. Sweating like
a horse.

Well, don't know how much longer we'll be training as bombardiers because they told
us yesterday that they don't want average bombardiers anymore. They say they've got more
bombardiers than they need. So they're really going to get tough. I can't figure it out, they
go to all the trouble of training us, setting up bombardier schools, etc., and then they tell you
they don't need bombardiers. Oh well, this is the Army, Mr. Lull!!!

We can only afford to take the cream of the crop. Air Crew demands and gets the
very best. Not the second best; not the third best. It must have the best.[1]

They usually let you graduate with a circular error of 230 feet. Now if you have that score
you've got to be a lot better.

Circular error is a measure of a bombardier's proficiency. In training the student
bombardier drops many practice bombs and later in his training has to pass a test
on his accuracy. There is a bullseye or a small shack on the ground and the student makes several bomb runs from different directions and drops on the target.
Someone on the ground measures the distance from the center of the target to
the point of bomb impact and the average of these distances is the bombardier's
'circular error' expressed in feet.[2]

And on top of that we're the first class they're going to give special tests to every three
weeks. The purpose is to see if you've learned and remembered what you've been taught.
If you haven't learned, bang, out you go. Everything now is to eliminate as many
as possible.

The cream of the crop, Fred. Only the very best will do.

I gather from that that they are doing a pretty good job in this war or otherwise they
wouldn't be so hard on us. All the fellows are joking about it. We've all quit worrying about
it. We're all saying we want a soft office job in the air corps now. No kidding – no one is
counting on making the grade now.
Well you don't want to hear all our troubles, but I thought I'd start breaking the news
gradually and if it does happen you won't be surprised.
I was so sleepy by this morning I could hardly get up. This night work is getting us.
I got the soap. Thanks a lot. Don't bother to get anymore.
What kind of weather are you guys having there this year? Wish we had some of it
here!! Fog and cold weather in June. Can't believe it. It's not California!!!
This Sunday I'm going to rest all day and study.

Friday we go out and learn all about the planes we are going to go up in Monday. Learn how to use the radio, interphone, how to operate the camera to photograph the other student bombardier's bombs as they hit the target.

Two students go up with the instructor and pilot.

Can't get over my ride in the Flying Fortress. It was really fun!!

I wear my good shoes all the time now as these G.I. shoes are too hot for me. Rubber soles. You know what rubber soles do to me!

Well I've got to get back to work.

Just after dinner:

Just had dinner, so am finishing this up. We've got to fall out in a few minutes to go down to the trainer until 10:30.

Love,
Fred

★★★

5/26/43
Santa Ana

Dear Mom,

Here it is Wednesday morning. Boy are we busy. We have to go to a show this morning. 'The Battle of Britain.' There are a lot of things for us to do today. Hardly any time to do any personal things. Have to pack our stuff tonight. There is no reason for the early part of this letter except I'm going to write you the log of our journey into the unknown. Everybody is guessing where we'll go. As far as we know we're not going on buses. That leaves Victorville out. Quite a few fellows from our squadron are being left out. They're being held over for awhile. Nobody knows why. Boy are they a sad lot.

I bought a few post cards yesterday. They're all addressed so I can send them when we arrive at destination unknown.

Thursday (5/27/43) I'm writing Thursday's news as we're on the train, Friday. Please excuse this writing as I'm swinging and swaying with the rock of the train as no doubt you can gather by this time. We got all lined up Thurs. morn at 11:30 and the trucks picked us up at 12:00. We had a convoy into Santa Ana to the railroad station. Our train was waiting. We went through Riverside, San Bernardino, and had dinner in Barstow. We have a special train. There's not much to write about on the train as nothing is happening. Went to bed at 9:30. Pretty tired! I had an upper berth. Very comfortable.

Friday (5/28/43) Woke up at 7:00 this morning. We were somewhere in Arizona. We had breakfast at Ash Fork at 10:00. We had to set our watches up one hour. Mountain Time. We passed Williams, Arizona a little while ago. The sign said 64 miles north to the Grand Canyon. Wish we could take a trip there (you and me)!

Passing a lot of hilly country with lots of pine trees. The conductor said we'd have lunch in Winslow. That's where you lived isn't it? Hunted rabbits, etc. Also said we would have dinner in Gallup, New Mexico. Our guess is we're going to Roswell or Albuquerque.

We had lunch in Winslow. It's the best place we've stopped yet. No wonder you liked it. Just before we hit Winslow we ran into some rain. Had dinner in Gallup, New Mexico. Three hours out of Gallup we passed the rain.

At Gallup our train split up. Half went one way and the other half went the other way. As soon as we left Gallup they told us where we were going because there were no more stops on the way. Our guess was correct. It was Roswell, New Mexico. That's down near the Mexican border and not too far, I think, from Texas. We're supposed to arrive at 6:00 tomorrow morning (Sat.). It will probably be a little later. We've had a 2 day and night train ride.

The meals have been good all the way. We've had to pay for our own meals. They allow us $1.00 for each meal. Get paid for it later.

The scenery is all the same – barren and hilly. You remember the red clay! The train just stopped for a minute and then started. They've been doing it all the way. Lot of the places we see from the train have out-houses.

Well, this brings events up to date, it's 8:30 now and I'm going to get the porter to make my upper berth up

Sat. (5/29/43) Woke up at about 6:30 and we were in some jerk-water town, about 150 miles from Roswell. Arrived in town of Roswell at 11:00. It has a population of 10,000 people. The train took us right out to the base which is 4 miles from town. As soon as we arrived on the base they gave us lunch. Boy what a difference. A lot better than Santa Ana. You eat cafeteria style. The tables have tablecloths.

Next they gave us our bedding and barracks. There are five fellows in our room. All my best friends from Santa Ana.

They gave us another big physical examination. They aren't taking any chances.

We're about ½ block from the airfield. I've never seen so many Flying Fortresses in my life. Boy are they big! We don't get to fly for about 3 weeks. They gave us flying boots, gloves, cap, and jacket. The cap looks like a baseball players cap. It keeps the sun out of your eyes when you're flying.

Well that's all that happened up to the time I sent you the telegram. Sent it straight wire so you should get it Sat. night.

I don't want many more train rides!!

Let me have all the news when you write.

Sunday morning 6:15 (5/30/43) Just was wakened by the Flying Fortresses taking off. It's a beautiful day today. There was a light thunderstorm late yesterday evening.

I know how you feel but please don't let yourself go. You know it won't help you a darn bit and it will make me worry if I know you're worrying. Take care of yourself so when I do come home you'll be right in the pink of condition.

This is all I can think of for now so I'll write more soon!!

Your son,

Fred

★★★

The Norden Bombsight – 'No wonder it's such a big secret'. (Author's collection)

6/1/43
Roswell, New Mexico

Dear Mom,
What a day! Boy has it been hot. You get so dry. All you do is drink water, water, and more water!!
*   We had our first look at the bombsight today. No wonder it's such a big secret.*

The USAAF, dedicated from the start to precision bombing, went to war with the highly accurate – and highly secret – Norden bombsight, a device considered so vital to the USAAF's success that the bombsight was fitted with an explosive self-destruct device powerful enough to blow the nose off the aircraft.[3]

In addition to the presence of the self-destruct device, the USAAF also developed the bone-chilling 'Bombardier's Oath' that cadets were supposed to swear to:

Mindful of the secret trust about to be placed in me by my Commander in Chief, the President of the United States, by whose direction I have been chosen for bombardier training … and mindful of the fact that I am to become guardian of one of my country's most priceless military assets, the American bombsight, … I do here, in the presence of Almighty God, swear by the Bombardier's Code of Honor to keep inviolate the secrecy of any and all confidential information revealed to me, and to further uphold the honor and integrity of the Army Air Forces, if need be, with my life itself.[4]

Tomorrow we start on the bomb trainer. Our day will end at about 10:00 at night. That is we go to school until that time. Then we come back and go to bed and still get up at the regular time.

On the bomb trainer you go into a hanger and they have machines set up that are just like being up in the air in a plane bombing. It teaches you to do it right before you go up in a plane. It's time for lights out so I'll add to this tomorrow.

                                                    Good night.

Wednesday: Here it is Wed. night. What a day. We started the trainer today. I've never seen anything like it. Boy it does everything that happens up in the air. No wonder our bombardiers are getting better hits than the Germans and Japs. The bombsight is really a beautiful instrument. Not everybody is fortunate enough to see one.

Newspaper clipping from Fred's scrapbook:

Bombsight does all but think. (The following story has been approved for publication by the Technical Service Command of the Army Air Force. – Ed.)

By George D. Drissey; Chicago, Dec. 13 – (UP) – The Norden bombsight is so efficient that after it has been set on a preconceived target the plane would continue toward its objective even though all the crew had been killed, it was disclosed today at a public showing of this heretofore secret weapon of the United States air force …

The bombsight is comprised of two units – upper and lower. The lower part is the stabilizer which holds the craft on its course through the ships' rudder during the bombing run.

The upper part is the 'sight' itself. The two function as a unit, although there are 900 parts to the lower unit alone.

Most important of the sight itself are the telescope, the computer and the gyro. The computer is called the brains of the sight by engineers, who said its mechanism is approximately 40 times more accurate than the finest watch.

The function of the computer is to solve various mathematical problems which confront the bombardier just prior to the bombing run.

It answers questions as to ground speed, altitude and atmospheric conditions almost instantly.

In effect the three way team plays this way:

The computer dopes out various conditions and circumstances, including the curvature of the earth.

The stabilizer seizes on the set course for the bombing run. The 'sight' fixes its eye on the target and follows it to a predetermined spot, loosing its load of distruction [*sic*] at the exact moment planned in advance.'[5]

The Norden bombsight, an engineering marvel of staggering complexity, was mass produced with precise measurements of its parts. A feat made more remarkable for the lack of advanced electronics and computers so available to modern industry and the need to coordinate the research, theory, design and manufacturing of the bombsight among more than 161 contractors, sub-contractors, corporations, companies, and agencies.[6]

I'll have to cut it short as we've got plenty of studying to do tonight – Tomorrow we go to ground school for 4 hours, then the trainer for 4 hours, then athletics for an hour and then dinner. After dinner from 8:00 to 10:30 we have the trainer again. Probably get to bed about 11:15 or so. What a schedule. It gets worse later on. You fly at night and day.

Send a check for $3.50 for income tax. It has to be paid as long as we have money in the bank.

Also please send me a jar of Bingo-salicylic acid. I don't know how to spell it. The name is in the little drawer in the desk. It's for my ringworm. It costs about 40 cents. If you can't find the name Dr. Randel knows it.

Tell everybody hello for me.

Well dear that's all for now so until next time, Dear John.

Good night,

Fred

P.S. We get the rest of last month's pay about the 10th. I'll send a post office money order and you can deposit it.

★★★

6/5/43
Friday morning
Roswell, New Mexico

Dear Mom,

It's about a quarter to nine. I'll try to sneak a letter out during the dry lecture we're hearing on aerial engineering, etc.

We left the hanger last night at about 10:30 and got to bed at 11:30. Kind of tired today. We have to go again tonight. Same time and everything. One of the fellows has a friend that is an instructor on the trainers. Boy is he lucky. He got to be with his friend. It surely will help him.

The days are really hot here. It was 100 degrees in the hanger yesterday. All you do is drink water, water, and more water. You've never seen such sand, dust, and wind, and low humidity. Your thirst is never satisfied.

I don't care what anybody says about California. It's the only place to be.

Just a minute I'll have to quit now as the period is just about over.

Later, much later!! (in fact 12:15 at night). We just got home from the trainer and studied a little for the tests tomorrow – we have 5 of them. We've been on the go for 18 hours today. Sunday we have to be on the trainer from 2:00 until 6:00. Some Sunday!!

In the day time we get home from school (6:15) just in time to go to athletics and then dinner and back to the trainer.

Our instructor said today they've only had one casualty here in the last year. Boy that's darn good.

Don't worry Mom. Don't worry Mom.

Please write everyday and don't send airmail, every other day. Just a line everyday is worth more than airmail letters.

Dear, I'm so tired. Please excuse me for breaking this off.

Love,
Fred

P.S. They told us if we get through this course here we should be very proud as they've toughened the course more than it was a year ago. They say they want quality and not quantity. From that statement I gather things are looking good over this world.

Good night

The folks at home have little conception of how much a letter means to the boy in the Service. The fact that he does not answer immediately is no indication that the letter is not appreciated. It must always be borne in mind that the cadet in training puts in a long day. Many's the time he returns to barracks with the firm resolve to answer that letter, only to tumble wearily into his bunk and dream of home instead of writing.[7]

6/6/43
Sat. night
Roswell, New Mexico

Dear Mom,
Another big day today. We had five tests today covering our first weeks work in ground school. They lasted 4 hours.
They were on the:

Trainer theory	*87%*	
Theory of bombing	*90%*	*These are the grades*
Aerial engineering	*93%*	*I received in these tests.*
Aircraft landing code	*80%*	
Theory of bomb sights	*93%*	

Well we've had about 6 hours each on the trainer now. I always thought a bombardier's job was easy and nothing to do. Well, I've found out differently now. When you're on a bombing run or trainer both your hands are going 50 miles an hour. Your eye is busy and you've got a million things to think of and do in a very few seconds.

Fred is becoming a bombardier. His test scores in this report card-like letter home to Mom are to his credit, and his description of the flurry of activity required while on a bombing run puts into practical terms what happens in the nose of the bomber. What does it mean, though, to put theory of bombing, aerial engineering and theory of bombsights together with the practical manipulations required of the bombardier? If Fred had been able to send home this description of the role of the bombardier, his mother, no doubt, would have been impressed because it is clear that the bombardier is not a second-class citizen of the air crew:

> Accurate and effective bombing is the ultimate purpose of your entire air-plane and crew. Every other function is preparatory to hitting and destroying the target.

That's (the) bombardier's job. The success or failure of the mission depends upon what he accomplishes in that short interval of the bombing run.

When the bombardier takes over the airplane for the run on the target, he is in absolute command. He will tell you what he wants done, and until he tells you 'Bombs away', his word is law.

A great deal, therefore, depends on the understanding between bombardier and pilot. (The pilot expects) the bombardier to know his job, the problems involved in his job, and to give him full cooperation. Teamwork between pilot and bombardier is essential.

Under any given set of conditions – ground speed, altitude, direction, etc. – there is only one point in space where a bomb may be released from the airplane to hit a predetermined object on the ground.

There are many things with which a bombardier must be thoroughly familiar in order to release his bombs at the right point to hit this predetermined target.

He must know and understand his bombsight, what it does, and how it does it.

He must thoroughly understand the operation and upkeep of his bombing instruments and equipment.

He must know that his racks, switches, controls, releases, doors, linkage, etc., are in first-class operating condition.

He must understand the automatic pilot as it pertains to bombing.

He must know how to set it up, make any adjustments and minor repairs while in flight.

He must know how to operate all gun positions in the airplane.

He must know how to load and clear simple stoppages and jams in machine guns while in flight.

He must be able to load and fuse his own bombs.

He must understand the destructive power of bombs and must know the vulnerable spots on various types of targets.

He must understand the bombing problem, bombing probabilities, bombing errors, etc.

He must be thoroughly versed in target identification and in aircraft identification.

The bombardier should be familiar with the duties of all members of the crew and should be able to assist the navigator in case the navigator becomes incapacitated.

For the bombardier to be able to do his job the pilot of the aircraft must place the aircraft in the proper position to arrive at a point on a circle about the target from which the bombs can be released to his target.[8]

You asked about a bombardier being a co-pilot. Sometimes later on (much later) a bombardier flys the plane.

The water is so hard here you can't lather soap. Will you see if you can get me some Kirk's Hard Water Castile soap or any soap that will lather in hard water. Please send quite a few bars as it won't be wasted.

Well dear can't think of anymore to say so I bid you good night.

Love,
Fred

★★★

6/6/43
Roswell,
New Mexico

Dear Mom,

Don't have much to say, but thought I'd drop a card (I mean a line) as long as I've a little free time. Well we didn't get up until 7:30 this morning. Walked over and had breakfast and then went by the post office. After breakfast we G.I.'d our rooms and barracks. We scrubbed the floors (I mean bleached them) washed windows, dusted all rafters and shelves, etc.

> This is the army, Mister Green –
> We like the barracks nice and clean;
> You had a housemaid to clean your floor
> But she won't help you out anymore. (Reprise)[9]

Next we went over and played tennis for about 4 hours. I got a little sun burned. Came back, cleaned up and wrote some letters.

Talk about storms, a thunderstorm just blew up. Boy is the wind blowing and it is hailing and raining.

I know less now about the world news than I did at Santa Ana. What is going on in world now?

A fellow here wanted to buy my Parker '51' for $20.00. No sale! I like it too well!!

Well I'm going over and eat dinner, come back and study some and try to go to bed early tonight and be able to start in fresh tomorrow morning.

Love,
Fred

★★★

6/8/43
Tuesday morn.
Roswell, New Mexico

Dear Mom,

Just a quick line before breakfast. I just made my bed and am all dressed and waiting while the rest of our room wakes up.

Last night I took it easy as it was the first time we've had to relax. I told you I think that we're going to be on the trainer nights all next week. Oh will we be tired!

Would it be possible to call next Sunday morning? Let me know.

Yesterday I was the best I've been so far on the trainer. Sat. I wasn't so hot. A little rest Sunday did the trick.

And wear it she did – see the photograph of Louise and Fred on p. 186. (Author's collection)

We've surely got a swell instructor. He's got an English accent (slightly). He seems a lot nicer than some of the other instructors that the other fellows have. There are 4 of us to 1 instructor. Four of us from the same room.

We started some new subjects yesterday in ground school so we'll have more tests this coming Saturday. Some fun!! Hope I can get as good grades as I did last Saturday. It came out 90.6% average.

You can wear this pin on your coat. It's just a little something to make you think of me.

Love,

Fred

P.S. I like the clippings you send in your letters.

Fred's letters are an interesting reflection of the lexicon of the 1940s. Something is 'the nuts', 'gosh', 'jerk-water town', 'some fun', 'wouldn't that knock your teeth out'.

Here and in other letters 'swell' is the adjective of choice – a 'swell group of fellows', a 'swell instructor'. At first blush, 'swell' seems archaic, if not adolescent, as a descriptor of people, places and events. But 'swell' was in common usage during this era, and those who used it included service men and women like Fred who wrote letters home and even General Eisenhower, who upon his return home after the war, exclaimed that it was 'swell' to be back in the United States.

Perhaps it is best left to one of the giants of the GIs' world to put 'swell' into meaningful perspective. The cartoonist Bill Mauldin, regarding the reactions of some people to his drawings, wrote:

> If it means that people are interested in seeing how the dogfaces look at themselves, that's swell. If it means that people at home are beginning to understand these strange, mud-caked creatures who fight the war, and are beginning to understand their minds and their own type of humor, that's even more swell, because it means that the dogfaces themselves are beginning to be appreciated a little by their countrymen.[10]

6/9/43
Roswell, New Mexico

Dear Mom,
First of all I want to answer your many questions.
     Yes, you wear a parachute every time you go up in an Army plane. It's not too smart to be without one. Another thing, they haven't had a man bail out of a plane here in over a year. That is the kind of plane I go up in. It'll be another week and ½ yet before we go up. Secondly, there are two ways to get out if you have to.

Don't worry Mom. Don't worry Mom.

Yes, I enjoy the clippings!
     Did the pin get there in one piece? Please excuse this writing as I've got to hurry so I can study for Saturday's tests.
     I can't write for a couple of days as I'm going to be very, very busy, but I'll write as soon as possible!!
     So far I'm doing o.k. Just got to keep on the ball.
     Let me have all the latest dope!!

All my love,
Fred

★★★

6/13/43
Sunday afternoon
Roswell, New Mexico

Dear Mom,
Been playing tennis all morning. Got sun burned again. Doesn't hurt though! Went to bed at 11:45 last night. Gosh what a town (pardon me for calling it a town). Cowboys all over the place, what a bunch of hicks. There's not a darn thing to do there. You've never seen such farmers. Some of the fellows that went in with me couldn't believe it was a town. Had dinner there however. All there is to do is drink and I don't go for that, so I came back here and went to bed. Got up this morning before everybody in our room and creeped around so I wouldn't wake them up and then went to breakfast. Some of the fellows and myself are going to the show here this afternoon. The picture is 'Bombardier'. Should be pretty good. Pat O'Brien, Randolph Scott. It was taken at Albuquerque.
     Starting tomorrow we really have a busy week lined up. We'll be going to school until 10:30 every night. Going to be pretty rough. A week from tomorrow (Monday) we're supposed to go up for the 1st time.
     Didn't go to the bombing contest today. They say it was pretty good.
     It sure sounded good to hear your voice last night!!!! Just take care of yourself, that's all I ask!!
     I'll try to drop a line tomorrow.

Love,
Fred

They quickly moved beyond what briefly seemed like a summer camp experience at the Classification Center to a rigorous schedule of training, classroom and flight instruction and the ever-present requirement that the barracks be 'GI'd' and their uniforms be clean and hung according to regulations, buttons polished and shoes shined. Somewhere in between scrubbing, cleaning, polishing, attending classes, squeezing into the trainers, flying, eating and sometimes even sleeping, there was 'athletics'. Physical body conditioning was as crucial to develop and maintain as was knowledge about the theory of bombing – a hard sell to many while they were completing their push-ups.

The schedule was as intense as the subject matter was demanding – from reveille at 0515 to taps at 2200. Reveille could be as early as 0400 if you were pulling MM, and 'lights out' could occur whenever the army said it was time to turn out the lights – struggling back to the barracks and crashing into bed after midnight was not uncommon.

> *6/15/43*
> *Tues. morning*
> *6:15*
> *Roswell, New Mexico*

Dear Mom,
This is the only chance I've got to write so here goes. We got home from school at 10:45 last night. Boy am I tired this morning!! We've got this whole week to go the same way. Oh, oh!!
We went to the show Sunday afternoon. 'Bombardier' – it wasn't a very good picture. After the show, had dinner and then walked over to the flight line and got a ride in a B-17 Flying Fortress. I was up in it for 4½ hours. We went all over. It's really a beautiful airplane. I've never seen anything so big inside.

Although the B-17 was not the biggest bomber of the USAAF during the war, it was, for Fred, beautiful and big, inside and out. With another set of eyes, though, the inside spaces were cramped and required a fetal-like position for the ball turret gunner. The tail gunner rested on his knees and shins for hours at a time on *prie-dieu* like benches, one for each leg, with prayer perhaps wedged somewhere between the gun sights and kneecaps. The space between the left and right waist gunners was so narrow that they often bumped into one another while firing their guns in combat. Just forward of these positions, the radio room was not even the size of a small closet.

The bomb bay was large enough to carry a bomb load of 6,000lb with an 8in-wide catwalk that spanned its length and offered a view of the gulf of space beyond the plane when the bomb bay doors were open.

The bomb bay area was also the location of the relief tube, which required that crewmembers who had to relieve themselves advise the ball turret gunner through the plane interphone of the oncoming torrent so that he could rotate the gun barrels away from the exit of the tube on the underside of the aircraft.

Radio room. (Author's collection)

The 8in-wide bomb bay catwalk. (Author's collection)

Failure to follow this procedure was sure to bring a string of invectives from the scrunched-up gunner.

The cockpit was crowded with instruments and controls, with just enough space for the pilot and co-pilot to sit in seats with their legs at near-constant angles. The seats offered little more comfort than straight-backed wooden kitchen chairs.

In front of and below the cockpit, the navigator sat at a table not much larger than the surface of a briefcase, and in the nose, the bombardier had a seat placement that demanded of him a Quasimodo-like humpback contortion during the bomb run.

Cockpit. (Author's collection)

In 1944, the price tag for a B-17 was a little more than $204,000.[11] It carried a crew of ten, had a wingspan of nearly 104ft, and was armed with thirteen 50-calibre machine guns, including the two located in the new chin turret of the B-17G model. Its four 1,200hp Wright Cyclone engines could power it to fly at a cruising speed of 160mph with a 35,000ft ceiling.

> In the air or on the ground with its 1,200 h.p. engines in sync, there was a certain thundering rendition of sound pleasant to the ear and unique to the aircraft. Even at 160 mph cruising speed, there was nothing serene about the cry of the engines. They labored in concert with each other and when they didn't it didn't take a pilot or flight engineer to know trouble loomed. Every man on the crew got to know the comforting, pulsating rhythm of those power plants.[12]

A total of 12,726 B-17s was built, including 8,680 B-17Gs, the model Fred flew in 1944.[13]

A couple of other fellows went up in another plane. They got airsick. Boy did they feel lousy. In the afternoon the air around here gets pretty bumpy so they got sick. Thank the lord I've never gotten sea or air sick yet. Wait until Monday, we'll have plenty of sick boys around here. They've been told to bring paper bags every time they go up. I wonder why? Monday is the first time up for most of them and it'll be in a lighter and much smaller plane than a B-17. We go up in AT 11's.

Time out for breakfast
Just got back from breakfast. Cantalopes (can't spell it) were very good. Starting today I'm taking salt tablets about 3 times a day. You sweat so much and lose so much salt you've got to take 'em to keep up your strength and pep.

We think we're busy this week, wait until next week. There's a rumor out that we have to be at the trainers at 6:00 in the morning and then after a couple of hours of that then we'll go up and practice in the planes. Plus ground school. It's been four months now that I've been here. Boy have we been on the go! Never a minute of rest. It would be worth it to get the measles or something to go to the hospital for a rest.

All the guys around here say those lucky soldiers! They really don't mean it though because there's not one of 'em that would trade his place here with a soldier. We've taken so much and gone too far to not keep on now.

… the infantry is the group in the army which gives more and gets less than anybody else … They don't get fancy pay, they know their food is the worst in

A bombardier's position in a B–17G. (Author's collection)

But for Fred, it *was* beautiful *and* big. (Author's collection)

the army because you can't whip up lemon pies and even hot soup at the front, and they know how much of the burden they bear.[14]

Well I just can't think of anything to say. Oh, I got the newspapers yesterday.

When I get back to California I'll never leave it except to go up north.

Gosh it's time to go to school so I'll write as soon as possible!!

Your little boy,
Fred

A framed copy of this advertisement was part of Fred's wartime memorabilia: 'Every man on the crew got to know the comforting, pulsating rhythm of those power plants.'

★★★

6/19/43
Sat. morn.
Roswell, New Mexico

Dear Mom,

Just a few quick lines as I'll have a little more time in a day or so. Yesterday our instructor took us out to the plane and showed us everything about it and what we have to do. They're really good planes we're going up in.

At about this same time, a B-17 based in North Africa was returning from a mission to Italy. It had been badly damaged, both engines on the same side were shut down and it was two hours late returning to its home base. Finally, it was spotted limping home just barely above the sand, and yet it managed to land safely.

> That night, with the pilot and some of the crew, we drank a toast. One visitor raised his glass: 'Here's to your safe return.' But the pilot raised his own glass and said instead, 'Here's to a God-damned good airplane!' And the others of the crew raised their glasses and repeated, 'Here's to a God-damned good airplane!'[15]

Last night we found out our schedule for next week. Well we get up at 4:25 in the morning and go to the trainers and then we fly from 8:00 until 11:30, then school and other stuff thrown in. You can see we're gong to be pretty busy!!

I'm not going anywhere tonight or tomorrow (Sat. or Sunday) because I'm too tired! We didn't get to bed until after 12:00 because we had to study for the tests today (Sat.).

We've been here three weeks now. Sure doesn't seem that long.

Well I guess we're lucky in a way because we get to fly in the morning instead of the afternoon. That means that there is less chance of getting air sick due to the very rough afternoon air.

We've got to go to the trainers now so I'll write more soon.

All my love,
Fred

★★★

6/20/43
Sunday afternoon
Roswell, New Mexico

Hi Dear,

Here it is Sunday afternoon. Hot as usual. Gosh it doesn't seem as if we've been here 3 weeks now.

Two of the fellows across the hall from me went to town and the show last night with me. We bought some note-book paper, a small note book, and a clip board. A clip-board is a wooden board about 10 inches wide and 12 inches long with a clip on one end. Very handy to write on when you're flying. Well we start flying tomorrow morning. That will decide probably whether we make the grade or not. I don't mean just going up tomorrow, but the whole flying time.

We took five more tests yesterday. We'll know tomorrow what we got in them. They were pretty tough.

I'm not doing a darn thing today but rest. (Not even tennis).

This last week tired us all out.

I see the pictures in the Examiner are showing Amie's [sic] fanatical religion is on the go again. Can't see why people are so nuts as to fall for her line.

Aimee Semple McPherson, Sister Aimee, combined religiosity and evangelistic ardour with Hollywood production values that defined her message, as well as her style. She preached the Gospel in flowing white robes and the latest Marcel hair style, with chorus and orchestra backups, to capacity congregations in her 5,400-seat Angelus Temple in Los Angeles, the 'City of the Angels'.

She crossed the bridge of social class differences commingling parishioner cultures and races when delivering her Pentecostal messages of faith, healing and redemption. Her soup kitchen fed the poor and needy during the Great Depression, and she took to heart raising money for war bonds, selling $150,000 worth in one hour during a rally in June 1942. Yet, to some, she reached a level of Gospel theatrics that defined her as eccentric: *'Can't see why people are so nuts as to fall for her line.'*

Less than a year after expressing her commitment to the war in both the Pacific and in Europe in her 'Praise the Lord and Pass the Ammunition' sermon, the frail and badly arthritic woman with a calling died at the age of 53 from an overdose of barbiturates in Oakland, California.[16]

How is Gabriel Heatter, or do you listen to him anymore?

Jack Benny's picture 'Meanest Man in the World' is on next Sat. Looks as if it will be a good picture.

Oh, would you, when you're downtown next time, ask them at Schwabackery Frey's why a Parker '51' pen scratches a little when it writes, also how long would it take to have a new point put on it?

Listen kid, you take care of your cold and get well. So you are getting a little summer weather now. About time isn't it?

In another couple of weeks we'll have an idea of where we stand approximately. (I hope!).

It surely rained here a couple of nights ago. There are always clouds in the sky.

Well, can't think of anymore for now so I'll write as soon as we have our first bombing run.

Love

Fred

P.S. I lost my pencil the other day and someone brought it back to me. Good thing I had my name on it. It's too much bother for you to send cookies to me dear. Anyway they have plenty of cake and pies here.

★★★

6/21/43
Monday noon
Roswell, New Mexico

Dear Mom,
Just finished lunch. Well we got up at 4:25. Had breakfast then went down to the trainer's
bldg. We were on the trainers until 8:00.
*   Then we drew our parachutes and Bombardier's kit, etc. We wear the chest type of chutes.*

The bombardier's kit is a cloth case containing computers, tables, and pertinent
working materials for use in maintaining bombing records and calculations. It
is provided for every student and graduate bombardier through regular supply
channels. It includes: C-2, G-1, J-1, and E-6B computers; set of dropping angle
charts for use with the E-6B computer, stop watch and wrist watch; pen-type
flashlight; bombing flight record holder; tools; drafting pencils; eraser, dividers,
Weems plotter; parallel rule; transparent triangles; bombing tables.[17]

We went out to the plane, got aboard and started to get everything all set up in the gun
house before the pilot and our instructor arrived. We didn't know until this morning if
we were going to have our same instructor or not. Each instructor had 4 students on the
trainer, but only 2 on the plane. Boy was I lucky because I got my instructor. I was up in
the nose before the take-off working on the bombsight when he came aboard. He crawled up
to the nose and said, 'Am I stuck with you two guys yet?' He's really a swell fellow. My
roommate and I are his two students.
*   Well we then went back in the ship and strapped on our safety belts and the pilot*
took off.
*   Boy there's nothing like it. Riding up in the nose and using the bombsight. It seems a*
lot easier up in a plane than it does on the trainer. We were up at an indicated altitude of
9240 feet. A couple of times the pilot was going over 200 mph.
*   We don't start dropping bombs for a couple of days yet. We're just getting used to the air*
and procedure we are supposed to go through. We do everything but drop bombs.
*   It was pretty calm today, but wait until we fly in the afternoon, then it really gets rough!!*
*   We don't know our grades from the test we had Saturday, but we did find out one.*
*   I got 93% in the computer. Do you know what a computer is? Well you figure altitude,*
temperature, air speed, drift, and all kinds of math problems on them. It also tells you from
what direction your wind is coming and the wind force.
*   I'll let you know the other grades in my next letter.*

More later
Love,
Fred

P.S. This is no kidding or bragging but my instructor said to me after we came down that I
did pretty good. I did just what he wanted me to do and the way he had taught me.

★★★

6/22/43
Tuesday
Roswell, New Mexico

Dear Mom,

Boy is it hot!! It's 3 o'clock in the afternoon. We're in ground school. We'll be here until 6 o'clock this evening.

Had a swell time flying this morning. We flew over Carlsbad Caverns. It's only about 70 miles by air from here.

I found out my grades yesterday for last Saturday's tests. I got two 100s and two 93s making an average of 96.5% for last week. Over the three weeks period my over all average is 93.5%. This coming Sat. the tests are going to be a lot harder than usual. (If that's possible).

True Airspeed Computer, Type G-1. (Courtesy of Gary Hammerstrom)

Aerial Dead Reckoning Computer, Type E-6B. (Author's collection)

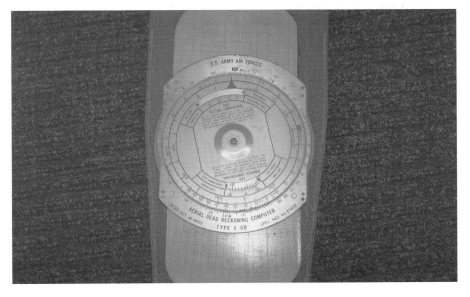

We're on our 4th week. Each 3 weeks is considered as a unit.

We've been living across the street from a pilot squadron. They live in pretty good tents. Well they graduated today as Second Lieutenants. They moved into our <u>nice</u> barracks and we moved into their tents Some fun! I don't think it'll be so bad because we aren't in our barracks hardly at all. Anyway it'll be cooler at night and morning. The tents have wooden floors and good heaters, etc. Who wants to use heaters?

Well we've got another hour of this class. It will then be 6:00 and then we go back to the tents and go to athletics. Athletics are over at 7:05 then we go to dinner at 7:30. Some fun, eh kid?

Here it is 8:30 in the evening.

Tell me more about Smitty (a high school buddy). What did he have to say and so forth? How long was he home?

Oh by the way, will you please send me some air mail stamps as I can't get to the post office to get any.

I like to send my letters to you fast!! Received both your letters today. One mailed the 21st and I got it the next day, the 22nd. Pretty fast.

You have no idea how much fun it is to skim over the land at 200 mph. I mean about 1000 feet up.

Today when I made my last bombing run and I gave the pilot, 'o.k. to turn Sir', he peeled off into something I don't know what it was, but when we leveled out we were doing over 200 mph. I was sitting right up in the nose and getting a big kick out of it.

Well, I've got to clean up and study and go to bed.

Your <u>little</u> boy,
Fred

★★★

6/24/43
Thursday afternoon
Roswell, New Mexico

Dear Mom,

Here it is 3:00 again! I always seem to get to write you at this same time.

We dropped our first bombs today. After the bombs leave the plane you just pray and mentally try to move the bomb over so it will hit where you want it to.

The Norden bombsight worked well under ideal conditions. During a mission with flak and fighters all around we didn't have ideal conditions. Under ideal conditions it was said you could drop a bomb with the Norden bombsight into a pickle barrel. In the reality of a mission that pickle barrel would have had to have been a ½ mile wide.[18]

We bombed from 4,000 feet today. That means we had a pressure altitude of 4,000 ft. and an indicated altitude of about 8,340 feet.

Two of us go up with the pilot and instructor. The other cadet bombed first today. While he was dropping his bombs I took pictures of them as they hit. We use movie cameras. You lay down on the floor of the plane and there's a hole to put the camera through.

A lot of the guys get sick from looking down through the camera hatch and stuff. One guy sure had tough luck. He exposed all his pictures, dropped something off his camera, knocked the door open, and on top of that he got sick!

I didn't do too hot, but didn't do as bad as some of 'em did. It was just practice today. In a couple of days they start counting.

You think each Saturday that next week you can relax a little, but the courses are just as hard if not harder. Boy it's hard to stay awake in the afternoon in classes. It's so hot and we're dead for sleep.

They talk about your free time! They're out of their heads!!! Here it is 4:45. We've been listening to 'Causes of Errors'. Some fun.

Sleeping in the tents isn't bad at all. A lot of fresh air.

I'll add more to this if I have time after dinner.

There's no more to add as I didn't receive a letter from you today and so there are no questions I can answer for you.

Love,
Fred

★★★

7/5/43
Monday afternoon
Roswell, New Mexico

Dear Mom,

Received both your letters today. What in the dickens made you sick, the street car? You mean to say you walked all the way from Pico and Broadway home? Boy I bet you were tired!!

How about me calling you at Mrs. Murray's sometime. You name the time on Sunday I could call. Don't forget you're an hour later there than it is here. When it's 10:00 here it's 9:00 there. Let me know.

Well I passed all the tests Saturday. I got 93%, 92%, and 81%. That means that the hardest part of ground school is over, I think. Now all we have to do is to hit our bombs in good.

We bombed from 15,400 feet today. It was slightly cold up there, plus that we wore oxygen masks. Boy that's a long way up, it's 2 miles.

This has been one of our hottest days. It's supposed to cool off in a month or so.

Had a pretty good time yesterday showing the town folks around. They still had the hay seeds in their hair.

Didn't leave the post at all Sunday. Just rested in the evening. Didn't have the ambition to go to town to see a show.

I'd like to let you know from time to time how my bombing scores are, but that's a military secret. They won't let us tell anybody. All I can say is that so far I'm under the wire. Starting tomorrow we start dropping our record bombs. We would have started sooner except for the bad weather. I keep adding to this as we have breaks between classes. After every hour we get 10 minutes to have a drink, have a coke, etc.

Say how's Gabriel Heatter lately? Or do you listen to him?

I said earlier in this letter how hot it was today, well it's 8:00 in the evening now, still plenty light and the wind is blowing, clouds and a few drops of rain.

How much do we still owe on the refrigerator? Just wondering.
Well, can't think of anymore so until next time, 'Dear John.'

Your son,
Fred

P.S. You go up and see Dr. Randel for your health and don't forget to pay him.

★★★

7/7/43
Wednesday
Roswell, New Mexico

Dear Mom,
Didn't get a letter from you yesterday but got one today.

We bombed from 15,000 feet today. Did pretty good. Tomorrow I go up solo. Oh boy, that means we have no one to blame but ourselves if anything goes wrong.

Boy was I cold today when I was taking pictures out of the camera hatch. Had on gloves, heavy flying jacket, oxygen mask and earphones. We have on more equipment than you can shake a stick at.

No, I don't have time to read the Examiner, but thanks a lot anyway.

Speaking of the picture 'Bombardier' it isn't a bit like what we do. We don't even fly in those kinds of planes. It's just a lot of horse feathers. The boys here really had a big laugh over it.

These two pages are out of a magazine. These are the kind of planes we fly in .

Well dear it's 9:00 now and I have to get to bed as 4:00 rolls around in a hurry and tomorrow is a big day.

Love,
Fred

★★★

7/13/43
Tuesday morn.
Roswell, New Mexico

Dear Mom,
Just finished breakfast. It is 9:15. We don't get up until 8:20. We get to bed at 1:00 in the morning. You know how I like that. Somebody open my eyes. Although it doesn't bother me as much this morning as it did yesterday morning.

It's really beautiful flying at night. The targets are lit up so you can see them, but I'm having a lot more trouble with night bombing than I did with day bombing.

Last night I was the second one to bomb and as I went up to the nose the pilot slapped me on the rear end. He's really a swell guy. He wanted me to do good. After I dropped my first bomb the pilot called me up and asked me whether it hit. I told him. Then he said let's get the next one in.

My eyes seem tired at night. We have just a little more time now. We start school at 2:00 in the afternoon and finish at 6:00, then fly at 8:00. In the morning we eat, drill, have athletics, etc.

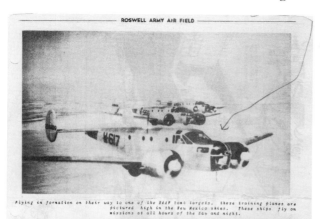

ROSWELL ARMY AIR FIELD

Flying in formation on their way to one of the RAAF bomb targets, these training planes are pictured high in the New Mexico skies. These ships fly on missions at all hours of the day and night.

'These are the kind of planes we fly in.' (From Fred's wartime scrapbook)

Post Tech Library Is Good Spot To Frequent

A valuable spot for cadets of the RAAF to visit frequently is the Technical Library. Available there are the latest manuals on technical matters concerned with bombardiering, and many detailed and inside descriptions of operations in Britian, Africa and the South Pacific.

Most of the material on the shelves of the Tech Library is confidential and some of it is secret. However, all of the manuals are available for cadets.

Bombardier School officials here are unanimous in their recognition of the value of the library. An invaluable aid to the cadet's extra-curricular education, the publications provide excellent information on enemy techniques and equipment, as well as revealing an insight into how our own equipment performs under combat conditions.

The Tech Library is located in Building #3, Area #2, directly south of the Clothing PX.

As pretty a salvo of bombs as was ever dropped is pictured here as training ships of the RAAF "lay an egg" on a target.

(From Fred's wartime scrapbook)

"He's training to be a bombardier."

(From Fred's wartime
scrapbook)

Yesterday we started navigation and bombsight maintenance in ground school. Those are the last subjects we take in ground school. They last for 3 weeks.

Well I just wanted to drop you a line so you would have word also I wanted to get this over to the post office before 10:00 so it will go out in the early mail.

Love,
Fred

★★★

Saturday July 17, 1943
Roswell, New Mexico

Dear Mom,

Here I am in bed. It's 8:45. I'm supposed to be C.Q. (Charge of Quarters) for a kid that's getting married tonight. I'm in the orderly room. There's a radio in here. You can't get anything on it hardly at all.

Talk about thunder, lightning, and rain, boy we've got it tonight. It's been hot as heck all day. Then this storm blew up tonight. I've never seen it storm as much before.

We didn't fly tonight as we fly tomorrow afternoon at 4:00 until 8:00. That's the time we'll fly for the next week. It'll be better on this new schedule.

They've been building a swimming pool here and now it's finished. Cadets can use it on Sundays.

What the heck are they digging in front of the house?

Nothing new has happened so I'll end this edition until the mail comes tomorrow (Sunday) and then I can answer your letter.

Your son,
Fred

★★★

7/19/43
Monday Evening 9:30
Roswell, New Mexico

Dear Mom,

Don't get worried if you don't get a letter from me every other day. Sometimes it's just impossible to even drop you a card. Now that we're on this schedule I can sneak out a line in the evenings. We're down at the flight line at 4:00 and get back here about 8:45. Have dinner, clean up and have about 45 minutes before lights out.

So soap and stuff is getting hard to get eh? Oh well, you poor civilians.

Nothing new has happened here since my last letter. Sunday I went swimming in our new pool here. Boy it really felt good. The first swim I've had in a long, long time. (In fact (since) last summer.)

One of the boys in our tent had word today he's the father of 6 pound 1 oz. baby girl. Boy is he happy. He lives in San Francisco.

Well I guess this week they'll really start the washing machine. Today it was really rough upstairs. We bounced all over the sky. We also ran into some clouds and rain. Just spots of them.

Well it's just starting to rain a little bit. Probably won't be much. I think we'll lose another man from our tent this week. That will leave 4 men in our tent. Oh well, that's life. Hank and I have been kidding about getting our furloughs at the same time and flying home together when we wash out. Oh well there's always the 'Fighting Finance' for we ex-bankers.

I'm glad to hear your flu is o.k. now! Those heat treatments are really good.

We had a shot for desert fever. Didn't bother me a bit. Just a precaution.

Time for lights out dear. I'll write real soon again!!!

Your boy,
Fred

★★★

7/23/43
Friday
Roswell, New Mexico

Dear Mom,
There's not much to write about this time.

Boy did I have fun yesterday. On the way back to the field the pilot let me try to fly the plane. I had it going right and left, up and down. I was a pretty sloppy pilot. They are twin-engine planes. It's a lot different than trying to fly a single engine plane.

Didn't get a letter yesterday. I'm writing this before school this morning. I'll finish it after flying this afternoon. Maybe I'll have more to add. Your letter today may have some questions for me to answer.

What do you think of my dividend check? Big, eh? Just keep the card. Put it in the safety deposit box whenever you're near the bank.

Received your letter. What's the idea of the air mail envelopes? What's the idea, you had no gossip in your letter. You're not slipping are you?

7:45 Just finished dinner.

Boy am I tired! Starting Sunday night we're on night flying again. Saturday we're going into town for dinner and a show. Sunday I'm going swimming all day here on the field. Just going to relax and take it easy.

Well dear I've got to take a shower and study and get to bed.

Write more Sunday afternoon!

Love,
Fred

P.S. Well tomorrow marks the end our 8th week here. 2/3 of the way through and just 4 weeks or 1/3 more to go.

★★★

7/27/43
Tuesday morning
Roswell, New Mexico

Dear Mom,
Just got up and waiting to go to breakfast. It's now 8:30. We didn't get to bed until 2:00 this morning. Boy was I tired and sleepy.

The whistle just blew for breakfast. Be right back.

Here I am back. Pretty good breakfast. We just finished cleaning up the tent, waiting to go to drill. After drill we have athletics, then lunch, and last but not least ground school until 6:00. I guess we'll go up to 15,000 feet again tonight. That's where we went last night. It was 4 degrees below zero.

You can hardly move around while you're taking pictures up there at night with all the junk you have on. All kinds of wires, earphones, coats, etc.

Didn't have a letter from you yesterday. Maybe this morning. (I hope so!)

We're all just praying to get through our final exams on navigation and bombsight maintenance on Saturday. Each test will last 4 hours.

It was really beautiful last night. Not a cloud in the sky. The stars were shining brightly.

We're supposed to get our uniforms out of the store this week and have them tailored. Boy that's being too optimistic on their part.

I can't think of anymore to say now, so I'll wait until your letter gets here.

Just received both of your letters mailed on the 24th .

Boy it looks as if Italy is finished.

Needless to say, this is a one-topic city today. Some Londoners heard late last night, and the rest of them early this morning, the news that Hitler's 'utensil,' (Mussolini) as the British Broadcasting Company's announcer disdainfully phrased it, had fallen off the Axis shelf. Although it is far too early for anyone to say what the news will mean to the Allied timetable, it's safe to guess that most families will be bringing out the monthly ration of Scotch tonight to celebrate what to even the most cautious looks like the beginning of the end.[19]

Well dear I'm out of news. So until next time, 'Dear John.'

> *Love,*
> *Fred*

★★★

8/1/43
Sunday morning
Roswell, New Mexico

Dear Mom,
Waiting for the mail. Got a nice long letter from you yesterday. Went into town last night for dinner and a show. Had a <u>big</u>, juicy, K.C. steak. (Jealous?)

Well if I graduate, when you get here I'll take you and we'll have one. It's at Mrs. Lu's place. It's the best place in town (clean and very cool).

This week we fly in the afternoons and next week it will be from 11:30 at night until 3:15 in the morning (you'll see I'll enjoy that).

The graduating class sure looked sharp yesterday. We're the upper classmen now. Boy we'd have given anything to be in their shoes!!

I can't say yet as to when you should start for New Mexico. If I get by this next week then you can get your train ticket. You can always cancel it if anything happens.

There also might be the chance of you coming here with Hank's dad and mom. They're driving here I'm pretty sure.

I see by the paper coffee is going to be off the ration list. That will suit our family.

You're quite a bit early on that Lieutenant Fred S. Lull stuff. We haven't graduated yet and even if we do we don't know if we'll be 2nd Lts. or Flight Officers.

Today we have to go down to the trainer building for 4 hours to learn how to work a different type of bombsight used for low altitude bombings. Sometime this week we'll bomb from 500 feet.

Sounds as if it's really getting hot at home. It's good for your cold and stuff. Have you seen Doctor Randel lately? Tell him and Mrs. McNerney hello for me please!

They give us $250.00 for uniforms when we graduate. So far I've spent $180.40, that leaves $69.60 I can use later on. We don't get the dough until the day of graduation.

I didn't send as much this time as I may need a little more (don't think so, though). So if you need more you know what to do!!

I think pretty soon it's about time for our safe deposit box rent to come due. It's only about $2.00. You had better ask about it next time you're in there.

Evening: (9:25)
Just got back from town. Hank, two other fellows and myself went into town for a show. After the show we went into one of the local drugstores and had light refreshments. We all had large root beers and pineapple sundaes. What a mixture!

Hank was saying tonight that his dad and mom will drive here and you can come with them. I'll know more later on so I'll let you know as soon as possible.

This Roswell is really a dead town. There's not a darn thing to do. You know, I haven't had a sick day since I had my shots at Santa Ana. I weigh 160 pounds.

Hank is sitting here in our tent writing his letters.

Gosh, I've run out of news so until your letter gets here tomorrow I'll end for now.

Love,
Fred

P.S. I can hardly wait to see you!!!

★★★

8/3/43
Tuesday morning
Roswell, New Mexico

Hi Dear,
I wrote you yesterday so I'm just starting this one. I'll mail it tomorrow morning.

Had a swell letter from Dan yesterday. His darn letter had me almost on the floor. I laughed so hard, thought I'd split a rib. You know how he can make me laugh.

Glad to hear Dr. Randel is going to give you a good physical check-up. Boy I bet he is busy.

I didn't fly yesterday as we had a little mechanical trouble. I'm quite a bit behind in dropping bombs. The Flight Commander was kidding me yesterday about it. He said we'd have to look up a B-17 and let me drop all my bombs at once. The kidding aside, though, I'll probably have to fly 2 missions a day pretty soon to catch up.

This is all I can think of for now so until tonight or when your letter gets here, 'Hasta la vista.'

Later: Your airmail letter just came. Boy it looked like a book. Your sleeping pills are doing you some good.

I always liked your ironing myself. Nobody could iron shirts like you did.

Oh, as for my final grades, I got 95% in bombsight maintenance and 87% in navigation.

How about calling Sunday, August 8th at 10:00 in the morning (your time)? The time here will be 11:00.

I don't understand what you meant by the statement, 'does it feel good to be that cold after all the heat.'

Hank told his mom and dad not to come here because it's so indefinite what we do after graduation. By that I mean we have to wait for orders after graduation on Saturday morning. You don't know what or where they are going to send us – to navigation school, instructor school, furlough or not. The class that graduated before the last class got only 3 days. This last class got 10 days. You don't know what you're going to get. The reason he told them not to come is that if we get 10 days he can get home quicker than they can get here by car. Also, he'll have more time with them at home. He also told them if they didn't come here and he didn't get 10 days they could come to see him then at his new station as soon as he got there. It's up to you to decide what you want to do. If you want me to come home it would be a lot easier for you also I could get home quicker. Another thing, if we don't get 10 day furloughs then I'm having you come here to live. If we graduate I'll try to get an airplane home, either an army plane or regular airlines. Please let me know what you think is best and what you want to do. I might know more later on.

Love,
Fred

★★★

Dear Mom,

Just a few lines tonight. Right now we're in night school. We have to go tomorrow night and next week also. Don't know for how long. We go from 7:00 until 9:00. In the mornings we have skeet shooting from 8:15 until 11:30. Boy it's a lot of fun.

Today on the way out to the target the pilot asked me if I wanted to fly. I said o.k. and I put in the rudder pedals on the co-pilot's side and locked in the stick and took over. On the way home he let me fly. Boy do I stink. Our radio went out so he asked me if I thought I could keep the plane straight and level. I said I thought I could so he climbed out of his seat and went to the back of the plane to see if he could fix the radio. Can you imagine me sitting all by myself up in the front trying to fly a two engine plane? Well, I did it for a few minutes. He had me trying turns, etc. I wished they would have made me a pilot. I'll learn to fly some day.

Been pretty hot the last few days. Last night it thundered a little, just a little rain.

The navigator school in Sacramento is for Celestial Navigation. That's for the cadets that are going to be navigators. We're just going to learn dead reckoning navigation.

So Doctor Randel is expecting a baby eh?

Well dear this isn't much of a letter. It's just a few lines of the latest news

Well, I'm looking forward to our telephone conversation Sunday.

Your boy,
Fred

★★★

Dear Mom,

Just a few lines before night school begins. Received both of your letters today. One regular and one airmail.

Night school begins at 7:00 and is over at 9:00. We go back to the tents and rest awhile and at 10:30 we fall out for the flight line. We get back at about 4:00 have breakfast and go to bed. By then it's about 4:30. We get up at about 8:30 or 9:00, have lunch at 12:00, then skeet shooting from 1:00 until 4:00. After that we have athletics and dinner. Then it starts all over again.

This was not sport shooting or target practice at the local country club or shooting range. From simple trap shooting, where the clay plates always flew in the same direction, they moved on to skeet shooting, where the target moved at different elevations, rising and falling, moving away from them. Instructors taught them how to stand, aim, how to lead a flying target. Those who had grown up learning to hunt pheasants in the field had an easier time of it. The basis for this training was held in the belief that if you could hit a moving target with a shotgun, you could bring down an enemy plane.[20]

We've been pretty busy. This night school is the nuts.

Just got home from night school and am going to rest for a few minutes.

Later: 8:30 in the morning.
Fresh as a daisy this morning.

We have to fly today at noon besides tonight again. Boy are they keeping us busy winding up our bombs. We're flying day and night now.

Can hardly wait for a week from Saturday. Just looking forward to coming home. We'll have a good time fooling around.

Gosh there's nothing much to write about as we're on the go constantly.

So if I don't write as often in the next week you'll know why. Anyway it won't be long before I'll be seeing you.

We're just getting ready to go to the flight line now. Then we have to go again at 11:00 tonight. You can't win!!!

Time is flying (not fast enough though!!). More later!!

Love,
Fred

P.S. You got my last money order didn't you?

Chapter Four

Officer, Gentleman, Bombardier

WESTERN UNION TELEGRAMS

AUGUST 15, 1943 5:21 AM
DEAR MOM JUST FOUND OUT TODAY ILL BE A
SECOND LIEUTENANT IF I GRADUATE MY INSTRUCTOR
TOLD ME HE RECOMMENDED ME FOR AN INSTRUCTOR THAT
DOESN'T MEAN ILL GET IT BUT IT'S A CHANCE LOVE=FRED.

AUGUST 20
DEAR SON MY THOUGHTS ARE WITH YOU TODAY
I AM WAITING FOR YOU ALL MY LOVE=MOM.

AUGUST 20
DEAR FRED THIS IS A GREAT DAY HOPE TO SEE
YOU SOON KEEP EM FLYING= BLUE AND NEVA

AUGUST 20
DEAR FRED WISH WE COULD BE WITH YOU, BUT WE
ARE ALL THINKING OF YOU AND WISH YOU ALL THE
LUCK IN THE WORLD. LOTS OF LOVE= TOPS

AUGUST 20
LOOKING FORWARD TO YOUR BEING HOME AGAIN BEST OF
EVERYTHING I KNOW YOU MADE IT LOVE=AUNTIE ROSIE.

The Roswell Army Flying School

of

Roswell, New Mexico

announces the graduation of

Bombardier Class 43-12

Saturday morning, August twenty-first

nineteen hundred and forty-three

at ten o'clock

Post Theater

Fred A. Lull 2nd Lt. a c

HEADQUARTERS
ARMY AIR FORCES WEST COAST TRAINING CENTER
1104 West Eighth Street
Santa Ana, California

21 August 1943

SUBJECT: Temporary Appointment

TO: Second Lieutenant FRED STUART LULL
       Army of the United States
       (Los Angeles, California)
       RAAF, Roswell, New Mexico

1. The Secretary of War has directed me to inform you that
   the President has appointed and commissioned you a
   temporary Second Lieutenant, Army of the United States,
   effective this date.
2. This commission will continue in force during the
   pleasure of the President of the United States for the
   time being, and for the duration of the war and six
   months thereafter unless sooner terminated.

By command Major General COUSINS:
>   (signed)
>   THOS. A. LEE,
>   Major, Air Corps
>   Actg. Asst. Adjutant General

HEADQUARTERS
ROSWELL ARMY AIR FIELD
Roswell, New Mexico

21 August 1943

By direction of the President, ea of the fol-named Aviation Cadets having completed the prescribed course of tng at the Roswell Army Air Field, Roswell, New Mexico, upon acceptance of his apmt as 2nd Lt (AUS), is asgd to Duty with the AC, and is with his consent ordered to Active Duty at the Roswell Army Air Field, effective 21 August 43, and will remain on Active Duty until reld. by competent orders. Ea Officer will rank fr 21 August 43.

Lull, Fred Stuart
(others)
>   By order of Colonel HORTON
>   A.S. Fetterman,
>   1st Lt., Air Corps,
>   Assistant Adjutant.

HEADQUARTERS
ARMY AIR FORCES WEST COAST TRAINING CENTER
1104 West 8th Street, Santa Ana, California

21 August 1943

PERSONNEL ORDERS

NO. 45

EXTRACT

Pursuant to authority contained in Paragraph 8 a (1) (B) AAF Regulation 50-7, 5 February 1943, the following-named Second Lieutenants, Army of the United States (Air Corps), graduates of Class WC 43-12, AAF bombardier School, Roswell Army Air Field, Roswell, New Mexico, are rated Air Observer (Bombardier) under the provisions of Army Regulation 95-60, 20 August 1942, and Paragraph 3 k (2) (a), AAF Regulation 50-7, 5 February 1943.

Fred Stuart Lull
(others)

By Command of Major General COUSINS

HEADQUARTERS
ROSWELL ARMY AIR FIELD
ROSWELL, NEW MEXICO

21 Aug 43

The fol-named Officers (2nd Lts unless otherwise indicated),
AC, graduates of 12-week course in Bombardier Tng, are reld
from asgd this sta, are asgd and WP on 21 Aug 43 to 29th GP,
Gowan Fld, Boise, Idaho, rptg upon arrival to the CO thereat
for asgmt and dy. A ten (10) day lv is auth but in no event
will Officers rpt later than 2400 4 Sept 43. Ea o will have on
his person his Officers' Identification Car (WD AGO 65-1), two
(2) copies ea of his travel orders, flying status orders, and
aeronautical rating orders for presentation to appropriate
individual at new sta.

LULL, FRED S.
(others)

By order of Colonel HORTON:
RICHARD M. BECKER,
Captain, Air Corps,
Adjutant

Somewhere in the crowd of newly commissioned second lieutenants, their friends
and family there was probably heard full throttle with the crowd, or perhaps as a
quiet whisper to oneself, or only in someone's head:

Off we go into the wild blue yonder, climbing high into the sun; Here they
come, zooming to meet our thunder, At 'em boys, Give 'er the gun![1]

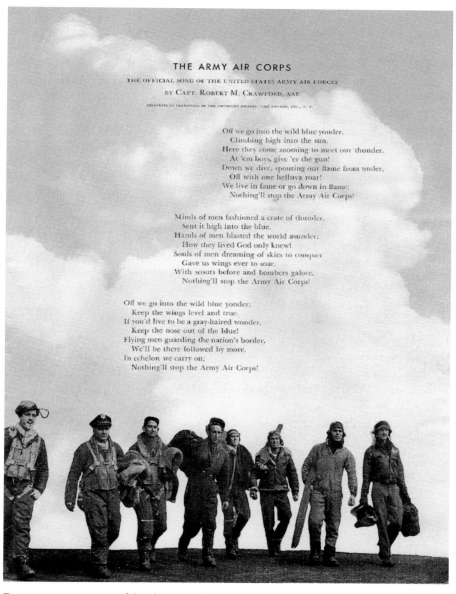

THE ARMY AIR CORPS

THE OFFICIAL SONG OF THE UNITED STATES ARMY AIR FORCES

BY CAPT. ROBERT M. CRAWFORD, AAF

REPRINTED BY PERMISSION OF THE COPYRIGHT OWNER, CARL FISCHER, INC., N. Y.

Off we go into the wild blue yonder,
Climbing high into the sun.
Here they come zooming to meet our thunder,
At 'em boys, give 'er the gun!
Down we dive, spouting our flame from under,
Off with one helluva roar!
We live in fame or go down in flame;
Nothing'll stop the Army Air Corps!

Minds of men fashioned a crate of thunder,
Sent it high into the blue.
Hands of men blasted the world asunder;
How they lived God only knew!
Souls of men dreaming of skies to conquer
Gave us wings ever to soar.
With scouts before and bombers galore,
Nothing'll stop the Army Air Corps!

Off we go into the wild blue yonder;
Keep the wings level and true.
If you'd live to be a gray-haired wonder,
Keep the nose out of the blue!
Flying men guarding the nation's border.
We'll be there followed by more.
In echelon we carry on;
Nothing'll stop the Army Air Corps!

From programme notes of the play *Winged Victory*.[2]

Chapter Five

Advanced Flight Training

9/4/43
Saturday night
Boise

Dear Mom,

Just a few lines to let you know what I know so far. As for the situation here I don't know a thing as yet. All I know is that it is B-24s instead of B-17s. The big plane I pointed out to you at Lockheed Friday was a B-24.

The town of Boise is a quiet little burg. After we took off Friday we were in Las Vegas 1 hr. and 30 minutes, then 2 hours later we were in Salt Lake City. It was a swell plane trip. Several people got air sick. (I don't mean it was swell because they got sick.)

We had to take the train from Salt Lake City to Boise. Boy what a train-ride. It took us 16 (14?) hours. We left at 12:00 midnight and got into Boise at 2:00 the next afternoon. We had a chair car so didn't sleep very well.

There's nothing more to add until I find out more tomorrow. So, good night dear.

Love,
Fred

P.S.: HBC means heavy bombardment crew. You can shorten Bombardment to Bomb.

★★★

9/5/43
Sunday
Boise

Dear Mom,

Here's the latest news. This morning we got up at about 8:00, had breakfast, and then started having papers and stuff signed. Boy I never saw so many things to be signed. Then we had our physical examination and had 3 shots. I got faint and a little sweaty, but I was o.k. though. (sissy!)

This Officers' Club is really sharp!

We'll only be here for 2 weeks at the most as far as I know. Here we get our crews together and then go to our first phase training station not very (far) from here.

The reason I'm writing in pencil is that I'm out of ink. Please send a bottle of Parker '51' (Blue) to me.

The food is really good. Served to us any time we like.

Boy does the wind and dust blow here. Just as bad as Roswell. Kind of chilly in the mornings and evenings.

We'll get our travel money tomorrow. I'm going to send it home in the form of a cashiers check so you can put it in the bank.

You never saw so many officers in all your life as there are here. Pilots, Bombardiers and Navigators.

From what I could see, Boise isn't much of a town!!

I'll write more soon.

> *Love,*
> *Fred*

P.S. Gene and I are in the same room.

★★★

> *9/7/43*
> *Tuesday night*
> *Boise*

Dear Mom,

Just a few lines as I'm all tired out tonight. We went to school last night from 6:00 until 12:00, then got up at 5:00 and spent the whole day out on the gunnery range. All day tomorrow will be spent out there also.

Have to go to a lecture on military intelligence tomorrow night, also a motion picture on the B-24. After learning to bomb with a Norden Bombsight they sent us here to bomb from B-24s. They have Sperry Bombsights. That means we have to learn plenty of new things. Some fun!

Frustrated. Perhaps even angry. Certainly disappointed. More than anything, Fred wanted to fly B-17s. If not that, then he wanted to be a bombardier in a B-17. So,

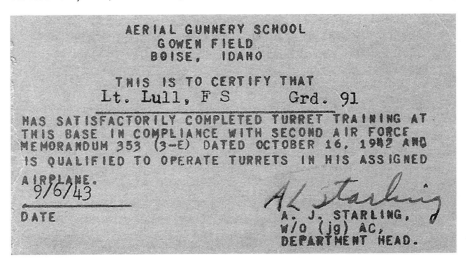

AERIAL GUNNERY SCHOOL
GOWEN FIELD
BOISE, IDAHO

THIS IS TO CERTIFY THAT

Lt. Lull, F S   Grd. 91

HAS SATISFACTORILY COMPLETED TURRET TRAINING AT THIS BASE IN COMPLIANCE WITH SECOND AIR FORCE MEMORANDUM 353 (3-E) DATED OCTOBER 16, 1942 AND IS QUALIFIED TO OPERATE TURRETS IN HIS ASSIGNED AIRPLANE.

9/6/43
_____
DATE

A. J. STARLING,
W/O (jg) AC,
DEPARTMENT HEAD.

after extensive flight and ground school instruction, his feelings about going to the B-24 and its Sperry bombsight are palpable.

The differences between the B-24 and the B-17 couldn't have seemed greater – the B-24 had short stubby wings placed high on the fuselage as compared to the B-17. Looking at it from the side, the B-24 seemed fat and clumsy and reminded some of a pregnant guppy. It had a triangle landing gear with twin tails sticking up in the air and doors that slid up the into the sides of the bomb bay like the front of a roll-top desk. But, it had a larger bomb-carrying capacity than the B-17 and, with a greater range, was able to penetrate further into enemy territory on its bombing missions. Although dubbed by some as the 'Flying Boxcar' or the 'Flying Coffin', it was vigorously defended by its crews against those who would dare to suggest that the B-17 was a better aircraft.

This check is part of the dough they gave me for my trip. They gave me $126.00 in all.

I'm having an allotment made to you starting October 1st. That means you'll get it Nov. 1st. It's going to the bank to go into our account. It's for you. Do as you wish. It's for $175.00. It's the best thing to have it go to the bank as it won't get lost or something if it were mailed to you.

A military allotment is a portion of the serviceman's salary that is automatically sent to someone of his choice, often a spouse, but in Fred's case his mother. Fred is concerned about his mother's financial status and their joint bank accounts and makes frequent reference to them.

Over 29,350 heavy bomber crews were formed … (with crew members) receiving a base pay, to which could be added flying pay and foreign-service pay. In 1945, a technical sergeant made $114 a month; with flying pay added, that went up to $171. Total pay for service overseas came to $193.80 a month. A captain earned $200.00 per month; if he flew, his pay climbed to $300.00. On foreign service, the total could be $320.00.[1]

This form is for you to fill out and have <u>notarized</u>. Guys that are married get it without having this form, but others have to have it filled out. It means about $80.00 more a month.

I filled in some stuff on this form in pencil, you can write it in ink then erase the pencil neatly. For the 2 people that you have to give their names, use someone who knows I've supported you. We need 2 people. Just do your best on filling it out then send it back to me after having it <u>notarized</u>. O.K.?

Well dear I've run out of news for now.

Oh, I may send my shoes home to be half-soled. Can't depend on them here. I may move before they have them finished.

Love,
Fred

★★★

9/10/43
Friday Afternoon
Boise

Dear Mom,
I was getting a little worried as I hadn't heard from you, but your letter came today. It took your letter 2 days to get here. It was a small book.
   I thought you would like 'My Friend Flicka'. It was beautiful color and horses, etc.
   How do you like the sound of the war news? I was sure surprised to hear that Italy quit.
   This makes the end closer and saves a lot of lives.

The capitulation of Italy could scarcely have come as much of a surprise, especially after Benito Mussolini, the Italian Prime Minister, had been overthrown nearly six weeks earlier.

Last night I went to the show with some of the fellows to see 'This Is The Army.' Thought it was better this time especially the 'Stage Door Canteen' number. (It's the one with the impersonations of Charles Boyer and Herbert Marshall, Lynn Fontaine, and Alfred Lunt, and Jane Cowell).

This is the Army, the government's own show written by Irving Berlin, was a monumental effort to shift from musical low gear to militant high gear. Designed, produced and plugged for 'morale,' it included a number of march tunes ... But the big hit of the show turned out to be 'I Left My Heart at the Stage Door Canteen,' a love song of the boy-meets-girl variety.[2]

I left my heart at the Stage Door Canteen;
I left it there with a girl named Eileen.
I kept her serving doughnuts
Till all she had were gone;
I sat there dunking doughnuts
Till she caught on.[3]

Today I went up in the pressure chamber. We went up to 38,000 feet. I was o.k. this time. You remember I didn't get over 5,000 feet in Santa Ana.
   Did you know civilians can only eat 2 meals a day on the train. Breakfast and dinner, no lunch.
   This evening I have to go on the bomb trainer to learn how the Sperry sight works.
   Can't get over the way we are fed here. Everything is so clean and our beds are made for us also. Tough eh?
   They have slot machines here. I've lost about $2.00, but I matched some of the boys and won $4.50. That's the extent of my gambling.
   I'll probably know how long I'll be here as soon as I get assigned to a squadron.
   It's been kinda hot the last couple of days.

'Dear John,' this is all for today, so until next time,

> Love,
> Fred

★★★

9/24/43
Friday
Boise

Dear Mom,

From what you say the weather is changing. From hot to cold and vice-versa.

My pen got there in pretty good time. I sent it Friday or Sat. and you got it on Wednesday.

You did the right thing dear about getting the pen fixed! That's swell what they're going to do about it, make the ink flow better and put in a new point. I guess you really talked them into fixing it in a hurry.

Still no news dear only I have the bomb trainer tomorrow night (Saturday) from 7:00 to 11:30 in the evening.

Gene flew last night until 4:30 this morning also he flew yesterday. Guess he dropped about 40 bombs. He's really busy.

I won't mail this yet. Add more later and mail it tomorrow (Saturday) because you won't get it until Monday anyway.

Saturday morning:

Just finished talking with you. It just took about 3 minutes to get you. It sure sounds good to hear your voice! Even if we don't have anything to say it makes me feel good just to hear you!

I got up this morning at 6:30. Gad, what a terrible hour. It is dark at that time.

Yesterday we saw 'My Kingdom for a Cook' with Charles Coburn. It was a pretty good comedy. As I told you on the phone I always like Marjorie Main.

I'll finish this when the mail gets here.

We're going to listen to the Notre-Dame/Pittsburgh game today. U.S.C. is playing U.C.L.A. also today. How about sending me the sport page of the Herald Monday? Monday is the day the write up will be about the game.

Gosh that haze and gas must be bad! That really effects your asthma.

Well dear this is all for now.

> Love,
> Fred

★★★

10/2/43
Saturday
Boise

Dear Mom,

Thank you for sending the picture and getting a frame for it.

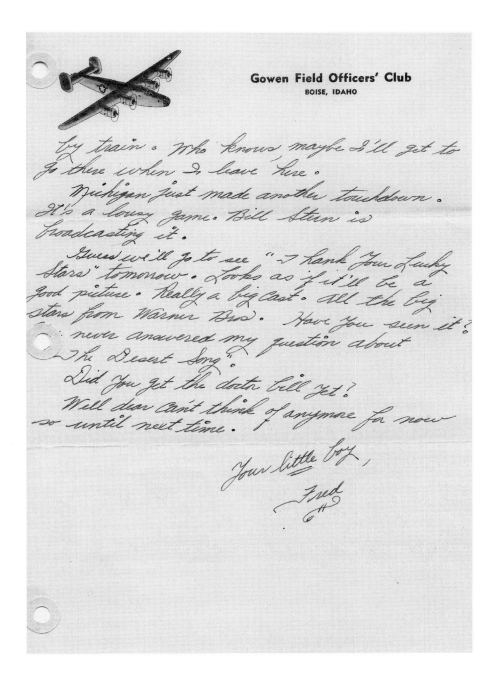

Gowen Field Officers' Club
BOISE, IDAHO

by train. Who knows, maybe I'll get to go there when I leave here.

Michigan just made another touchdown. It's a lousy game. Bill Stern is broadcasting it.

Guess we'll go to see "Thank Your Lucky Stars" tomorrow. Looks as if it'll be a good picture. Really a big cast. All the big stars from Warner Bros. Have you seen it? You never answered my question about "The Desert Song".

Did you get the doctor bill yet?

Well dear can't think of anymore for now so until next time.

Your little boy,

Fred
6th

Received my pen Thursday afternoon. Been going to school for the last few mornings. It's all on navigation. As I said before I'll probably be assigned before long.

My dear, I'm going to be on a B-24 Liberator, not a B-25 Mitchell. The picture on this paper is a B-24.

Right now the Northwestern/Michigan game is on. U.S.C. plays California today at Berkeley. Be sure and send the paper (sport section) from Monday's paper.

It's a cloudy day. Maybe it's going to rain. Sure hope so, but it hardly ever rains here, so they say. It's still plenty hot however. Yesterday it was about 100 degrees. The mornings and nights are really cold.

Yesterday afternoon another fellow and I went into town and bought things. I bought a trench coat ($18.00), a flight cap (to you an overseas cap). We had a lousy dinner and then went to a show. It was also lousy. (Deanna Durbin in 'Hers to Hold'.)

Gene left yesterday morning for California. I told you it was Muroc Dry Lakes. He should get there Sunday sometime. He went by train. Who knows, maybe I'll get to go there when I leave here.

Michigan just made another touchdown. It's a lousy game. Bill Stern is broadcasting it.

Guess we'll go to see 'Thank Your Lucky Stars' tomorrow. Looks as if it'll be a good picture. Really a big cast. All the big stars from Warner Bros. Have you seen it? You never answered my question about 'The Desert Song.'

Did you get the doctor bill yet?

Well dear can't think of anymore for now so until next time.

Your <u>little</u> boy,
Fred

★★★

October 12, 1943
Tuesday morning
Boise

Dear Mom,

Just a few lines to bring you up to date on the situation here.

Yesterday we had a hot rumor about being moved out of here. It was unexpected. So we got going to find out if it was true. Found out that it was. So the first thing I did was to call you up so you wouldn't start for here. We don't know where we're going yet, only rumors. Some of the places are, California, Washington, Florida, and the East Coast. We'll know tomorrow morning (Wednesday) at 8:00. We're supposed to leave Thursday as far as I know now.

Gee I hate to disappoint you. Imagine you were all set to leave, etc. Grady answered the phone. He said you were leaving Tuesday (today). Boy I found out just in time and stopped you just in time also!!

I'll let you know as soon as possible where I'm going to be.

Received my longies yesterday. Thank you for sending them!!

Boy the last few days have been really cold. An icy gale blowing plus some rain. Last night and this morning there was plenty of frost.

Sure hope we go to California or Washington. You'd like Washington, wouldn't you?

There's no use in answering this letter or writing to me until I arrive at my new field.

Oh, before I forget I got a swell leather jacket yesterday. It's the best thing they issue.
Last night Ted and I saw the picture 'Claudia' on the post. It was a very good picture.
The other day we saw Betty Grable in 'Sweet Rosie O'Grady.' Pretty good.

Guess this means another train ride.

Guess my summer clothes are home by now. That takes a lot of weight out of my stuff.

Well dear can't think of anymore for now so until you hear from me.

Love,
Fred

P.S. You'll probably hear from me before you get this letter.

★★★

WESTERN UNION TELEGRAM:

1943 OCT 13
DEAR MOM NEW ADDRESS IS 395TH BOMB GP H EPHRATA
WASHINGTON LETTER SOON LOVE=FRED

★★★

10/13/43
Wednesday

Dear Mom,
Once more I start a log of my journeys. Lull's travelog!!

Let's start with yesterday. Nothing happened as usual except we went to the show and then I washed my hair, took a shower and read the 'Shadow' magazine before I went to sleep. This morning we had a meeting at the Officers' Club to find out where we were going and what time we were leaving and arriving. Found out it was Ephrata, Washington. Looked at a map and it seems to be in the middle of the state. We leave tomorrow (Thursday) at noon and should arrive Friday sometime. We go by Pullman. Besides going for nothing we collect .05 cents per mile which should come to around $30.00 or there abouts. That's not hard to take.

I'll probably have a letter when I arrive there because I sent you a telegram this morning about 11:00 and you should have it around noon time.

I'm sure glad I found out in time to stop you from coming here. That would have been good, you coming here and me going farther up into the great northwest.

Spend all summer in the desert and now they send us north for the winter. Boy I bet it's going to be cold!!

There was a change in plans – Fred goes to bed expecting to head north-west to Ephrata, Washington, and wakes up to find that he is heading south-east through Denver.

Friday night:
Please excuse this writing from now on as we're on the train.

It always sounds good to hear your voice on the phone!

Yesterday afternoon we went into town and saw 'Stage Door Canteen'. It was really a good picture!! Came back to the field early. Finished packing and went to bed early. Got up this morning early, we were down at the depot at 11:00 and the train left at 12:30. Boy you can have my share of this train riding. It's now 9:00 and we haven't gone very far. We're supposed to be in Denver around noon tomorrow. These train companies really clean up on their meals and stuff.

We've been playing Hearts all evening. Got a letter from you yesterday. It was the one you were telling about getting your ticket and coming by bus. So far there hasn't been any good scenery. Isn't this writing terrible. Hope you can read it

It was with heavy heart we bid a reluctant farewell to the enchanted land of Idaho. (Who's kidding).

Well Mom, this is all there is for now. Will start in again tomorrow.

Saturday Morning 9:00
Just got up a little while ago and had breakfast. Boy this train food is lousy. Don't think I'll eat any lunch. Everybody is running to the toilet this morning. That dinner last night must have done it. It was chicken fricassee. Right now the train is stopped here somewhere in Wyoming. It stops every so many minutes.

If I ever have my choice of traveling it will never be by train. Bus or airplane or car. Trains are so dirty also.

We have 2 Pullman cars therefore we're luckier than most of 'em. There are some cars up in front with Sailors and some cars behind us with enlisted men. Of the whole bunch we're the best off.

Someone said the airfield we're going to is near a town by the name of Gene Autry. I think that's about 12 miles out of Ardmore.

We got into Denver last night (Sat.) about 5:30. We had an hour there so I dropped you a card. I already told you what a swell dinner we had there. A real big steak. Denver was the best town we have been in. Nothing more happened during the night. Played Hearts and went to bed about 10:30. Had a stopover of about 5 hours during the night.

When we woke up this morning we were hooked onto a fast passenger car. Boy it was really o.k. The dining car was very nice plus it had all the modern streamlined cars on it. We only stayed with that train until we arrived in Newton, Kansas where they hooked us onto the rear of another train. That's all we've been doing, getting hooked onto the rear of other trains.

On the train out of Denver there were 3 cars of cadets going to Santa Ana. Boy they were really eager to find out about Santa Ana.

Sent you another card from Newton, Kansas today (Sunday).

Had another good steak dinner here also.

Pardon, but the porter just came around to make up the berth. I'll finish this later.

Monday morning:
Here I am again dear. Went through Oklahoma City last night about 11:30. It's just 11:45 in the morning now. We arrived here this morning at 4:00. They had trucks to pick us up. The train stopped at a town called Gene Autry. It has about 50 people or so. It's about

1 mile from the air base. As far as I know the town of Ardmore is about 10 miles from here. Boy we're really out in the sticks here. The ground is all red clay. You know how that is! Don't know anything about it yet.

This field hasn't been in use for a long time. 65 pilots arrived here a day ago. We arrived today (65 bombardiers). Tomorrow 65 navigators are supposed to get here. There are only 3 B-17s here so far. They are moving plenty more down here from Washington.

As you can gather things are very unsettled here. Nothing is certain. We'll probably sit around here for sometime before doing anything. Everyone here is very nice.

Well dear I want to get this in the mail so you will hear from me. Will write more real soon!!!

> *Love,*
> *Fred*

It is probable that Fred meets his pilot, Alfred (Al) Manz, and navigator, Richard (Dick) Webb, at this base. In the letters that follow, he refers to both by name.

> *10/19/43*
> *Tuesday*
> *Ardmore, Oklahoma*

Dear Mom,

There's nothing new to write yet. We had a physical examination this morning and haven't done a darn thing since.

Boy this base isn't up to what we've had at Boise. The Officers' Club isn't half as big or as nice. No stationary or anything. I'll have to speak to the general about that. The wind blows here quite a bit. It's nice and green around here must rain quite a bit.

Gene Autry has his ranch right next to the base. Of course he isn't here now. Looks as if it would be quite a nice place.

Went into the town of Ardmore yesterday afternoon to pick up my luggage. It looks like a pretty good-sized town.

Called up the U.S.O. today and asked them about apts. and rooms. All apts. are gone, there are some rooms left. Going in tomorrow and see about getting one for you. If I can, you can get your reservation to come here. I'll let you know.

Dependents would sometimes follow their husbands or sons to the training bases, especially if the men were to be stationed there for some time. Because the air bases were often away from major cities and towns, housing for the dependents was difficult to secure, at best, and the living conditions were less than amicable:

> We don't take our training all in one place, you know. Every six seeks or so we move on. Sometimes the field is near a big town, and if it is, the town is jammed. Sometimes the field is smack out in the middle of the desert and the town is just a collection of shacks. You'd be living in tourist camps and flea-bitten hotels. You'd be alone all week – just sitting and waiting for those four hours we could have together – maybe. It's no good, Dot. It's a rotten life, believe me. I won't let you do it.[4]

Well my little petunia, you flower of the South. How do you like that stuff? I've got to get an interpreter. As I sit here among the honeysuckle drinking mint juleps (is this me talking?).

I think it's pretty warm here.

Darn it all they've still got slot machines here. They must know my weakness.

Did I tell you this used to be a glider base.

Guess in another week they will be moving in lots of planes. You know I always wanted B-17s. Now don't tell me you don't know what B-17s look like!

Fred

Think the reason they shipped us out of Boise is that the Colonel couldn't find a place to sit down in the Officers' Club on account of us loafers.

P.S. Now to get down to some serious loafing. Our time is two hours different now. When it's 10:00 there it's 12:00 here.

There is a sense of relief in this letter. Fred will get his wish fulfilled – assignment to a B-17, and it looks like there is a possibility that Louise will be moving to the area, at least temporarily, while he is in training at Ardmore.

Chapter Six

Rattlesnake Bomber Base and Beyond

Fred's base prior to the following letters was in Ardmore, Oklahoma. There are no letters from Fred to his mother during his almost three-week stay there, 18 October 1943 to 7 November 1943. It seems as though his mother was able to make her way to Ardmore and that Fred was able to find someplace for her to stay, although there is no correspondence to this effect – except for a brief reference in a letter dated '11/7/43'. The first several letters appear to have been sent to Mom who stayed in Ardmore for a time after Fred was sent to Pyote Army Air Base, Texas.

11/7/43
Sunday night
Pyote, Texas

Dear Mom,
This is the first chance I've had to write today. We didn't take off until 9:00 this morning. Boy was it a cold trip!. It took us 2 hrs. and 35 min. to get here (Pyote Army Air Base, Pyote, Texas).

Boy you've never seen such an isolated place as this is. Boy there's nothing here. It gets worse and worse! (If possible.)

A sign on the base made all aware of the ominous danger of this 'isolated place':

BEWARE RATTLESNAKES

1. WEAR BOOTS OR HIGH-TOP SHOES OR LEGGINGS
2. WEAR PROTECTIVE GLOVES
3. WATCH WHERE YOU STEP
4. WATCH WHERE YOU REACH[1]

Pyote Army Air Base became known as Rattlesnake Bomber Base for obvious reasons:

When the dust cleared some four months after the initial construction phase had commenced in September, the Suggs Company and the Corps of Engineers had created a full-fledged city where only snakes and jackrabbits had recently dwelled.[2]

One veteran of the base building period in late 1942 recalled that it became a daily routine to scrape up what remained of the snakes after bulldozer's blades and jittery men with shovels had dispatched them by the hour. Once placed in huge piles, the snakes' carcasses would be liberally soaked with a combination of diesel oil and gasoline and then set afire.[3]

Isn't this sloppy writing. Sitting on my bed.

As far as I can gather the closest town is called Monahan and is 17 miles away. Don't know what it's like. Will try and find out tomorrow all about it. Just what there is there, etc.

Fred consistently misspells the name of the town, 'Monahan', omitting the 's'. His distaste for Texas in general and Monahans specifically apparently knew few bounds.

You should get this letter Tuesday as it's too late tonight for it to go out.

When we arrived here we had a million papers to fill out and other stuff to do. They also gave us another big physical examination and I had a typhoid booster shot. Gosh, there's not much to write or say as I just left you last night. I hated leaving you there after you making that long trip and only getting to stay a little over a week. I know it's hard on you, but look at it this way, you got to see me and it did me good to see you. But if I know you feel bad and get yourself all worked up it gets me just as bad as it does you.

There are some things you can't control, Fred, one of those being how your mother feels. She will remember the articles she's read in the newspapers about the loss of planes and their crews and she'll 'feel bad' and will get herself 'all worked up'. She will remember the pictures of bombers in the air she may have seen in the newspapers or *Life* magazine and will know that you are in one of them, perhaps in mortal danger. Those feelings will create a sense of foreboding of the dreaded telegram from the War Department telling her that her son is injured, dead or a prisoner of war. She will carry those feelings everywhere, and she will 'feel bad' and will get herself 'all worked up.'

Don't worry Mom. Don't worry Mom.

I'll write tomorrow again. I'll probably find out more by then. So for now just sit tight until I find out.

Good night.

Love,
Fred

★★★

11/8/43
Monday night
Pyote, Texas

Dear Mom,

Just got back from town. (Pardon me if I call it a town.) Monahan is dirty — you've never seen anything quite like it. I walked around and didn't see anything at all. The town of Pyote is even worse if that's possible.

Didn't do a darn thing today. That shot yesterday kinda made me feel not quite up to snuff today.

We'll probably get going in a day or so. They give you one day off every nine days. They also work night and day here. 24 hours a day.

Heard Gildersleeve last night. He was pretty good.

I hate for you to make that long trip home but it looks as if it's the only thing we can do for now. Better get your ticket up in front this time. Write me when you're supposed to leave and then I'll write your letters home.

Love,
Fred

★★★

11/10/43
Wednesday
Pyote, Texas

Dear Mom,

Didn't write yesterday as nothing happened.

There's not much to write today either. Got up at 8:00 this morning and got some things done, had a haircut, picked up some papers, etc. Came back had lunch and then rushed down to the flight line. Didn't fly, but we'll probably fly in a couple of days. Our crew is almost complete now.

We have to go to the gunnery range at 6:00 in the morning. We'll be there for six hours. Then we'll go to ground school until 6:00 at night.

It's been pretty cold in the mornings. Yesterday morning it was 27 degrees. That's kinda cold, don't you think?

By the time you receive this lousy letter you'll probably be all set to start for home. Gosh that's a long trip!!

Again, I repeat, I've never seen anyplace so desolate and out in the sticks. The only things that are near are the main highway and railroad tracks.

Will you excuse this poor excuse of a letter this time? I just don't have anything to write about yet.

Love,
Fred

★★★

                                                        11/11/43
                                                        Thursday night (8:00)
                                                        Pyote, Texas

Dear Mom,

Gosh darn I was disappointed today. Got your telegram today about 3:00. Did you go thru Pyote at about 1:00? Did you stop for awhile? If you would have gone thru here Wed. or Friday I could have been in Pyote to see you. Guess you left Wednesday night. Sent you a short letter last night. It was addressed to Ardmore. It will probably be forwarded home to you. Did you have any trouble getting a ticket?

The latest rumor today is that we may move from here at the end of this month. Boy I'm really getting to see the country!!

Still haven't received my check for last month yet. It'll catch up to me some time. The $175.00 should be at the bank by now, or some day soon.

We have to get up at 2:45 in the morning. We fly the early mission. Some fun!

What did you think of Pyote as you passed thru? Isn't it terrible!!

Tell everybody hello for me.

Well this just about ends my day. So far nothing much has happened in this quiet, god-forsaken spot.

The coyotes howl at night.

                                                        Good night,
                                                                Fred

Those weren't the only critters on the prowl through the night:

A sign on a bulletin board in the officers' quarters warned: 'Empty your shoes in the morning; scorpions may have crawled into them at night to stay warm'.[4]

                                                        11/13/43
                                                        Saturday
                                                        Pyote, Texas

Dear Mom,

Received your letter and 3 cards yesterday. The Pony Express only gets in here over a week or so. No kidding the mail from the West comes once a day and the mail from the East comes once a day. It goes out of here the same way. Deluxe service!

Guess what show they're showing today? 'In Old Chicago' with Alice Faye, Tyrone Power, and Don Ameche. Guess it's over 5 years old. Next Friday and Sat. they're showing 'Lassie Comes Home'. It's supposed to be a very good picture. Something like 'My Friend Flicka'.

We got up yesterday morning at 2:45, ate breakfast and then went down to the flight line and flew until 11:00. Left about 2:00 and then we had our day off, from 2:00 yesterday until 2:00 today. We have one day off once every nine days and then you can't do anything.

Last night 4 of us went to some little town around here to a high school football game. Well I've seen the real Texans again. Dirty, sloppy, and ignorant ones. Last night at the

football game they had their bottles and were drinking from them all during the game.
Some of the older ones had no teeth and were chewing tobacco. It was pretty cold by the
time we got back.

Got up this morning at 9:00 had breakfast, bought Life and Time magazines and then
I'm writing this letter to you.

You are probably home now as I write this letter, or you will be home some time today.
Bet you're glad to be away from the cold wind in Ardmore! Glad to hear you got on a good
bus for a change! What were you doing getting on the wrong bus? That was swell of those
people across the hall being so nice to you.

We have to fly tonight from 5:00 until midnight. Then tomorrow we don't fly at all just
go to school from noon until 9:00 at night. Nice quiet days, so restful!!

You ask about the radio. Well it won't play here. The kid in the next room has one and it
won't play either. Reception is very bad here. It's o.k. at night and the funny part about it
is that mine plays good, day or night, on batteries. Took it into town to see if they could tell
me just why it won't play.

Guess she was anxious to rent after we left. Good thing she gave you your dough back
though!

Had a woman bus driver last night and she nearly scared me to death. She'd look
around and take her hands off the wheel, etc.

Rumors are flying around here fast and furious, but they probably don't mean a thing.
I'm getting tired of moving around.

Bet it feels good to be home after your hectic trip and camping out in Ardmore. Tell
everybody hello for me and you can check up on our balance. I'm anxious to hear from you
about the trip!

Love,
Fred

★★★

11/17/43
Wednesday night
Pyote, Texas

Dear Mom,
Received your last 3 cards today also your letter.

Boy, no kidding, we've been plenty busy. Just finished school a little while ago. We started
early this morning.

Yesterday afternoon I went in to town to get my radio. It works swell now. A couple
of wires had come loose. In the day-time around here it's almost impossible to get radio
reception.

As much as Fred dislikes Monahans and the surrounding area, he seems loath to
offer anything good to say about the fact that someone in town had the materials
and skill to repair his radio. How about a little even-handedness for the people of
Texas here, Fred?

Well I guess that rumor is correct about us leaving here. It will be the first of next week if we go. Our co-pilot was made a first pilot today. He came from Ardmore with me. He wants me to be on his crew. We're going to see the major in the morning and find out if I can. If I can, that means I'll stay here.

Boy it really gets tiresome being up in the air 5 hours at a time. The other night we were supposed to be finished at 5:30. Well our tire blew out and we had to stay around until 9:00 to see that they changed it right. Got to bed about 10:30 and had to get up at 2:45 to fly the early morning mission. I was just dead tired yesterday afternoon.

The constant adversary – fatigue. From early on in his training and throughout his operational missions, Fred tells his mom about being tired as a result of training, flying, combat: 'I was just dead tired yesterday afternoon'; 'This makes the fourth straight day we've flown at high altitude. It really tires you out using oxygen so long'; 'It's almost midnight and I'm just dead on my feet tonight'; 'My rear-end is dragging on the ground'; 'Our whole group is restricted to the base. The reason is that everyone is so tired they just couldn't go to their damned old ground school'. After the eighth combat mission: 'Every chance they give us to sleep we sure take advantage of it! Last night I had 13 hours of sleep, but day before yesterday they woke us up before 2:00 in the morning so you can see we sleep every chance possible.'

And after the twenty-first combat mission: 'Dear, I'm dead tired so I'm going to end abruptly.'

While it is a truism that men engaged in heavy bombardment are chosen because they possess the attributes of youth and stamina, there is a factor of inescapable fatigue.[5]

But, don't worry Mom. Don't worry Mom.

That was surely nice of the bus driver to slow down and let you stop to see if I had been in Pyote! Who asked your nationality at Pecos? Gosh, that's too bad you had to wait for 11 hours in Dallas. How come your bus was held for inspection? So you walked from Arizona to California! Some walk eh kid!! Also how come you went by way of San Diego?

Your first letter said I had two little towns to wander in. Maybe you didn't get a good look at them!

I don't need a watch dear. Mine is plenty good.

I'm glad that my allotment finally got there. After this it should be there about the 5th of each month.

Tomorrow we fly from 5:30 until midnight. We don't even get to eat our meals at a regular time (that is most of the time).

Well, I'm out of news from this end. I'll write again, quick like!!

Love,
Fred

★★★

11/23/43
Tuesday morn.
Pyote, Texas

Dear Mom,

Didn't write to you yesterday as I talked to you on the phone. It just does me good to talk to you and hear your voice. You sounded a little tired though.

After our talk yesterday we flew from 1:00 until 8:00. Boy did we have fun. We fired 50 caliber machine guns from the air to ground targets. The nose was so smoky neither the navigator nor I could hardly see or breathe. We had a Captain riding as Co-Pilot yesterday and he said my shooting was pretty good.

As I told you on the phone be sure and see 'True to Life' with Dick Powell, Franchot Tone and Mary Martin and Victor Moore. I never laughed so much in my life. So did everyone else. Every line was almost a laugh line. Another good picture is 'Lassie Come Home'. It kinda makes you want to cry. Everyone liked it too.

Gosh there just isn't anything more to write today. Maybe I can write more when your letter gets here today.

On second thought, think I'll just send this as it is and write another letter later. O.K.?

Love,
Fred

★★★

11/25/43
Thursday morn.
Pyote, Texas

Dear Mom,

Brought my writing stuff along this morning as we are flying formation today and there won't be any bombing. I've dropped 50 bombs now here at Pyote.

It's kinda cold up here and lots of clouds over us and under us, but we're between them. It rained a little on us. I'm all over the navigator table.

We flew until late last night so couldn't write you. This letter will probably get home Monday. Isn't this a fine way to spend Thanksgiving Day! Next one we'll have at home!

Hope you have a nice dinner at Aunt Frances' today!

If you want one of those new Eversharps (pen) buy one. I didn't know they were putting out one something like a Parker '51'.

I'll quit for now and write more when we land and get your letter that will be waiting at the post office.

Here it is dear about 6:30 this evening. We landed in the rain. Not bad though. Came back to the B.O.Q. (Bachelors' Officers' Quarters) and cleaned up and went to dinner. They had turkey and all the stuff that goes with it, but it still wasn't like what we have at home.

As for any Xmas presents for me if anybody asks you, socks (wool, olive drab) handkerchiefs or a nice wallet are all I can use or need.

Bought a pair of shoes the other day for $3.41. They're just to work in. They're not bad though. They're cadet shoes, low cut, brown colored. Don't need a coupon to buy them as I bought them from the Q.M. (Quartermaster).

This is the first rain they've had in months. It's just a heavy California fog, but if it stays this way we won't fly tomorrow.

Our schedule for tomorrow calls for getting up at 6:30, go to school from 8:00 in the morning until 5:00 in the evening and fly from 8:00 that same night until 2 or 3 in the morning. That's a 21 hour schedule. Think we're going to ditch the school schedule. All they'll do is take our passes away and that doesn't mean a thing here as you can't go anywhere anyhow. Besides we'll only be here until Sunday I think.

> *Good night,*
> *Fred*

★★★

11/26/43
Friday night
Pyote, Texas

Dear Mom,

Wrote you last night so don't have very much to write tonight. We don't have to fly tonight as the field is closed in due to the weather.

So it's cold home eh! It's plenty cold here also.

The boys want to go into Pecos tonight for dinner and a show. I'd rather stay in but they won't hear of it.

The hottest rumor is that we're going to Dyersburg, Tenn. Boy that's deep in the heart of the South. Farther and farther from home.

Later: (In fact, next day, Saturday). Well we flew this morning at 6:00. Boy was it cold. It was below zero at 6,000 feet. I had my heavy boots and clothes on. Before we took off there was some snow falling. On the way home last night it snowed. Not very bad though.

Sure been busy today we leave tomorrow (Sunday).

What kind of talk is that about you making your expenses so I can have more money when I come home? Get those ideas out of your head! (This comes straight from the boss!!)

You had better start to buy your Xmas presents now before it gets too late.

Well dear we found out where we're going. Dyersburg, Tenn. Some fun!! Just think how lousy that is; cold and snow etc.

Gosh, I'm out of news now. Oh, did I tell you some jerk took my good hat from the mess hall? Now I'll have to buy another one. I would rather have given him the money and kept my hat.

It's clear as a bell here tonight. Someone said they saw a train pull in today and it was covered with snow.

We flew up to Carlsbad today. It was surely pretty. All covered with snow.

On the way back one of the planes there came up along side of us and flew along with us for awhile until our gunners started to track 'em with the machine guns in the turrets. Guess they thought someone might slip and let go with some bullets.

> *Good night,*
> *Fred*

★★★

11/29/43
Monday

Dear Mom,

We left Pyote last night at 6:00. Boy we've just been creeping along. Here it is 1:30 in the afternoon and we're just a little ways out of Fort Worth. We arrived at Ft. Worth at about 9:00 this morning and had breakfast at the (Milan) Cafeteria. It was really a swell meal. From what I could see Ft. Worth is a nice place.

Supposed to arrive at Dyersburg tomorrow morning (Tuesday) at 5:00, but as far as I can see we won't be there until in the afternoon sometime.

Dyersburg is about 50 or 60 miles from Memphis.

So far the weather is clear and pretty but sort of chilly.

It's hard to write as this darn train rocks and sways.

I slept in an upper last night. My pilot and I matched to see which one of us would sleep in the upper. I lost and so I climbed up and went to sleep.

No kidding the engineer on this train must be a plow jockey. I never had such a rough train ride! During the night it was so bad it woke us up and the guys sure were cussing!

Should be in Dallas pretty soon.

Bought a Time *magazine in Ft. Worth and clipped this article about FDR Jr. out for you to read, also one about James Roosevelt. When some people say things about them they just don't know what they're talking about. It also said that the only thing that gets the President mad now is when someone tries to get at him through his sons.*

I'm really getting to be the old traveler now! Before we've finished I bet we come to California some time. (I sure hope so!!)

Gosh it's so darn hard to write on this train. I'll stop for now and write more later.

Later: (Tuesday afternoon)

We're almost in Dyersburg now. Left Memphis about 1:00 or so. Sent you a card from Memphis while we were eating breakfast and lunch combined.

There are a lot of hills and trees here in Tenn. But still I'll take California!!

We crossed from Arkansas to Tenn. over the Mississippi River.

The trees and grass are all sort of brown. Is it supposed to be winter or autumn?

Nothing more has happened except this morning when I got up I couldn't find my pants for a long time. Looked and looked for them. Everyone was helping me. They had fallen down during the night and had been kicked clear down to the other end of the car beneath someone's berth. I was beginning to get worried as it was almost time to arrive in Memphis for breakfast, but could have borrowed a pair from Al or Dick (our navigator).

Memphis seemed kinda old and dirty near the train station. Guess the main part of town is better.

Well, I'll sign off again until after we arrive and get settled.

Tuesday Night:

Just finished a shower and getting to bed. Boy I've never seen it so cold. You'd freeze to death and I'm not kidding. Tomorrow morning we have to take another physical examination and fill out our pay vouchers.

It seems that each place gets worse. Don't know how I'm going to stand a winter around here. Got to buy a short coat. Coal smoke is so bad it makes your nose run.

This is really a big base. From what we have found out so far it's really going to be a rugged schedule.

Guess what, I heard Gabriel Heatter tonight at 8:00. Bob Hope is on now. Yes, I've heard Ginny Sims.

This address I gave on the envelope isn't correct. Just send it to that address though. I'll let you know as soon as possible what the correct address is.

I wrote a check for $23.80 to the Officers Mess. I'm out of dough so I'll write one for $10.00 tomorrow and that will last me until I get my check.

I'll say goodnight for now. More tomorrow night.

Love,
Fred

BOMBARDIER NAVIGATOR PILOT COPILOT ENGINEER BALLTURRET RADIO WAIST GUNNERS TAIL GUNNER

(Courtesy of Frank Halm)

Chapter Seven

They Become a Crew

The crew will live together, fight together, eat together and play together. No single individual will be shot at more than any other, and they will all suffer when one of them is injured. And, there is the chance that they will die together. The ties that bind these ten men as a living fighting unit are tighter than those in just about any other endeavour or organisation of the war or in peacetime.[1]

> *12/4/43*
> *Saturday night*
> *Dyersburg, Tenn.*

Dear Mom,
Don't know what to write tonight. Maybe just a few lines to say good night.

Got your telegram this afternoon. Again they addressed the telegram wrong. This time it was Fred F. Lull. You'd better print my middle initial!

Boy it came just in time. I almost bought a box of Christmas cards today. Also glad to hear there's another book on the way.

Turned my pay voucher in today. Should get the check about the end of next week. By that time it will be about the 11th of the month. How time does fly.

My pilot hasn't felt any too good today or yesterday so he went to see about it and they stuck him in the hospital. Don't know how long he'll be there, maybe two days or three weeks. He said it was Nasophneyngitis or is it just the flu?

Didn't fly today, just went to ground school all day and late this afternoon. I took my navigator down to the bomb trainer and was teaching him how to operate the bombsight, etc. Boy it's a job to try and show them (him) how!

Going to take a shower now and then get into bed and listen to the radio. I'll write on this letter tomorrow night and mail it.

Good night.

Sunday:
It's about 1:30 now and time for John Charles Thomas and John Nesbitt.

Had a Xmas package from Stella today, a box of candy. Some kind of apple stuff.

Going up to the hospital in a little while and see how Al is (the pilot). Saw Gildersleeve last night. 'Gildersleeve on Broadway.' A lot of laughs in it. Peavy was in it also. Going to see 'Thousands Cheer' today.

What do you think of Roosevelt's travels? Sounds pretty good. Saw a picture of Elliot meeting him in Cairo. A bunch of the fellows were talking the other day. Everyone of them think F.D.R. is the only one to be President and deal with Churchill and Stalin at the peace table. They all say Roosevelt is the only one that is shrewd and smart enough to deal with them.

This damn coal smoke just about gets me. It gets all over your face and clothes. Things are dirty and black.

Ever since I got my wings I haven't drawn any flight pay so I was 3 months behind. Flight pay is $75.00 per month. You are allowed 3 months to make it up so I think I am a little over time and may lose $75.00 (that's one month's pay).

The voucher I turned in the other day will get me this much:

> *$327.00*
>   *75.00*
> *$402.00*
> *−175.00: this is the allotment*
> *$227.00: this is what my check will be.*

I'll get 227.00 and you will have $175.00 at the bank making a total of $402.00.

There's a remote chance that I might collect that other $75.00. That wouldn't be bad at all.

Think the bank balance is about $500.00 and something. As soon as my check comes I'll send about $170.00 more home and that will make it close to $700.00 in the bank.

No mail this morning maybe some this afternoon from someone. Everyone should have had my change of address yesterday (Sat.).

This is all for now, more tonight!

Just got back from the show. It was very good. 'Thousands Cheer.'

Right now I'm listening to Jack Benny. Didn't know Phil Harris was back on the program. Fred Allen comes back the 12th of this month.

Gee whiz, I just can't think of anymore to write tonight.

Good night dear,

Fred

P.S. Jack Benny is pretty good tonight. Dennis is singing 'A White Christmas'. Makes me think of you.

White Christmas … (was) a nostalgic remembrance of home and holiday peace and goodwill to savor when the war was at its worst.[2]

I'm dreaming of a white Christmas
just like the ones I used to know,
Where treetops glisten
And children listen
To hear sleigh bells in the snow.[3]

12/8/43
Wednesday night
Dyersburg, Tenn.

Dear Mom,

Boy, I received all of your letters today. One from Pyote, and two from home. I read them over about 4 or 5 times. Really enjoyed reading them! Sounds as if you've been pretty well on the go.

As for the situation here we haven't been up in the air once yet. Been here a week yesterday. Today it's been raining and for the other days the clouds and mist haven't been over 300 feet off the ground. Some weather!

It wouldn't surprise me at all if this keeps up that they would send us to Florida. Don't count on that though. (Right now it's just pouring)

As soon as the weather permits us to fly the navigators will be plenty busy trying to find their way around here. All this country looks the same. Jack Richardson was right when he said he hated the South. It's so damp!

Oh yes, before I forget, went into Dyersburg yesterday afternoon. It's about 10 or 12 miles from here. No kidding it looked dirtier than Memphis. Coal smoke covers everything. They have a great big statue of a Confederate soldier in the town square. It's in memory of the Confederates in the Civil War. Only stayed about 2 hours. There wasn't a darn thing to see or do. Stopped in at the café in town and had a cup of coffee and a piece of pie and the waitress told me it usually snows around here Christmas time.

Had to laugh to myself about your bacon sandwich as I always told you not to eat before going to bed as it made you sick. Working out in the yard will do you some good. Gets you outside in the sunshine.

You get one of those fountain pens if you want one and like them!!

Guess the Christmas cards will be here tomorrow or the next day. Think they were a swell idea!! Christmas trees are going to be rather hard to get this year and pretty expensive.

The shows in Dyersburg are all old run pictures such as 'Artists and Models Abroad' with Jack Benny.

They finally gave us a Co-pilot today and a radio operator. Sent them from Salt Lake City.

The crew is being filled out with the arrival of new members. As they become a team they begin to learn about one another – their idiosyncrasies, their responsibilities in the plane and how they will survive together. On the other hand, one wag suggested that members of the crew were fairly stereotypical:

You can always tell the gunner by his cold and steely glare.
You can always tell the bombardier by his manners, quite debonair.
You can always tell the navigator by his pencils and papers
and such.
You can always tell the pilot, but you can't tell him much.[4]

Sounds like the postman keeps track of my travels. The other night I just traced them all on a map in dark pencil from the time I left Los Angeles for Santa Ana up to now. Quite a distance!!

So you think you've made $100.00 dollars eh? It surely would be nice if he did pay off for finding him a house to live in. That ain't hay.

Al (pilot) is 25 years old and he is from Wichita Falls, Texas. Very quiet and the home type like me. He's just been married for a short while. Dick (navigator) is 24 years old and an old gad-about. Don't know much about the co-pilot yet.

Fred was the youngest of the crew in the cockpit and the nose of the plane. The pilot, a 25-year-old married man, had those prerequisites that allowed for the sobriquet of 'The Old Man' – a term reserved for the leader of the group, the pilot, the skipper, the boss.

I should be there to trap all of your little pets (mice?) in the traps. What are they doing just sitting there daring you to get them?

Well, I'm just about written out for now. Hadn't heard from you for some days until today and I was kinda lonesome for your letters. All three of them came today and I felt like a new person again.

Your <u>little boy</u>,
Fred

P.S. I was thinking about my scrapbook and annuals the other day and was wondering if you had looked at them. They bring back those wonderful high school days don't they?

★★★

12/13/43
Monday Night
Dyersburg, Tenn.

Dear Mom,
Didn't get a chance to write to you last night as we were so busy yesterday. In my last letter I said the weather would be bad for another week well it cleared up day before yesterday and we flew yesterday. Talk about cold, it was really cold yesterday where we were. We flew at 20,000 feet for four hours. The temp. was −18 degrees or 18 degrees below zero. Some fun! The water that leaked out of our oxygen masks turned to ice as soon as it hit our leg, etc. My crew is due to land at 6:30, 10 minutes from now. I got out of flying today as I wanted to get some trainer time in and have my oxygen mask refitted. They were to fly at 20,000 again today for 4 hours in formation.

Received both packages today. Those cards are really beautiful! The wedding cake was hard as a rock.

Tonight the Officers' club is having a stag here on the post. I'm in the Club and they're all drinking beer and eating here. The show is later on at the post theater.

It sure takes a long time for your mail to get here. At least 4 or 5 days. Received your letter from South Gate yesterday and the one mailed the 8th today.

I'm sure happy you bought your fountain pen. Those are beautiful pens and they write very smoothly. Your writing with the new pen looks a lot nicer and smoother.

Yes, I heard 'Take It or Leave It' that night when the sailor said that about the beans. Everyone really laughed.

You spend that whole $100 on yourself if you want to!! (Hope he sends it.)

Your letter from South Gate beat the one mailed after it.

The fellows just came in from flying and they said it was 22 degrees below today at 20,000 feet.

I'm not quite sure what the balance is. How about letting me know once more. I couldn't make out your balance. Is this right $346.35 + 150.00 = $496.35 for a total.

The food is really good tonight here. I'm an old drunkard. I had ½ bottle of beer. That's all I could take. They can have it. (We're just not good sports are we dear!)

Right now everyone is singing around the piano, etc.

I'm just about run out of conversation for this time. Oh, had a letter from Smitty yesterday. He's teaching some classes and in a short time he said he expected to be a Staff Sergeant.

Al (pilot) doesn't feel any too good yet. He had quite a bad cold. The fellow in the next room had a fever of 104.6 when he was in the hospital last week.

Goodnight dear.

Love,
Fred

★★★

12/16/43
Thursday morn.
Dyersburg, Tenn.

Dear Mom,

Please excuse writing as I've just got the paper (from the W. Len Hotel, Memphis, Tennessee) on my knee. It's about 11:00 now and the stores don't open until noon so we stayed in bed late.

We arrived here in the big city about 6:30 last night. Got a room here at the hotel then went over to the swanky hotel, The Peabody, and had dinner at their sky room. Very very nice. Music with the dinner. We tried to get a room at the Peabody but they were all sold out. After dinner we met some other fellows we knew and went to the show. It was 'Jack London.' Not bad.

Going out to have breakfast in a few minutes.

Mike our co-pilot went to Nashville and Al, Dick and I came here. We got a room with 3 single beds. This morning I just soaked in the bathtub. Oh, this will get you. After the show we had a hamburger and a cup of coffee. Well this morning we were all running to the toilet. I had to go about 4 times. I bet that was some hamburger!

We were lucky and caught a ride right from the base to here. Don't know if I'll stay here tonight or not. Think I'll go back though. Guess Dick will stay here again tonight.

In the last letter I said it was snowing. Well when we woke up in the morning it was clear as a bell, but brother was it cold. The wind was like ice. Yes, before I forget, it was supposed to go down to zero or 5 degrees above last night here in Memphis.

It was certainly a pleasure sleeping in a real bed last night.

What a shopping trip. I felt weak and sort of dizzy and had to leave my shopping tour rather suddenly and run for the hotel and the bathroom. Felt much better last night; had dinner and went to the show. It was 'The Gang's All Here' with Alice Faye, Phil Baker, Carmen Miranda. Not bad. Caught the 10:30 bus out of Memphis and arrived here at the field at about 12:30.

Bought Smitty a wool pair of gloves. They have leather on the palms. Not bad gloves. Don't know if Smitty will like them or not, but I just couldn't think of anything to get him. As for your present I just couldn't think of anything at all.

What I did get you, you already have but this is supposed to be very good stuff.

That was a beautiful Christmas card you sent me!!!

It's almost time to get to school. Today it's from 12:30 until 3:30 and then we fly nights for a while. Gosh I hate night flying. That means getting to bed about 2:00 or so in the morning.

Well, I'll finish this in the morning and mail it. Probably get some mail this afternoon.

Oh, before I forget, the reason the radio worked some times when you moved the dial is that the filter condenser was burned out. Had it fixed.

Later: Didn't get a chance to check the afternoon mail so will get it in the morning. Didn't fly tonight, but will tomorrow night. Went to the show and saw Bettie Davis and Miriam Hopkins in 'Old Acquaintance'. Very good!

Bet everyone is glad you're having rain. Probably need it.

It doesn't seem as if it's been a month since you started home.

Right now I'm listening to Jimmy Durante.

Well, here I am again, out of thoughts so good night dear.

Love,

Fred

★★★

12/24/43

Friday Eve

(Xmas Eve)

Dyersburg, Tenn.

Merry Christmas Dear,

Just a few lines tonight to thank you for the swell socks and wallet. Is the address book for me? The reason I asked is that your name is on the inside cover. It looks like rain or snow here tonight. Nothing yet though.

Missed the President's speech today. Hope I can hear the rebroadcast. Guess he's not going to fool with the railroads. Everything is fixed so the government can take them over if need be.

We received word a few minutes ago we don't have to fly tonight as the weather has closed in and it has started to rain. I went over to the Club and almost broke my neck. The ground and everything is all frozen. You slip and slide all over. Did you ever see it that way?

They had Christmas songs at the Club. They're beautiful!

I sure missed you. Think I had a tear or two in my eyes during the singing. Next year it will be different!!

I'm dreaming of a white Christmas
Just like the ones we used to know (Reprise)[5]

*Right now I'm listening to a world Xmas program. Bob Hope, Bing Crosby, Lionel
Barrymore and others. It's very good! Hope you heard it also.*
    *Missed F.D.R.'s speech, but heard it on the world Xmas program. I've never heard
anyone that talks like he can! Did you hear him?*

But on Christmas Eve this year I can say to you that at last we may look forward
into the future with real, substantial confidence that, however great the cost,
'peace on earth, good will toward men' can be and will be realized and ensured.
This year I can say that. Last year I could not do more than express a hope. Today
I express a certainty – though the cost may be high and the time may be long.[6]

Saturday (Xmas Day)
*Got up about 9:00 and had breakfast. Got a life raft out and went over to the Club. Boy it
rained all night and it's just pouring here now. Mud is knee deep.*
    They had a swell meal at noon-time. Thought you would like to see the menu.
    After lunch went down to check my mail. Had some cards and a box of hard candies.
    *Going to the show this afternoon, 'The Vampire Returns.' Doesn't that sound
wonderful! Oh well, it will kill time.*
    This evening they're having a buffet supper at the Club and an orchestra.
    *Did you hear Lionel Barrymore this year in 'A Christmas Carol'? I missed it.
Remember how we've listened to it every year.*
    *Your wool socks are really going to be the thing in this country. Those are nice slippers
and handkerchiefs.*
    *Later: Just got back from the Club. They had very good eats. Cold turkey (white meat)
for sandwiches, etc.*
*Listened to the music awhile and now I'm in bed writing an end to this letter and listening
to the radio.*
    I'll write tomorrow night.

Love
Fred

***

12/30/43
Thursday morn.
Dyersburg, Tenn.

Dear Mom,
*Just a few lines this morning before I go to school in a few minutes. It's 11:30, have to eat
and be in school at 12:30. Just got up about an hour ago. We didn't get to bed until 3:45
this morning. We were up in the 'Wild Blue Yonder' flying.*
    *Think we're going on a cross-country tonight to Indiana and Illinois if the weather
permits.*

Yesterday was the first bright, clear, sunny day we've had in a week and now this morning it's completely closed in.

Didn't get a letter from you yesterday so I'll have to wait until today to check and see if I have one. When I get your letters it makes it easy to write as I can answer your questions and ask some of my own.

There's a hot rumor out now if the weather continues to be bad here we'll move back to Pyote, Texas. I'd like that a lot better!!

This is a strange comment from someone who professed as much dislike for Pyote as Fred did. Could it be true that he thought Pyote would be better, or is this just a note of facetiousness?

Well, I'll close for now and finish tonight before we go down to the flight line.

Later: (Flying was called off on account of weather.)

Just got back from seeing 'The Heat's On' with Mae West. Make it a point to miss it! Boy was it lousy.

I never knew anyone who liked purses better than you do. I'm mighty glad you liked the perfume. As I said before I just couldn't think of anything.

Boy I'm glad to hear that your lip is o.k. as it had me worried also!! Sure sorry to hear you had such a headache. Better take care of yourself for the boss, kid!!!

Well, it's about time to end this masterpiece of writing for this installment.

Love,
Fred

★★★

1/1/44
Saturday
Dyersburg, Tenn.

My Dearest One,
Happy New Year!

It's about 3:00 in the afternoon and the U.S.C./Washington Rose Bowl Game comes on at 3:45. Boy sure glad I can hear it!

Our 48 hour pass started at noon today and lasts until Monday, but I'm not going anywhere as Memphis would be so crowded you couldn't get a room. So I'm just going to rest as we're going to be extra busy for a while because of all the bad weather.

Yesterday my crew went on a cross country all over Arkansas. It was high altitude so I didn't go as the flight surgeon restricted me to low altitude only until my cold clears up. I went to the doctor this morning and had him look my nose and ears over as my sinus has been hurting all week. He said my cold had settled in my sinus. That's why it hurt.

If I'd gone yesterday I'd have to use oxygen at 20,000 feet and that's no fun with a cold plus the fact that your ears would really hurt on the way down trying to clear them. Enough of my trouble eh!

One more thing before I finish with yesterday's flight. One of the ships had 2 engines out; one was on fire and the other quit so he landed at an airfield in Ark. You see how safe these B-17s are — they'll fly on two engines if necessary.

Don't worry Mom. Don't worry Mom.

Boy they really had a brawl here last night. They were just bringing in the New Year. Never saw so many bottles in all my life. Had a good orchestra here also. That's about all they can do as there is nothing to do for miles around. Even the townspeople say there's more life here on the post than in town.

What I said about going to Pyote isn't to stay there; we'd just fly down there and stay for a few days, if we go at all.

Fred's sigh of relief is almost audible, even now.

Hope your $100.00 doesn't fall through, but when did we ever get anything through chance!

Did you notice the new address? It's been that for a long time, but I was too lazy to change it.

I'll close for now.

Your loving son,
Fred

P.S. I'm going to call you tomorrow (Sunday). Payday was today.

★★★

1/5/44
Wednesday
Dyersburg, Tenn.

Dear Mom,

Now is the only chance I have to write so here goes. Just got out of ground school a little while ago. Got up at about 10:15 this morning as we didn't get to bed until after 3:00 this morning. The weather was a little better so we flew 5 hours. We go to eat in a few minutes and report down to the flight line. This schedule is the one I hate most as it keeps poor little me up so late at night. It's pretty cloudy out now. Don't know how it will be by the time we're supposed to take off. In my last letter I said some crews were going to fly down to Pyote and back. Well they got as far as Kelly Field, Texas and were told to land as the weather was getting bad so they're still there. The barracks seems kinda empty without them as they are from our flight and live in the same B.O.Q.

You figured the bank statement wrong; 2 bonds at $150.00 instead of $200.00 I still don't know what the correct balance is now that the holidays are over and this month's allotment should be there plus the $70.00 more I sent you.

Boy all I can say is you're certainly getting your share of rain and storms this year!!

Wait before you buy any more bonds. What I mean is until you send me the up-to-date correct bank balance. I haven't or won't write any checks so it will be just yours.

Guess who's supposed to be here on the field tonight? Max Baer and his brother Buddy Baer. They're putting on an exhibition boxing match. Probably won't get to see them as we'll probably fly.

I took my Parker '51' down to the P.X. and they're going to send it away to be fixed. It goes to Wisconsin. It's going to be cleaned, new point, and fix the leak in the barrel. Someone borrowed it and I think they dropped it and caused the leak. That's all that could have caused it.

At long last I'm over my cold.

We lost the engineer out of our crew yesterday. He put his application into the cadets about five months ago and now they called him. We kinda missed him last night flying.

Before I forget, did you hear Jack Benny Sunday night? I didn't but he usually does that play about the 48 states and Columbia. It's always very good. I think Fred Allen's program is about the best on the radio.

Heard a good joke the other day:

Quote, 'Take that star out of your window Mother, your son is in the A.T.C. (Air Transport Command).' The A.T.C. just ferries planes and supplies and personnel, etc. Nothing dangerous, but they are needed. It's just a pretty good joke.

> *Love,*
> *Fred*

★★★

It's not likely that she took 'that star out of the window'. (Author's collection)

January 6, 1944
Thursday
Dyersburg, Tenn.

Dear Honey Child,

Hey this is pretty good I wrote you yesterday at this same time. They let us out of ground school early today. They covered 3 hours of lectures in one and we got out 2 hours early.

Boy the sun has really been shining today. It's really clear and blue out. These kinds of days are so rare around here. Took one more picture today; 3 more to go on the first roll. Think we start flying days Monday. I sure hope so! Then I can take some pictures of my crew in their flying stuff.

Received your great big envelope today. So you forgot to put stamps on the New Years letter! Is my dear little Mother getting screwy?

Boy was it cold last night. My hands nearly froze off. I dropped 9 bombs last night. The first since we left Pyote. Had two close ones. One hit about 60 feet and the other hit about 75 feet. There was one awful strong wind last night and we had a lot of drift therefore it makes bombing much harder.

I'm afraid we'll have to bomb from 20,000 feet tonight. I hate that. How about you dropping them for me?

When I dropped those 2 close bombs last night the pilot called over the interphone and wanted to know who was dropping those bombs, Webb? Webb is the navigator. Do you get it? He was joking.

The moon was beautiful up there last night. It was like some of the nights we used to have at Roswell. The Mississippi River is beautiful when the moon is shining on it!

No, I'm not wearing heavy underwear. Those socks are darn nice! I should wash them myself, shouldn't I, with Ivory Flakes or something as the laundry would shrink them so much.

So you're wearing slacks eh? They had better look good and not be traipsing around town. You know me kid.

Well, I'll close for now. This was just a note. You'll receive this about Monday I think. You should have one on Sat. also.

Your loving son,
Fred

Fred's expression of distaste for women's slacks and what he thinks is appropriate dress for women is not something new for him. Slacks began to be worn during his days in high school and, as one of the school's leaders, he and others were interviewed in 1939 by the Poly High School student newspaper regarding this terrible trend in women's fashion:

Slacks on Campus out of Place, Say Students. Slacks, besides giving a bad impression to outsiders, are looked upon with disapproval by the majority of Polyites. Here are some opinions of prominent persons on the campus. Hal Holker, ASBO president, says, 'Slacks are all right in their place, at home, in the mountains, or the beach, but school is definitely not the place for them. They cheapen a girl. I personally do not like them for school wear because their use hurts the reputation of both the school and the girl.[7]

One of the 'prominent' girls interviewed for the story chimed in, 'It lowers the respect of other fellows and girls for the one who comes to school in slacks. It is just as out of place as a playsuit at a formal affair.'

And from our hero, 'It looks terrible. I definitely disapprove of them', says Fred Lull, Senior B president.[8]

It seems that Fred was not the only man who thought women wearing slacks was distasteful and inappropriate – a thought not likely to be lost on his mother after his comment in the letter. A rebuke, is a rebuke, is a rebuke, even if it does come from your son, or maybe especially if it comes from your son, a would-be style critic.

Presumption of establishing clothing appropriateness for women reached beyond house, home, and student newspaper during these years. Even the Mayor of Los Angeles had his say. On 23 April 1942 letters started pouring into City Hall two days after Mayor Fletcher Bowron expressed his disapproval of the city's female employees wearing slacks to work.

Bowron had weighed in on a City Council debate on the matter, saying: 'Slacks are fine for women workers in defence factories but good taste and good sense will dictate that they are out of place in City Hall'. *The Times* reported:

> The mayor went on to say: 'Don't let us use the war to undermine these things we like to consider feminine and lady-like. I am not old-fashioned, but I don't like to see masculine women much more than feminine traits in men.'
>
> Bowron's words provoked veteran City Hall secretary Dorothy Foster to walk into the City Council chambers in trousers, *The Times* said. The newspaper quoted Foster as saying that 'as wartime apparel they increase our efficiency and save us money.'[9]

There you have it, Fred. If slacks are good enough for women defence workers and the likes of Dorothy Foster, they're good enough for Mom.

January 7, 1944
Friday
Dyersburg, Tenn.

Dear Mom,
Didn't receive a letter today as the mail-room was closed as they were rebuilding it. Will probably get two tomorrow.
We're not flying tonight as the weather has socked in again.
Boy what a country this is down here! Weather at home was never like this and it is plenty cold.
We flew on a cross-country navigation mission to Atlanta, Georgia last night. On the way back we flew at 20,000 feet. It was really cold up there last night.

I don't have much more to write tonight so will let this letter go until tomorrow night. Good night dear!

Sat. Night:
Here it is 10:30 in the evening. Haven't done a darn thing since I started this letter last night.

When I woke up this morning boy was it snowing. Guess it snowed all night and it's been snowing most of the day. Tonight it's almost clear out! The moon is shining some. Everything sure looks beautiful; so white and clean. We didn't fly tonight as it had become icy on the runways so I had to put some trainer time in. I'm all finished on that trainer, I hope. Took the radio operator and one of the gunners down with me and tried to teach them something about the bombsight and bombing.

My darn feet get so cold in the darn snow!

I see you're back on your old writing paper. It doesn't weigh so much and you can write more. The other stuff was too heavy.

Well, I'm going to sign off for now. I'm going to turn the light off and listen to the radio. I'll be asleep and when Dick comes in he can turn it off.

Good night honey child!

Your loving son,
Fred

★★★

January 9, 1944
Sunday Afternoon
Dyersburg, Tenn.

Dear Mom,
As we didn't have ground school today I was really lazy this morning. Didn't get up until 11:30. Can you imagine me doing that?

The sun was really bright all day today. The snow has been melting very fast. Took some pictures of the snow today. Got one more to go on the roll. Mike, our co-pilot had his camera also. Should have some good pictures.

Honest to goodness last night was the coldest night I ever had to endure. It was so cold I couldn't sleep hardly at all.

Bet the ground will become all slushy and muddy as the snow melts.

Later: Monday afternoon:
Here I am again. Just got out of ground school a little while ago. Haven't had very much mail in the last week from anyone and none from you for 2 days. Found out the reason for it today. The mail condition here is terrible. They've got about 10 sacks of mail they haven't been able to sort. So tonight they're going to have a mail-sorting bee and get it all done so I should have some mail out of it.

It was beautiful last night flying. The whole countryside was covered with snow. The moon was shining on the snow and it made it almost bright as day.

Here, and in a similar sentiment in the letter of 6 January about flying over the Mississippi River, Fred comes close to being poetic about flight. There is a sense of joy, perhaps awe, at the vistas flying opens up for him:

Oh! I have slipped the surly bonds of earth
and danced the skies on laughter silvered wings.
Sunward I've climbed and joined the tumbling mirth of sun split clouds
and done a hundred things you have not dreamed of,
wheeled and soared and swung high in the sunlit silence.
Hovering there I've chased the shouting wind aloft
and flung my eager craft through footless halls of air.
Up up the long delirious burning blue,
I've topped the windswept heights with easy grace
where neither lark nor eagle flew.
And there with silent lifting mind
I've trod the high untrespassed sanctity of space
Put out my hand and touched the face of God.[10]

Last night it was colder on the ground than at 8,000 feet. That happened because of a temperature inversion. I dropped 12 bombs last night. Don't know what we're going to do tonight. May bomb again. Don't know though. We go on the afternoon schedule tomorrow (Tuesday). Instead of flying five hours they're going to make us fly 6 hours starting tomorrow.

Well I'll close for now. When I get the mail tonight I'll probably have a couple of letters from you and then I'll have something to write about.

Love,
Fred

★★★

January 11, 1944
Tuesday night
Dyersburg, Tenn.

Dear Mom,
Haven't heard from you in three days. Guess the reason I didn't hear today is that I couldn't get to the mail room, as it doesn't open until afternoon and we fly from noontime until after 8:00 at night. We started on the day-shift today. Gosh I've just got to get over there tomorrow and get my mail.

They give us the worst schedules they can think of. If we can't get our mail tomorrow because of the schedule we're going to see the Major and put in a big protest. We boys have to have our mail!!

Don't have anything to write tonight but I want you to have a letter before the weekend. I'll probably write tomorrow also if I get your letters.

Last night I dropped twelve bombs from 20,000 feet. Boy was it cold!! You can't imagine how high that is until you get up there and look down.

I also dropped 8 bombs today from 20,000 feet.

Tomorrow we may fly down to the Gulf of Mexico for air-to-air gunnery, etc. On the way down squadrons of P-47s will pick us up and escort us to certain targets.

I just wanted to drop ya-all a line to say everything is o.k. and to say good night.

Love,

Fred

★★★

January 13, 1944

Thursday night

Dyersburg, Tenn.

Dear Mom,

Didn't get to pick up my mail today, but received 3 letters from you yesterday. Boy was I glad!!

Our day is so long now! Here's how it goes: 7:00, up for breakfast; 8:15 until 11:30 for ground school. 12:15 until around 9:00 or 9:30 at night, we fly; and then if we're lucky we have dinner. Right now it's 11:15 in the evening and I just got back from dinner about 20 minutes ago. I just had to drop you a few lines before going to bed as I didn't write last night. Please excuse this hasty, sloppy writing. Will probably get 2 letters from ya-all tomorrow if I can check my mail.

Today we flew up to Kansas City, Kansas, to Tulsa, Oklahoma and back here. We had certain targets to camera bomb in them. We flew the whole mission at 20,000 feet. This makes the fourth straight day we've flown at high altitude. It really tires you out using oxygen so long.

As a member of a heavy bomber team, in combat you will be living and fighting in a world where man has no business – from three to six miles above the environment for which nature designed you.[11]

Glad you got to see 'Lassie Come Home', Knew you would like it. You and I both like those kind of pictures. Also you will like Dick Powell's picture, 'True to Life.'

Pretty fancy using green ink aren't you kid!!

Isn't it ever going to quit raining in dear old California?

Tell Mrs. Davidson I'll take her up on that T-bone steak.

So you bought 2 $100.00 bonds eh! Pretty good.

That picture of the dogs is the cutest thing I've seen in a long time. There's nothing like little puppies is there?

The importance of mail to those in the armed forces was not lost on corporate America during the war. This letter, as part of a magazine advertisement, uses the back-home/down-home pull of a far-away son to his mother to press the message of what the war is all about, to garner readers and, hopefully, to encourage the purchase of its product:

May 2, 1944

Dearest Mom,

So old Bess has pups again! That reminds me of so much. She had her last litter two years ago – just about this time of year – when everything was so fresh and new. That's what I want to get back to, Mom! – what all of us are fighting to get back to – that world back home where a fellow can give the sort of welcome he ought to give to a litter of setter pups in the spring. To watch them grow up with all the other new, young things in a world that's bright and free.

Good old Bess! Pat her sweet old head for me and tell her she and I have a date – some autumn day – to teach those youngsters of hers what bird-dog pups are born for.

God bless you all

Your loving son,

Bill

The product: Polk Miller Products Corp., Richmond, VA, makers of Sergeant's Dog Medicines.[12]

It's almost midnight and I'm just dead on my feet tonight so will you excuse me for tonight? I knew you would.

Love,

Fred

★★★

January 14, 1944
Friday Night
Dyersburg, Tenn.

Hello Honey Child,

Not much to write tonight as I wrote ya-all last night. Received 2 letters from you today.

We were called back from our flight today as a freezing rain was moving in so that's why I've got a little free time tonight.

Didn't do very much today except drop one bomb before we were called back. It was a darn good hit. It was 10 feet from the shack.

This is not a tragedy, but we had a plane that made a crash landing the other day. They couldn't get their wheels down so had to come in without them. I saw it land. It was a beautiful job. No one was hurt, not even a scratch.

Don't worry Mom. Don't worry Mom.

Boy you're having quite a struggle with that darn old gremlin germ 'flu' aren't you? Take care of yourself. Glad that you finally bought your sweater.

Yes, I finally have your bank balance and our bonds straightened out.

Hey that fire really came close didn't it? I can just see you all excited and shaking. Fire is one thing that really scares you!!

We haven't had any time off in so darn long. We don't get a day off until the 23rd or 25th.

I'm finally going to take that roll of film over tomorrow and get it developed.

So much of this high altitude flying lately because of the extreme cold has my hands kinda red and chapped. I'm using Jergens lotion on them though!

Filled out my pay voucher tonight. Boy how time does fly! Of course it's two weeks before payday. After this payday our balance should be a little over or around $500.00.

Please tell everyone hello for me. Had a letter from Smitty today. He's fine I guess. Good night dear.

> *Love,*
> *Fred*

★★★

> *January 17, 1944*
> *Monday night*
> *Dyersburg, Tenn.*

Dear Mom,

This is just going to be a brief note tonight as it is late. Didn't get to check my mail yesterday or today. I'll get it tomorrow even if I have to miss school!!

Yesterday we flew 1,000 nautical miles. That was from here to Little Rock, Ark, to Hot Springs, Ark, to Jackson, Mississippi, to Chattanooga, Tenn., to Nashville, Tenn., and then back here to the base. Finally had dinner about 11:00 last night. We just finished dinner 20 minutes ago. The time now is 10:45.

Boy they're really driving us. My rear end is dragging on the ground. This is worse than cadet life!!

The hottest rumor has it we'll get a leave about the 28th of this month. That's just about 10 days away. Don't count on anything though, because you know as well as I do you can't trust the Army. Think I'll try and put in a reservation with the airline soon. If I don't get them I can always cancel it. I might be able to get a ride with the Ferry Command from Memphis to Long Beach (for nothing). All we can do is hope! (I know you'll do plenty of that!)

Hey, watch those cracks about me slooping up soap.

I'm sorry I didn't write yesterday, but we just haven't had a spare minute and I'm not kidding either.

Yes, Duffy's Tavern is a good program if one ever finds time to listen.

Your surprise should be ready pretty soon. Don't know what's holding it up.

A surprise? What have you done Fred? Is it nice to keep Mom wondering and waiting about this?

Will you excuse me for this time? I'll probably have something to write tomorrow night when I check the mail.

Good night.

> *Your loving son,*
> *Fred*

★★★

January 18, 1944
Tuesday
Dyersburg, Tenn.

Dear Mom,

It's 11:00 in the morning. Maybe you're wondering why I'm writing so early in the morning. Well I just got tired of going to ground school, so this morning I went on sick call. Just did it to get out of school. Picked up my mail — two letters from you.

I also called up the airline this morning in Memphis. It will cost about $200.00 round trip. They're going to try to get me a reservation for the 29th without a priority, but if we do get our leaves we'll be sure and get priorities so then it will be a lot easier to get a ticket. It would be pretty easy to get to Dallas, Texas from Memphis without a priority, but then without one it would be hard to go on to Burbank. One leaves at 3:00 in the morning also one at 8:19 in the morning and one in the afternoon at 2:11.

As soon as I get a chance I'm going to get to Memphis and go to the Ferry Command and find out if I can get a ride with them. I think if you fly with the Ferry Command you have to bring your own parachute. Wouldn't I look funny carrying a parachute home! (I don't care though! I could look like a tramp if I could only get home!)

I don't know what military training unit means, it's just the address of everyone here now. It's too bad you're not going to get your $100, but dear did we ever get anything that way?

Boy you could have knocked me over with a feather when I read Evelyn was a WAC. She's really doing her share if you ask me.

You'd better see about your eyes and those headaches. I can't have my loved one with headaches. It's just your brains pushing out. You shouldn't be so brainy.

Well it's time to get dressed for the flight line so I'll try to finish this letter tonight. Don't know what we're going to do today or where we're going yet.

Think we start flying the morning schedule tomorrow. That means getting up at 4:15 in the morning.

Later:
I'm just going to add a few lines tonight as it's 10:30 and we have to get up at 4:15 in the morning.

All we did today was to fly high altitude formation. After we finished that at 6:00 I flew the plane for about an hour or so.

Did you ever get the Kleenex and soap?

No, I didn't get to hear F.D.R.'s speech! Would have liked to though!

Do you still listen to Gabriel Heatter?

Gabriel Heatter, famous with the folks at home for his wartime radio broadcast that opened with 'There's good news tonight', was a source of comfort, support and hope for those who had sons, husbands, fathers and friends in harm's way on the war fronts of the Pacific theatre and in Europe. They eagerly tuned their radios to hear what the 'good news' might be every night, hoping against hope that they would indeed hear something that would sustain them until the war was over and their boy came home.[13]

*Guess I'll have to figure out my income tax pretty soon, now that you sent me the blank forms.
I'm going to close for now.*

*Love,
Fred*

★★★

*January 21, 1944
Friday night
Dyersburg, Tenn.*

Dear Mom,

Haven't written you for 2 days. This is my first chance to write. Haven't heard from you for
2 days, but received 2 letters from you today.

Busy isn't the word for what we've been lately!

Got a card from the Railway Express today saying I had a package in Halls, Tenn. It's
only a mile from here. Can't imagine what it is and who it could be from. Says something
about weighing 3 lbs.

Don't know when I can get it as our whole group is restricted to the base. The reason is
that everyone is so tired they just couldn't go to their damn old ground school. Therefore,
they restricted us. You don't learn anything in ground school anyway. Well now the rumor
is that we probably won't get any leaves. Still you can never tell. All we can do is hope and
pray. My ticket is reserved on the airliner home if we get our leaves. Won't lose anything as
I can always cancel it but it pays to have it reserved just in case.

I may as well tell ya-all about the surprise. It's just a big picture of me. Haven't received
it yet. Can't understand what's taking it so long.

Our days lately have been between 16 and 18 hours a day.

Gosh Charles is really getting around. Bet Aunt Frances is glad he's out of Italy and in
Ireland. Looks as if they're moving their paratroopers to England for the big invasion.

It will do Chuck good to get to Ireland for a while. He probably needs a rest.

Yesterday we were supposed to be in a big wing formation. We were to rendezvous with
other groups from Pyote and Alexandria over Little Rock at 20,000. Then all planes were
to fly to Jackson, Miss. for a big review for General Armstrong. It was to be the biggest
formation of B-17s ever assembled in the United States. We got almost as far as Little Rock
and one of our engines started to cause trouble so the pilot had to feather it (that means to
shut it off). Therefore we dropped out of the formation and headed back here for the field on
3 engines. These darn airplanes fly on only one engine if necessary.

The rest of the formation was attacked by P-40s, P-47s, B-25s, etc. it must have been a
swell show. We didn't get to see it.

Don't worry Mom. Don't worry Mom.

My Parker '51' should be back any day now. Hope so! This Schaeffer pen is very nice
though. It writes very smoothly.

Guess what I was doing today at 20,000 feet while we were flying high altitude
formation? I tuned in the radio compass and listened to all the soap operas. Heard 'The

Romance of Helen Trent', 'Our Gal Sunday', etc. Thought of you while I was listening.
Poor old Helen Trent is still trying to find romance after thirty-five.
   Well I can't think of anymore for tonight. You should have this letter Monday dear.

Love,
Fred

★★★

January 27, 1944
Thursday
Dyersburg, Tenn.

Dear Mom,
I just don't know how to start this letter. It's the hardest thing I've ever had to do. When I
phoned you the other day I thought there was a chance left that we would get a leave, but a
lot of things have happened since then. First of all I had no idea we were as near finished as
we were. So what happens, they tell us we're leaving here. Have no idea yet. I wanted to get
home so much I couldn't even think of it.
   Now today we find out they've broken up a lot of crews. By that I mean they've taken
different crewmembers and put them on other crews and put the rest of the crew in a pool
squadron. That means they'll just fill in on other crews. So far they haven't bothered our crew.

The bomber crew was a tight-knit family of men who relied on each other's courage and skill to successfully complete a mission. They had to know not only what their own responsibilities were in the airplane but also the duties and responsibilities of others, their temperament and what you could expect of them. 'Any misfits were identified and replaced.'[14]

Relying on this knowledge of one another often paid life-saving dividends:

We almost blew up when a piece of flak went into the #2 fuel tank and right away gas started gushing out over the wing. I radioed the pilot and told him to feather the #2 engine, right now. He didn't question me and feathered the engine immediately. Later in the flight when the pilot asked me why I wanted him to feather the engine, I told him what I had seen (from the ball turret). The pilot simply said, 'Good God'. We were within seconds of blowing up. This episode really showed me the trust the pilot had in me when I radioed him and told him to feather the engine. He didn't hesitate or question my judgment.[15]

It is not enough to master the exacting details of successful bombing. To be of maximum value to an airplane's crew you must know how to keep yourself physically fit to endure bone-wearying flights without dangerous loss of efficiency. You must know how to give first aid to wounded crew members, recognize the hazards of high altitude, know when and how to use oxygen, what to do if the airplane's oxygen equipment fails. You must know how to improve

Engine flak damage – 'We were within seconds of blowing up'. (Courtesy of Wilbur Richardson)

your vision for bombing at night, how to fight fires in flight. A confident knowledge of emergency equipment and how to use it is vital if you have to bail out or the pilot must ditch your bomber. You should know how to signal for help after a crash landing. In this global war, you also need to learn how to be healthy and strong in any kind of climate.[16]

The airplane is your home. Everyone has a duty and responsibility in the home. You become a family and rely on one another.[17]

The official superhero image of a bomber crew was parlayed into dogma for the masses and for those who were to go into the throes of battle. But ask a crewmember how they became 'tight-knit', and the response was less mechanical and more visceral and emotional:

When you die together a few times, you're bound together. That's what makes a crew so tight-knit.[18]

This afternoon we'll probably find out just exactly when we leave here, but they won't tell us where we're going.

Picked up the pictures in Memphis yesterday. Will send them home today. Will you please get a couple of frames for them. Just cardboard ones. The photographer up the street will have some to fit them. Do what you want with the small ones.

Don't know who would want it. I think the small colored ones are better than the big one.

We're leaving here this evening by train. Not sure where we're going, but I think somewhere in Nebraska. Don't know what my mailing address will be yet.

Lots of things can happen in Nebraska. We could go on submarine patrol, or go to radar school but no matter where we go or what we do I can do what I have to do if I know you'll take care of yourself and don't worry. It may be a little while before I can write so don't worry about that. We'll be on the train, etc.

They're going to send my Parker '51' home so just put it away. Then I'll have a spare pen when I get home. This one writes fine.

Can't think of very much to say for now dear only I just want to say that if I know you're o.k. and take care of yourself, I'll be o.k.

I'll close for now.

All my love,
Fred

Chapter Eight

Deployment

January 30, 1944
Sunday
Kearney, Nebr.

Dear Mom,

We arrived here (Army Air Base, Kearney, Nebr.) this morning at 2:30. They let us sleep until 6:00 then we had to get off the train.

This wasn't such a bad train ride. Spent 2 nights on the train. Well my travels have been added to again.

Came through Kansas City, Mo. and St. Louis and Omaha, Nebr. to here.

There's no use in sending any mail here as we won't be here but a few days. Still don't know what we're going to do or where we're going.

It's colder here than in Tenn., if that's possible.

Guess what's on at the show tonight? 'The Desert Song.' I wouldn't miss it for anything!

Ran into some of the fellows I knew in Bombardier School and also some fellows from Gowen Field and Ardmore.

Gosh there just isn't anything to write yet so I'll quit until tomorrow night. I'll write as often as possible and let you know what's cooking, but as I said before there's no use for you to write until I give you an address.

Fred

EXCERPTS FROM MOVEMENT
ORDERS/OPERATION ORDERS
4 FEBRUARY/5 FEBRUARY 1944

HEADQUARTERS ARMY AIR BASE
Kearney, Nebraska

4 February 1944
SUBJECT: Movement Orders, Heavy Bombardment Crew Number
FG-200-AA-26, To Overseas Destination

```
TO:    P    2nd Lt ALFRED (NMI) MANZ           O808571
       CP   2nd Lt MICHAEL V. PEDULLA          O697371
       N    2nd Lt RICHARD S. WEBB             O696181
       B    2nd Lt FRED S. LULL                O752877
       E    S/Sgt FRED C ZERBE                17060057
       R    S/Sgt ROBERT A. WHELAN            39553275
       AG   S/Sgt AARON (NMI) GORDON           6872346
       CG   Sgt ROBERT G. WILBUR             32588268
       CG   Sgt MICHAEL B. RYAN              32867429
       CG   Sgt JESSE (NMI) PRANGER          16088139
```

1. You are assigned to Shipment FG-200-AA, as crew
   No. FG-200-AA-26, and to B-17 airplane number 42-31723,
   on aircraft project number 92420-R. You are equipped in
   accordance with the provisions of the movement order.
2. You are relieved from atchd unasgnd 7th Heavy Bomb Proc
   Hq, this station, and WP via mil acft and/or rail to AAB,
   Presque Isle, Maine, or such other Air Port of Embarkation
   as the CG, ATC, may direct, thence to the overseas
   destination of Shipment FG-200-AA. Upon arrival at the
   Air Port of Embarkation, control of the above personnel is
   relinquished to the CG, ATC.
3. This is a PERMANENT change of station. You will not be
   accompanied by dependents; neither will you be joined by
   dependents en route to, nor at, the Air Port of embarkation.
   You will not discuss this movement except as may be
   necessary in the transaction of OFFICIAL business.
4. You will use APO 1280-AA (Followed by the numeral ending
   of your shipment crew number, referred to in paragraph 1
   above), C/O Postmaster, New York, New York. Upon arrival
   at final overseas destination, you will use the mailing
   address of the troops at that place. Advise your friends and
   relatives of your permanent APO by forwarding a completed
   V-Mail WD AGO Form 971; also notify the postal officer of the
   theater by forwarding a completed WD AGO Form 204.
5. In lieu of subsistence, a flat per diem of seven dollars ($7.00)
   is authorized for officers and flight officers for travel, and
   for periods of temporary duty en route to final destination,
   when necessary, in accordance with existing law and
   regulations. Payment of mileage is not authorized. Per diem
   will be suspended for such times as the individual is billeted
   and subsisted, as outlined in W.D. Memo, W35-2-42, dated 30
   September 1942. In lieu of subsistence, a flat per diem of seven
   dollars ($7.00) is authorized for enlisted men for travel,

and for periods of temporary duty en route to final destination
in accordance with existing law and regulations, if travel is
performed by air. For travel by rail and for periods of delay
en route to final destination, monetary allowance, in lieu of
rations and quarters, is prescribed in accordance with AR
35-4520. From time of departure from the continental United
States until arrival at permanent overseas station, payment
of per diem is authorized for a maximum of forty-five (45)
days. Officers are relieved of assignment to quarters in B.O.Q.
effective on date of departure. Married officers were not
assigned adequate quarters while at this station.
6. Equipment and baggage of crew members not carried en route
will be prepared and forwarded on government bill of lading.

GRENIER FIELD
MANCHESTER N.H.
STA. 16, NAW, ATC

OPERATION ORDERS
No. 10
The following named crew WP by air in the aircraft as indicated
below at the proper time from Grenier Field, Manchester, New
Hampshire, via North Atlantic Route to the European Theatre
of Operations, London, England, reporting upon arrival to
the Commander, 8th Air Force Service Command, Air Transport
Command Terminals of arrival, British Isles, for further
assignment and duty with the 8th Air Force.

Z PROVISIONAL BOMB GROUP
Shipment No. FG-200-AA
Project No. 92420-R
APO No. 12810-AA-44

B-17G	Crew# 26	#42-31723
Pilot	2nd Lt. Alfred (NMI) Manz	O-808571
Co-Pilot	2nd Lt Michael V. Pedulla	O-697371
Navigator	2nd Lt Richard S. Webb	O-696181
Bombardier	2nd Lt Fred S. Lull	O-752877
Engineer	S/Sgt Fred C. Zerbe	17060057
Radio Op.	S/Sgt Robert A. Whelan	39553275
Arm. Gunner	S/Sgt Aaron (NMI) Gordon	6872346
Career Gunner	Sgt Robert G. Wilbur	32588268
Career Gunner	Sgt Michael B. Ryan	32867429
Career Gunner	Sgt Jesse (NMI) Pranger	16088139

Note: 7 crews were identified for movement to the British Isles
in this set of Orders.

'It's really a beauty!'

Feb. 5, 1944
Sat. morning
Kearney, Nebr.

Dear Mom,
Well, a lot happened after I talked to you yesterday. First of all they gave us an airplane of our own, a brand new B-17 G with the new chin turret. It's really a beauty!

It's really a beauty!

The most noticeable change in the B-17G from its predecessors was the addition of the 'chin turret' – a rotating pod directly beneath the nose of the plane that featured twin 50-calibre machine guns operated by the bombardier. The 350 additional rounds of ammunition gave added protection from frontal attacks by enemy fighters and increased the plane's firepower to thirteen machine guns. In later models of the B-17G, the waist gun positions were staggered and enclosed with Plexiglas windows, which gave the gunners more room to manoeuvre during combat and helped with the reduction of freezing wind when they flew at extreme altitudes.

We packed like mad and loaded our baggage in the plane. As I write this letter it's really Friday night late instead of Sat. morning as I have on top of this letter. We're supposed to have a weather briefing at 1:00 a.m. and take off a little while later.

We also received shoulder holsters and 45s. Look like Chicago gangsters. Will close for now as time is very short.

My address is:
> *Lt Fred S. Lull*
> *A.P.O. # 12810-A.A.-26*
> *New York City, N.Y.*
> *This is only a temporary address.*

                              Love,
                              Fred

★★★

Sunday Morning

Dear Mom,

First of all can't say where I am. You'll notice from this envelope that they don't even have a name on the postmark.

It's beautiful here in the New England states. Snow all over everything. It's kinda cold, but it doesn't seem as cold as Tennessee, because it isn't a damp cold.

Saw the Great Lakes yesterday on the way here.

We won't be here but a short while, just long enough to rest and have everything checked o.k. Seeing that so far we have nothing to do today, think we will go ice skating here on the field. They also have skiing.

When I talked to you I knew we would leave pretty soon, but not like they sprung it on us the same evening. Didn't get any sleep at all until last night. It was quite a long trip.

By all chances I'll be there when you get this letter.

The way I understand it is that we go to school for 6 weeks to 2 months when we get there. Guess this darn schooling will never end.

We got our electric flying suits yesterday.

Dressing for combat turned slender athletic men into stout Michelin tire-like figures with the intent of protecting them against the cold and to the extent possible, the enemy fire that might easily shred through the layers of cloth and protective material. First came long lightweight woolen underwear to help protect against the minus 65 degree temperatures encountered when flying at 25,000 feet. Next, the electric suits, light-blue full length underwear supplements that reached to the ankles and wrists threaded with electric wires that ended in plugs that would eventually be connected to outlets inside the airplane. Flight suit coveralls followed, then heated gloves and boots, also with heater plugs, a Mae West life jacket for a water landing, and a parachute with heavy canvas straps over the shoulders and between the legs. Finally a helmet with throat mike and earphones that allowed for communication between all crew members regardless of the noise of battle.[1]

Well there isn't much more to say so I'll just say it again, take care of yourself and don't worry as we're going to get our break one of these days.

All my love,
Fred

P.S. Tell everyone hello for me.

Chapter Nine

England

V MAIL [with censor's stamp; see note in letter re. mail censor]
February 15, 1944
Stone, England

Dear Mom,

Tonight is the first chance I've had to write. Arrived o.k. Had a very uneventful trip; one I'd never trade for anything. Hope you haven't worried too much!! Can't say where I am until we get our permanent A.P.O. no. but it's darn damp and kinda cold here. You probably can guess where I am. If this means anything to you my pen leaked on the way over. Before I forget will you please send candy bars and cookies as soon as you can. Food is one thing you think about all the time. All I can say is that I was in Belfast Ireland. That is I visited there for an evening. Also, I think I know where Charles is. Not sure, but think he was about 50 miles from me. When there we ate with the R.A.F. officers and one of them told me where he thought Chas.' unit was. I'm going to look him up if I ever get the slightest chance!! This darn foreign money has me nearly nuts trying to figure it out. I still have the valentine I bought in Nebr. for you. It's too late to send it now but you know my thoughts are with you all the time!! Is this writing too small for you to read dear? Let me know. Also I think the best way for you to write is V-Mail as 2 weeks is the longest it will take to get here. You can write as much as you wish. As far as I know we go to school for 6 weeks here. So far the people I've met are very nice. I'll continue on another page. Hope you keep 'em straight.

Love,
Fred

Fred's six weeks of school was of a kind that was meant to give the newest crews as much practice and training as possible in flying conditions that were not available in the United States. The training consisted of learning large plane formation flying and what it was like to fly wingtip to wingtip and avoid mid-air collisions. Add gunnery and bombing practice and familiarisation with the English countryside, newly arrived crews were kept out of battle during these initial weeks of training in England.

Flying in formation required learning the different places a plane would occupy while flying in a group and how to maintain a distance that offered the most protection. *The Pilot Training Manual for the Flying Fortress B-17* stated:

> In flying the Vee formation, aircraft will be flown no closer to one another than 50 feet from nose to tail and wingtip to wingtip.[1]
>
> LeMay wanted planes to fly 25–30 feet apart, wingtip to wingtip. He wanted tighter formations. With formations this close, you had to be careful that someone didn't cut in front of you.[2]

Although the tighter formations provided better concentration of firepower against enemy fighters:

> … flying too close gave you very little room to take evasive action and was the cause of mid-air collisions.[3]

> I was in a six-plane squadron. We started out and everything went wrong that day. We were flying through clouds and the younger pilots did not know how to fly in formation well. When we came out of the clouds the plane on my right wing was way off to the right. He swung his plane over too sharply and came within four feet of the top of our plane. That's the closest I came to death.[4]

Results of a mid-air collision – 'That's the closest I came to death'.[5]

'Put your wingtip in the other plane's waist window.'[6] (Photograph by Roy Test; used with permission)

If 50ft of distance, wingtip to wingtip, seems close, particularly with a wingspan of nearly 104ft, and with Curtis LeMay wanting even tighter formation flying with distances between wingtips of 25–30ft, flying closer would seem almost suicidal.

> You're flying off someone's wing, and you don't take your eyes off the wing – that's all that exists. We were often the lead plane of a three-plane element, so being aware of where the other planes were was very important. The formations were tight – a common expression was to: 'Put your wingtip in the other plane's waist window.'[7]

Sheet #2

Dear Mom,
Here I go again on another sheet. Did my Parker '51' get home yet? Some snapshots will also come home. If you were here you'd be wearing your red flannels and I don't mean maybe. My letters will be between 10 and 14 days in getting home so don't worry if you don't receive them as regularly as you did before, but I'm going to write as often as possible!!! Airmail letters are pretty good in summer time but V-Mail is best now. A regular letter takes about one month. The shows here aren't too new but some of them aren't so bad. Gosh it's hard to write as there are so many things I can't talk about. Have you noticed that I censor my own mail? Boy the ocean looked cold and rough. Please tell everyone hello for me. You may have to use an eye glass to read the first page of this letter but from now I'll write larger. I'll close for now. All I ask is for you to take care of yourself and then I'll be o.k.
Love,
Fred

★★★

Friday Feb. 18, 1944
Stone, England

Dear Mom,
Missed writing to you yesterday but as nothing much happened you didn't miss anything.
You can see from the top of the page I'm in England. In my first V-letter I couldn't say, but
you probably knew where I was anyway.

Been into several different towns since being on this present post. The trouble is that both
times have been at night and with the blackout you just can't see 3 feet in front of yourself
and I'm not kidding. Everyone carries a flashlight. Pardon me, I should say 'electric torch' as
the British say. Everything closes very early. There's hardly anything to do at all in most of
these towns. Food is very scarce. People haven't seen rationing until they've been over here.
Our blackouts at home were a farce compared to these. These people haven't seen a streetlight
for over 4 years now. When you go into a town at night it looks as if it's a ghost town, but in
a small area there are thousands of people.

There is a slight reflected glow on the streets from the lights of automobiles and
buses, when any of these happen to be passing. But if no such vehicle is near, you
simple have to feel your way with your feet.

When I pull my curtains and open the window before going to bed … I can
see no more than if I were standing in the middle of the Sahara Desert on the
darkest night of the year, blind-folded and with my eyes shut. Looking down
from my sixth-story window, I can't see a single pin point of light anywhere.[8]

Did I tell you before that while we were in Ireland I drank tea just to keep warm?
Thank goodness we get coffee here in our own mess. The English use a substitute for
coffee. It's terrible.

By the time Fred and his fellow crewmembers arrive, England has been at war for
more than four years. Food, coal, clothing and other necessities of life are in short
supply and what is available is not of the quality that these newly arrived visitors
have come to expect. These fresh warriors need to learn that '… It is always impolite to criticize your hosts; it is militarily stupid to criticize your allies.'[9]

The food we get is pretty good. It's very tasty, nothing like I ever got at home though! The
milk is powdered, so are the eggs.
Sent a cablegram yesterday to let you know I was o.k. because my first V-letter won't be
there for awhile. By the way check and let me know which comes the fastest: V-mail or this
airmail letter. Just check the dates on them from the time they were mailed.
Learned a lot about censoring today. By that I mean I learned a lot of things I could say
and not say. For instance I can say I flew over here, but can't say from where I took off or
landed or how long it took. All I know is I'm glad we didn't have to ditch in the middle of
the ocean. It looked too cold and rough.
I've spent most of today censoring mail. Boy do you get some laughs reading some of
them. Some of the boys think they're pretty cagey and can fool you by just hinting and

stuff. Well it's just like I've hinted around in first letters to you. One letter I cut quite a bit off the end because the guy had told exactly what the weather was like so on the end of the letter I wrote 'the part I cut off was just about weather' so his folks wouldn't wonder what was censored. Ain't I sweet? (Don't answer). Officers censor their own mail, but once in awhile they spot check it.

> The gunners are inveterate writers of long, wordy and usually pretty dull epistles to the folks at home. Wordy and long because they try very hard not to talk shop and still know an urge within themselves to push out to their folks a little of the feeling that is with them every minute until they have finished their tour, one way or another; dull because the censor for military reasons will not allow them to speak of operations in which they have taken part, and those operations make up most of their lives now. Everyone in the hut writes letters; even the gunners who haven't anyone to write to write to someone.[10]

The cigarettes are very cheap for the boys, about 5 cents or in English money 3 pence. They are allowed 2 packs a week and one candy bar.

Boy it's going to be good to hear from you! Haven't had a word since I left Kearney, Nebr. It'll take awhile before your letters catch up with me.

Also in my last letter I didn't tell you I was in Labrador. Couldn't say so before, but now I can. I know you wouldn't like Labrador at all but I think it would be pretty in summertime. Oh, also one more place I've been to is Scotland. The hills of Scotland are beautiful. So green and rolling. The English countryside is just what we've always seen in motion pictures. In Ireland every piece of land is used. They have hedges all around their land. Once more I say there's no place like California.

You ought to hear them talk here. They use a lot of our slang. It sure sounds funny. In general it's pretty easy to talk to them. Streetcars are called 'trams'; trucks, 'lorries'; drugstores, 'chemist shops.' The first time we had dinner with R.A.F. boys the first thing they would say to you is 'Good Trip!' It sounds funny the way they say it.

> British slang is something you will have to pick up for yourself. But even apart from slang, there are many words which have different meanings from the way we use them and many common objects have different names. For instance, instead of railroads, automobiles and radios, the British will talk about railways, motorcars and wireless sets.[11]

One of the funniest things is to have them give you a destination to find something. They go on for hours giving many directions and then when they're finished they say 'you cawn't miss it.' It's a standing joke.

It became more than a standing joke. Two B-17s, one from the 94th Bomb Group and one from the 389th Bomb Group, and two B-24s (one each from the 93rd BG and the 448th BG) were named, 'You Cawn't Miss It'.[12]

The main thing I want to do while I'm here is to go to London. It's the only place over here that you can probably feel a little bit more at home in.

Went into town last night and saw a show. Pretty good but they cut them quite a bit. The English don't know it though as they're always shorter than at home. London is about the only place you can see a show uncut. Also in London a show costs about 10 shillings which is $2.00 in our dough.

I almost have heart failure driving with one of the Englishmen. The darn fools drive on the wrong side of the street. It seems funny to have the steering wheel on the right side, etc. One thing you never hear, the English complain about their tough time or whine.

There's a very good chance of my going back to where Charles might be for school. I mean I'll go to school near where he is, I hope!

From what we hear from rumors we may get a good deal here. Things are changing.

Did some of my washing the other night. Haven't had a chance to send it to a laundry as we've been on the move too much. Just for the fun of it look on the map and see where I've been since leaving Nebr. Maybe you can trace about where I've been if you're as smart as I think you are.

Mom it's getting a little harder now to think of anything more to write for this time. It'll be a couple of days again before I can write.

Once more I'm going to say if your eyes are still bothering you go to the doctor before you ruin them beyond the point where glasses will help!!!!

Any extra money we have after payday we can cable home free. Not bad eh!

One more funny thing and I'll quit. These Irish and English trains are really good. Just like you see in the movies.

Take care of yourself. My thoughts are with you always. Remember what I said over the phone about our break. We're bound to get it. I'm going to drop everyone a line or two on V-mail.

Good night.

Your loving son,
Fred

P.S. Hope this letter hasn't been too long and tiresome for you. It's such small paper though.

★★★

V-MAIL
Feb. 20, 1944

Dear Mom,
I'm also writing an airmail letter tonight. Just wanted to drop this V-Mail letter so you would have my new and permanent A.P.O.# and also my cable address. This letter will probably get home quicker than the airmail letter I also wrote tonight.

Love,
Fred

★★★

'The plane and crew found a home at Rougham Air Base near Bury St Edmunds.'The control tower at Rougham – 'Chairleg Tower'. (Courtesy of Wilbur Richardson)

Feb. 20, 1944
Sunday
Stone, England

Dear Mom,
Don't have much to write tonight, just wanted to say good night.
Also dropped you a V-mail letter tonight giving my new A.P.O. # and cable address. This is my permanent A.P.O. #.
Well since I last wrote you I've moved again. This time I think it's a permanent place for some while.

The plane and crew found a home at Rougham Air Base near Bury St Edmunds. It was to be their permanent station for the duration of their deployment.They became a part of the Eighth Air Force, 3rd Air Division, 94th Bomb Group (H), 331st Bombardment Squadron.

The group designation on planes was a large white 'A' on a black square on the yellow tail, the 'Square A'. Additional plane markings included 2ft red bands around the outer portion of the wings and the rear fuselage of the unpainted shining aluminium fortress and later in the year, for planes of the 331st Squadron, blue engine cowlings.[13]

This was a unit that would be called with pride and affection during and after the war: 'The Big Square A'.This was a unit that had distinguished itself in combat and received Distinguished Unit Citations for action over Germany, on 17 August 1943 and 11 January 1944.[14]

This was a unit with its own anthem:

When this war is over, the final victory won; When there are no more missions, and all the fighting's done; When airmen get together to toast the days of yore, You'll always hear the mention of the fame of Ninety-Four.[15]

We start to school Tuesday morning from 9:00 in the morning until 9:00 in the evening.

We're attached to an operational group now, and from what I've seen and heard things are pretty darn good.

This darn field is scattered all over the countryside. You have to walk about a mile before you can get to the mess hall or anyplace at all so everyone rides bicycles. Bicycles are the

The Men of the Ninety-Fourth.
(Courtesy of Frank Halm)

B-17G with 94th Bomb Group markings. (Author's collection)

thing both here and in Ireland. We're going to try and get ourselves one as soon as possible. I can just picture myself riding into the nearest town around here. I'll probably get all mixed up and ride on the wrong side of the road. I still can't get used to going on the wrong side of the road. Instead of signs saying 'main highway' they say 'major road'.

The food on our field here is darn good but keeping warm is the big problem. Coal is pretty scarce.

They really treat us swell here. Everyone gets to know each other because there aren't too many men here. Everyone gets together every night in the Officers' Club and talk, read, write letters, etc.

'Gets to know each other' – contemporary language – bonding, forming a brotherhood; what was it like then to 'get to know each other'?

There's not much I can say about what we're doing or going to do. All I can say is for you to follow the headlines and read Life magazine. They can tell you just what the 8th Air Force is doing. Every once in awhile Life has stories and pictures about the 8th Air Force in the E.T.O. (European Theatre of Operations).

You said before that you wanted to know what exactly I'm doing. Well I want to say a few things. First of all from our field today they sent over 30 ships and everyone of them returned. That sounds hard to believe, but it's the truth. The only man I saw or heard about being hurt had a black eye. He fell and hit his eye on a machine gun. Boy that's darn good for a day raid.

On the day that Fred remarks, 'Boy that's darn good for a day raid', a mission to Tutow, Germany, left with snow and ice on the runways. They flew in a tight

This photo, widely distributed to the media, including *Life* magazine, shows the near-beauty of contrails but neglects to mention their finger-pointing attributes to antiaircraft gunners on the ground and the problems these vapor trails cause for formation flying and navigation. (*Yank*, 17 March 1944)

formation, ready to defend themselves as crewmembers saw others in the raid get pounded by GAF fighters. However, flak was light and inaccurate, there was only slight damage to five B-17s and, as reported by the historian of the 94th Bomb Group, there were no losses or injuries.[16]

One more thing, dear. If you ever receive a telegram saying I'm missing it doesn't mean too much, because most of the guys that are reported missing turn up as prisoners of war. Sometimes it takes 4 or 5 months before they find out that they are prisoners so you can see it doesn't mean too much.

While we're on this subject, remember the Schweinfurt raid when we lost 60 bombers? That means 600 men were lost. Do you know how many finally turned up as prisoners of war? Over 400 turned up as prisoners. If anyone should ask me, I think that's remarkable.

This information would have done little to ease Louise's mind and heart to learn that only 200 of the 600 men lost on the Schweinfurt raid were killed in action and the remainder had become prisoners of war. She would not have known or much cared about the outcome of the raid if Fred had been among either group, the 200 killed or the 400 imprisoned. Her boy would have been gone, plain and simple. The fact that the raid had little effect on the production of ball bearings and various war-related industries also would have been lost on her, inconsequential to her loss.[17]

One last remark. American airmen, both officers and enlisted men are treated pretty darn good in German prison camps. Officers don't do a bit of work. Also their pay goes on and is paid

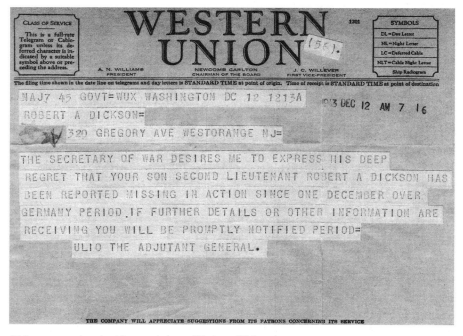

(Telegram reprinted with permission of Robert Dickson)

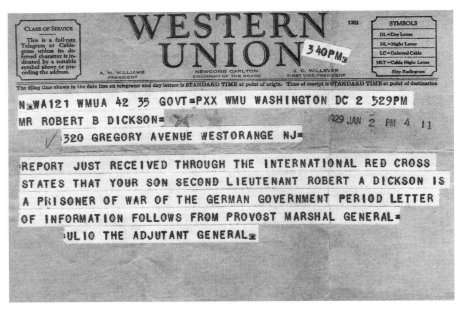

Notification of parents that their son was being held as a POW was done by telegram. My folks hated to see the Western Union guy riding his bicycle up the street because it was always the possibility that it was bad news.[18] (Telegram reprinted with permission of Robert Dickson)

them when they are released or exchanged. These things aren't easy to write or easy for you to read, but they're realities and I know you want to know just what the situation is and above all I know you can take it, Mom!!! Just remember now Mom if I'm ever reported missing don't give up hope because I'm going to be all right and come through this thing o.k.!!!

U.S. flyers were called terrorflieger (terror flier) by German civilians. They had been told, and probably to a large extent had witnessed, that the US Air Force was engaged in 'area bombing,' hitting churches, orphanages, hospitals, etc., rather than bombing strategic sites … and so the label terrorflieger.

Our bombardiers were always briefed on a specific aiming point on a target such as a factory, a railroad yard or military installation. Because of poor visibility, turbulence or maneuvering at bomb release, the bombs often went astray. Also, for a plane in trouble, one that was losing power, the first thing it did was to jettison its bombs to lighten the load and God only knows where they landed.

The Luftwaffe treated us fairly well as compared to German civilians – the civilians would ill-treat or kill U.S. crew – several crewmembers in the Stalags were seen with rope burns on their necks where the Germans tried to hang them. The German army rescued airmen from the civilians who would threaten, beat, and kill crewmembers they had captured.[19]

Well dear I can't think of anything more to say for tonight. This hasn't been a very pleasant letter, but I knew you'd want to know the facts and I sincerely believe in my heart you will feel better after reading this letter and have time to think it over. It will ease your mind and feelings a little I hope. Just believe; that's all that is necessary.

Love,
Fred

This one letter probably did more to give Louise cause to worry than any other letter Fred wrote during the war. It was a difficult letter to write, even more difficult to read and fully comprehend. The reality of the consequences of Fred's participation in the war, the possibility of injury, death or at least imprisonment, is brought home for the first time in this letter. Fred's explanation of these possibilities probably provide little or no comfort to his mother, but the frank presentation of what could happen in light of what had already happened on a specific mission seems to be as much an act of reassurance to himself as an attempt to ease his mother's fears and anxieties.

Don't worry Mom. Don't worry Mom.

Feb. 23, 1944
Wed.

Dear Mom,

Haven't written to you for a couple of days. Been pretty busy. I'm writing this before going back to school tonight. Just finished dinner. Boy the eats are pretty darn good here. This darn school business keeps us going like the dickens. From 9:00 in the morning until 9:00 in the evening.

Bought a bicycle the other day. Makes it a lot easier getting around now.

Notice on this next sentence I don't say when it happened, dates and names of places can't be used, but all I can say is recently. Well here goes. Recently I heard the engines of German planes overhead at night. A little later we could hear bombs hit and hear the antiaircraft guns firing. My guess is that it was quite a distance away from where we are. Sound travels pretty good at night when things are more quiet.

Dick (my navigator) paid 11 pounds or in our money $44.00 for his bicycle. Mine only cost 6 pounds or $24.00. They have more accidents with bikes than anything else. It seems funny doesn't it?

New crews were told by old timers that '... the bicycle was Hitler's secret weapon and that no one was a combat veteran until he had experienced having a tooth filled by the dentist using a foot-powered drill'.[20]

A lot of the boys are finishing up their operational tours and are going home now. Boy I'd like to be one of the lucky stiffs. When they get home they get quite a long leave and then are made instructors. You'll finally have your wish when I come home and they make me an instructor.

May I add here that I've seen quite a bit of rain and snow during my travels in England.

Boy it'll sure seem swell when I get some mail from you. Don't know how long it will be yet before it finally catches up with me. Probably won't be much longer.

Fred and his $24.00 bicycle.

Mom, you know how you've heard stories about bomber crews getting drunk, loud and boisterous after a day's raid. Well I haven't seen it happen yet. Most of them sit and play cards, listen to the radio, talk, and have a couple of drinks. I think that's pretty darn good.

They're too tired, too weary to be boisterous. Exhaustion trumps rowdy.

Heard 'Command Performance' last night after dinner before going back to school. Bing Crosby and Dinah Shore were on it. Boy the 'Old Groaner' is pretty darn good. Guess he goes on a lot of programs for the Armed Forces. Also heard Red Skelton the other night.

I usually can get up out of bed pretty easy in the mornings but since coming over here I just can't get the nerve to get up as it's so darn cold. Finally it gets so late and time creeps up and we're supposed to be at school and so I just fall out. Will quit for now and add some more later tonight when school is over.

Later:
Nothing more has happened so I shall sign off for this time. 'Dear John.'
Good night dear.
Love,
Fred

★★★

V-MAIL
Feb. 25, 1944
Bury St Edmunds

Dear Mom,

Right now I'm sitting in front of the so-called stove trying to warm my feet. Just got back from school. It's pretty hard for me to write, as so far we're not doing very much except go to school. It'll be a lot easier when I start getting some mail from home because you'll have questions for me to answer plus the fact I always have a lot of remarks and questions for you. Mom, you would be ashamed of me the way I'm eating over here. Don't get up in time for breakfast so make up for it at lunch and dinner. It's too bad Roosevelt had trouble over the tax bill but you've got to hand it to him for trying to get more taxes and cut down all these high profits, especially if he's going to run again. There's nothing political about that. He's doing everything he can to win this war and pay for it now and not years later on. Space is short here so I'll end for tonight.

Good night,
Fred

★★★

Feb. 27, 1944
Sunday
Bury St Edmunds

Dear Mom,

A few quick lines before going to dinner. Just got out of school and then have to go back after dinner. I've had another slight cold. That's one thing you can never get away from over here.

Got our money the other day for our expenses in coming over here. I collected $73.50. Not bad; in fact I made quite a bit on the deal. Going to wait until payday which is about 3 days away and then put what extra I have from my pay and add it to the $73.50 and buy a money order and send it home. In writing this brief bit of ramblings tonight I figure that by today or some day soon you should start receiving my letters. In fact by the time you get this one, regular mail service will be well under way.

Boy was I surprised last night. Was sitting around our stove (a fugitive from a junk pile) trying to get warm when the orderly came in and said there's a telephone call for Lt. Lull. Guess who it was. You guessed it, it was Hal Hoerner. It sure sounded good to hear him. Talked to him for about 20 minutes. He's going to try to get here as soon as he can. Gosh, Hal has been over (here) 18 months. That's quite a long time. He may get home pretty soon. We had some good laughs about things that happened when he was at the bank, etc. He writes to Giles about once a month. Giles is Mr Hall.

Time out for dinner:

Not a bad dinner; chicken and biscuits. The Army chicken never appeals to me very much.

The time is very short before I get back to school. There's not very much more I can think of. Are you taking care of yourself? You'd better be or when the boss gets home he'll really give you a good bawling out!!!

From the paper I see that ya-all had some snow and quite a bit of rain. Notice I said ya-all, I haven't quite lost my southern accent yet. By the time I get home I'll sound like one these darn Englishmen. Heaven forbid that.

They have a darn good newspaper called 'Stars and Stripes' over here for the Armed Forces. It keeps us up to date on everything both here and at home.

Started in the First World War and revived in the Second World War, first as a weekly newspaper in April 1942 and within a few months as a daily, *Stars and Stripes* the European edition was printed in *The London Times* building. The paper used as staff reporters soldier writers who were officially accredited as war correspondents with access to GIs in the field and generals at headquarters. Service men and women looked forward to the articles by Ernie Pyle and the cartoons of Bill Mauldin, Pulitzer Prize winners both, for their depiction of the life of the ordinary GI without frills or the interference of the brass hats.[21]

Glad to see that F.D.R. and Barkley have settled their dispute!!

You ought to see all the guys around here wearing their medals, etc. The Air Medal, D.F.C.s etc.

Your turn will come, Fred. Your turn will come.

> *Will sign off now.*
> *Love,*
> *Fred*

★★★

> V-MAIL
> *Feb. 29, 1944*
> *Bury St Edmunds*

Dear Mom,
Just a quick report tonight to let you know I'm thinking of you and that I'm feeling o.k. We've had one day now that reminded me of home except that it was a lot colder but the sun was out anyway. Took some pictures today and am going to try and take some more tomorrow. My letters to you are probably coming all mixed up. Some that are written later are arriving sooner than some others. Hope you get these in pretty good order. When we want a shower or bath we have to go about a mile so consequently we don't get as many as we're used to. The British don't go much for sanitary conditions. Guess we Americans are kinda spoiled as we are used to too many luxuries and conveniences. Another thing, I don't think they ever drink any water. No drinking faucets are around. It was a month yesterday since leaving Dyersburg. Well it's kinda late so I'll quit for now.

> *Love,*
> *Fred*

★★★

March 3, 1944
Friday
Bury St Edmunds

Dear Mom,

Didn't write to you last night so am doing so today before going back to school. We flew all yesterday afternoon.

Sent my laundry a week ago and it's not back yet, may come this afternoon. I'm out of everything so therefore I need it pretty much. Sent all my clothes to the cleaners last week. Got them this morning. They sure don't do them like in the States. Think they wash them in 100 octane gasoline. You have to hang them out to air and let the wrinkles come out of 'em before wearing.

There was ice on the road yesterday morning going to breakfast, so careful me knew it was there and slowed down and tried to turn carefully, but I fell clear across the road and tore my pants a little. Must have looked funny sliding with the bicycle on top of me!! These darn bikes are more trouble than anything else around here.

We had more guys in the hospital with broken arms and legs from riding their bicycles than from combat injuries.[22]

Let me know if you received these 2 money orders will you? Going to do my best to find out where Chuck is located!

Since coming over here one kinda gets sorta raunchy. By that I mean not as neat and tidy as before. There just aren't the facilities here to keep too clean. You'd think after all these

From inside the programme of this all-male GI show:
'The cuties dancing on this stage
Are pure and sweet and virgin
All stage door Johnnies please take note
They won't respond to your urgin'!'

A GI show act. (Author's collection)

years the British would have gotten shower and bathing facilities. I'm going to quit now
Mom. It's time for school. I'll finish tonight.

Later
Just got back from seeing a G.I. show. It was pretty good. It was a soldier show. Some of the
acts were pretty clever. Had a sandwich and cup of coffee afterwards and now I'm sitting by
old faithful (our English stove) finishing up this letter.

Well can't think of anymore for tonight. Boy when I get home I'll never leave it again.
Except when we go on a vacation!!!

Good night,
Fred

★★★

Sunday
March 5, 1944
Bury St Edmunds

Dear Mom,
Well yesterday I was 22 years old. Sure doesn't seem a year since I had my last birthday
at Santa Ana. Remember all the birthday cards I got!! Everyone sent me one. We just flew
around here yesterday and today.

Saw 'Falcon in Danger' last night. Tonight is Red Skelton in 'Whistling in Brooklyn.'
It's just a dinky little building for a show and the screen is just about ¼ the size of a
regular screen.

Never thought I'd miss mail so much, but haven't had a letter since 1st of February.
That's over a month. I miss yours more than anything! They should start getting here in

another week. That temporary A.P.O.# will take longer than the permanent one you have now. Boy I'm really out of touch with what's going on at home and how you are.

Everyone here is optimistic about the air war being over sooner than most people think. At the rate German airplanes are being shot down plus the fact that their airplane factories are being blown to bits by our bombers is what makes us think so. Once the German air force is out of the way things will really be simple.

A more intensive campaign was possible during the early months of 1944, reaching a peak of sustained effort during the period 20–25 February and maintained, subject to tactical considerations, until the end of May. The substantial damage to factories and assembly plants, coupled with destruction in aerial battle of German first-line combat aircraft by both bombers and escorting fighters on a hitherto unprecedented scale, was unquestionably the decisive factor in reducing the GAF to the point where it had no more than a nuisance value during the critical invasion period. This was attested by the remarkably low number of sorties directed against the Allied beachheads and shipping lanes.

The following figures give some appreciation of the war of attrition by the Eighth Air Force against the GAF. During the first months of 1944, 6,813 bombers dropped 16,522 tons on aircraft factories, and 8,257 bombers dropped 21,267 tons on airfields and airparks. In the same period 1,914 first-line enemy aircraft were destroyed by the bombers in aerial combat and 1,682 were destroyed or damaged on the ground as a result of bombing of air parks, airfields, and factories. To these figures can be added the impressive total accounted for by escorting fighters – 1,696 destroyed in combat and 761 in strafing attacks.[23]

I didn't know that they had so many snow flurries in England. Always thought it was a lot warmer and sunnier. Haven't seen any fog as yet.

From the papers I gather that we're doing pretty good in the Pacific with the Japs. Guess you're still getting some rain, but in a couple of more months summer will be there and then you can start sweating. Believe me I'd rather be sweating any day than always feel cold!

As I said before there just isn't much to write yet so I'll quit for this time. Just wanted to say goodnight to you Mom.

Love,
Fred

★★★

March 9, 1944
Thursday
Bury St Edmunds

Dear Mom,

Missed writing to you for 2 days. Will you forgive me? I knew you would.

Had another phone call from Hal this afternoon. We had a few more laughs.

Still nothing new has happened. The only thing that has happened is that 3 of our gunners have gone on a couple of raids. That is they flew with another crew. Dick, our navigator, went on the raid today. He also went with another crew. It's his first one.

By the way how do you like the way they've hit Berlin for the last 4 days!!

Berlin was being bombed relentlessly — 500 American bombers targeted the German capital the day before Fred's 9 March letter and a few days later, the Eighth Air Force launched another attack of more than 600 aircraft. [24]

Remember how Goering said bombs would never fall on Germany. Bet Gabriel Heatter is having a field day getting dramatic.

Sgt Whelan, our radio operator was telling me today how his dad listened to Gabriel Heatter all the time.

I'm getting to be quite an electrician now. Installed a light over my bed today with a switch on the wall and everything. Of course you might know the lights in the hut wouldn't turn out as I had done something to them while fixing my light. Finally Al, our pilot had to change some of my wiring and connections before we could turn lights out.

I have to buy a transformer for the radio before it will play here as the English electricity is different than ours. 50 cycles, I think.

Finally think I'm getting used to this cold and being damp all the time.

Please excuse this writing as I'm doing it in rather of a hurry so I can turn out my light so the boys can sleep.

I expect to go on a raid any morning now, Mom. After a raid or two then we go on our own crew again. Don't worry because everything is going to be o.k.

I'll close for now and write again tomorrow night.

Love,
Fred

★★★

[Undated; immediately follows 3/9/44 letter]
Bury St Edmunds

Dear Mom,

Didn't do a darn thing yesterday. Only went to school for a couple hours. Don't have to go to school today until 1:30 this afternoon. Go until about 4:00 and then we have some kind of a special meeting. Think some general is going to talk to us. We have to wear Class 'A' uniforms.

The other day we were flying around here at 22,000 feet. Didn't even have my electric suit turned on. The temperature was 32 degrees below zero. The reason I was so warm is that the sun was shining in on me in the nose and I was actually sweating.

Flew out over the English Channel. Wasn't very far from France. The water looked awful muddy, but seemed pretty calm.

We test fired our guns at altitude. Mine worked good. Boy these 50 cal. machine guns really kick around in my chin turret. I asked Smitty if he could imagine me cleaning, oiling and completely taking apart a 50 cal. machine gun and generally taking care of them. I know you can see me doing it. I'm so mechanical! Don't laugh too hard.

The student gets a 16 hour course that teaches him how the approximately 200 parts of a .50-caliber machine gun tick. He devotes five more hours to the secret sights. He gets 15 hours on sighting and sight harmonization, learns how to sight a spot through the gun barrel, finds out how to estimate the drop in the trajectory of a bullet and masters the various sight adjustments.'[25]

I've got my corner of the hut all fixed up now. Especially when I get the radio going.

The nut (aka a Nissen nut): Fred's home away from home was like all the others scattered over England, and in fact all over the globe where US armed forces served. They were metal buildings that looked like soup cans cut length-wise – cold in winter, hot in summer, with a few windows and sometimes two doors. Bunk beds lined each side, and there was a coal/coke-burning stove in the middle, which did little to heat the interior, especially at either end of the hut. Coal was at a premium (it was tightly controlled in Britain through rationing) and, according to Andy Rooney, scrounging and theft from base supplies was not uncommon.[26]

Aircrews stole coke or coal from fenced locked storage yards. When lots of coke/coal filled the area one could run a shovel under the fence and trash the pile of coke/coal to drag a few hunks out to use for heating. Our co-pilot arranged to buy bark or bits of wood from a local sawmill. It was stacked under our beds until burnt.[27]

Fred's hut, Swoon Inn, Rougham Air Base, Bury St Edmunds.

'The hut.'

In the trip over something went wrong with it so the boys in the radio shop down on the line are fixing it for me. Darn nice of them! With the radio I've got the best setup in the hut. The batteries are still good. Wish they'd wear out so I could throw them away. It would make the radio a lot lighter and easier to carry around.

A man approached death rather decently in the Air Forces. He died well fed and clean-shaven, if that was any comfort. He was at the front only a few hours of the day, instead of day and night for months on end. In the evening he came back to something approximating a home and fireside. He still had some acquaintance with an orderly life …[28]

Did I mention it before how un-modern the English are? Their electric lights look like the ones that Edison first invented. They just don't have anything that equals ours.

Gosh, you just can't spend money around here. There's nothing to buy and besides we haven't been off the field yet. Probably will get a chance when we get a 48-hour pass. I'll quit for now and finish up tonight. Oh before I forget, wrote to Charles again the other night. Sure want to find out where he is and go see him if possible!!

Later:

One of our gunners got a letter today. It was from New York. It was addressed to his permanent A.P.O# so I should be getting one darn soon.

I bet some of the letters you wrote when I first gave you my temporary A.P.O. # will get here long after the ones that are addressed to our permanent #. Boy that first letter is really going to be a wonderful feeling!!!!!!

Well, I'll say 'adieu' for now. Get the French!!

Love,
Fred

★★★

March 14, 1944
Tuesday
Bury St Edmunds

Dear Mom,

Haven't written to you for 2 days so will just send a few lines now. Still nothing new or exciting has happened. They got us up to go on a raid the other day but at the last minute it was scrubbed (cancelled).

I've been reading Sherlock Holmes the last few nights before going to sleep.

My name is Sherlock Holmes. It is my business to know what other people don't know.[29]

My new lamp makes it swell! The radio has a burned out filter condenser. Will get the radio in 2 more days. To pass the time in the evenings we usually go to the show. Pictures are rather old, but free.

We flew a practice mission around here today. It was pretty cold.

We should be getting a pass pretty soon and then I'll get to see London and Hal and try to find out Chuck's address.

It doesn't seem possible that we've been on this field a month this Sat. That doesn't include the rest of our time in Ireland, Scotland and England.

We have 30 missions to do. This is called an operational tour. It means we have 30 raids over enemy territory to do. Then after that we may come home as instructors, or take pilot training or we can stay here as Intelligence Officers, or fun jobs that are on the ground. All we would have to do then to collect our flying pay is to take a four-hour airplane ride around here every month.

German pilots and crew didn't fly 25 or 30 missions and then go home like we did. They flew until they were killed or the war ended, whichever came first.[30]

They put a notice on the board that some of us were late or absent from a meeting the other day. We're supposed to write a military letter to the major telling why we were late or absent. My crew is just going to ignore it. Maybe they'll get mad and send us home!

The writing of a letter explaining why the crew didn't attend the meeting smacks of command behaviour that is pure chickenshit:

> Chickenshit is so called – instead of horse – or bull – or elephant shit – because it is small-minded and ignoble and takes the trivial seriously. Chickenshit can be recognized instantly because it never has anything to do with winning the war.[31]

Besides I was there and not late either.

Incidentally there's another meeting tonight at 7:00. It's just about time for dinner so will stop for now dear. Bet we have meat loaf!

Love,
Fred

Chapter Ten

Operational Missions

Operational Mission 1: 16 March 1944 – Augsburg, Germany

Four hundred and one Eighth Air Force B-17s, twenty-five from the 94th BG (H), are included in the attack on Augsburg. An additional sixty-four B-17s attack other targets of opportunity in Germany. Eighteen are lost. ★

> Training in the States nowhere near prepared you for the slaughter of the first mission. It was like someone slashing at you with a big knife.[1]

Operational Mission 2: 18 March 1944 – Munich, Germany

One hundred and ninety-six B-17s, twenty-six from the 94th, participate in this attack on Munich aircraft plants, airfields and other targets of opportunity in the area.

By the time Fred and his crew flew their first combat mission the Eighth Air Force had:

> … become a mighty power capable of going where it (wanted), when it (pleased). (The) contribution of those early squadrons lives still in that they not only opened the way into darkest Germany but fixed undying traditions for American airmen.[2]

The costs of this dominance and these 'undying traditions' were more than dramatic; they were hellish. By 16 March 1944, the 94th had flown ninety-seven

---

★ Mission data are adapted from: *The Army Air Forces in World War II; Combat Chronology, 1941–1945*, compiled by Kit Carter and Robert Mueller; *Air War Europa; Chronology* by Eric Hammel; and *Lingering Contrails of The Big Square A; A History of the 94th Bomb Group (Heavy); 1942–1945* by Harry E. Slater. Three missions are listed by BG mission number rather than by specific location.[3]

combat missions and lost eighty-two planes with 820 crewmen (ten in each plane), killed, missing in action or prisoners of war. By VE day, 8 May 1945, these figures would climb inexorably, month by month, to a total loss of 156 planes and 1,560 crewmembers. These losses contributed significantly to those suffered by the entire Eighth Air Force for the whole of the war: 4,418 B-17s and 2,242 B-24s were lost with a staggering 43,742 airmen killed or missing.[4]

Early in the war, the USAAF command was committed to the concept of daylight bombing and the self-defending bomber. Fighter support simply was not possible for those bombers with targets well within the Continent. As bombers crossed the European coastline in these early days of the bomber war, fighter escorts reached their limits for gasoline consumption and left the bombers on their own. By flying in tight combat box formations, each plane in a formation gained protection from its brothers when attacked by enemy fighters, but paid the penalty when entering flak zones of the target. Being closely stacked and aligned in formation increased the possibility of losses – from any one or several flak bursts hitting more than one plane; the terrifying possibility of another plane hitting its comrade as it exploded; or as a damaged plane, with loss of flight controls, tumbled out of formation and crashed into another.

Additionally, through all of this, there was the need for the bombardier to concentrate – concentration made all the more difficult because of these combat distractions.

> It must be an inhuman concentration that can ignore a sky ahead rocking with ack-ack and shells streaming in from (fighters) in the rear – and see nothing but the target below. Major problems, aside from the ever possible bomber's blight, zero visibility, with the distraction by fighter planes, blasting antiaircraft fire, and the cones of blinding searchlights, that make instrument reading impossible.[5]

The percentage of American aircraft losses diminished as long-range fighter escorts became available and the GAF fighter losses continued to mount. However, GAF fighters and anti-aircraft artillery combined to exact a toll on Allied bombers, with a loss rate of 9.1 per cent in October 1943 to a low of 3.5 per cent six months later. Both percentages represented a significant loss of planes and their crews, and crewmen were aware of these loss figures and worried about them. One airman was 'kind of concerned' when, out of thirteen bombers sent out on a raid to Schweinfurt, only one returned.[6]

Being 'kind of concerned' may just be the epitome of combat-related understatement of the war. It's as if this airman knew Fred's mother or knew that he was speaking to all of the mothers of bomber crewmen and wanted to add his voice to the chorus of, 'Don't worry Mom. Don't worry Mom'. However, Louise and the rest of the mothers would have been more than worried; they would have been scared to distraction if they had been aware of these losses, especially those suffered on 14 October 1943, in the raid on Schweinfurt where there was a loss of twenty-six planes.

In considering a mid-range loss rate of 5 per cent, only twenty aircraft and crew out of an original group of 100 planes could be expected to survive to complete a thirty-mission tour of duty. Although separated by miles of space, combat conditions and environments that differed from fighting in and from wet, cold, muddy foxholes to -50°F temperatures inside a long silver tube in the air, Bill Mauldin's infantryman, Joe, expressed it best for both airman and soldier: 'I feel like a fugitive from th' law of averages.'[7]

> 3/19/44
> *Sunday*
> *Bury St Edmunds*
>
> *Dear Mom,*
> *Missed writing yesterday and the letter I wrote the other night was sure a poor excuse of a letter. It was just a note to say goodnight. We've been pretty darn busy. Today we were just lucky and don't have to do anything.*
> *I've been on 2 raids now.*

Fred and his crew have begun the journey to complete their required missions. The first, a grizzly and tortuous mission with so many lost, was truly a baptism of fire – a full emersion into combat.

> It was commonly believed that one's first mission should be a rough one, so all that came after that would seem easier.[8]

As Fred finishes missions and returns to base, he keeps a running total for himself through his letters to Louise by telling her how many raids he has been on or how many more he has to go to complete his tour of duty. In some letters, Fred will tell his mother how many missions he 'has in'; in others, how many he 'has to go.' At some point, there is a difference in the perception relating to mission completion – so far I've completed a given number; later, I've *only* got so many more to go. In the former, there is the sense of having completed a job; in the latter he expresses a feeling of needing to complete a task. And because of recent orders increasing the number of missions needed to complete a combat tour of duty from twenty-five to thirty, his sense of task completion must have tumbled.

Fred's report of mission completions to his mother nearly always takes on the vein of job completion and not the pessimistic view of still needing to complete a fixed number before it is his turn to stand down. 'Will I be able to do it?' 'Will I beat the odds of being shot down?' 'Are odds and luck even a part of the equation?' When one plane flying next to yours in formation is lost to flak and your own, although hit, is still airworthy and capable of completing its assigned mission, is this luck or skilled airmanship that keeps the plane aloft and on a steady course? Does it matter? Returning from a mission is the important part. Why or how is not as important as making it home alive.

For the generals though, it became a matter of pragmatics, effectiveness and efficiency combined with maximum effort of flying personnel. '… a combat crew must be very good or very lucky to complete an operational tour … we cannot expect them to do more efficiently.'[9]

Am sending this issue of 'Stars and Stripes.' Maybe you can tell where I was from it. Also dear I visited where your father was born (if I remember right).

Due to mail censorship of information about missions, aircrew often relied on *Stars and Stripes* to help them keep the folks at home informed about what they were doing and where the action was. Fred was not alone in this ruse to foil censorship strictures: 'I sent a copy of *Stars and Stripes* home with the #1, #2, etc., on the article that told about a mission. This way, my folks knew where I had been.'[10]

For some, it was 'mom' who was the inventive keeper of the track record of missions: 'Mom would find clippings from the newspaper that matched the dates of my letters – this way she could see where I was at and what I was doing.'[11]

When you go on a raid your day is really full. Get up at 2:45 in the morning, have breakfast, then to briefing, and then to your airplane and when you get back they interrogate you, then clean your guns, eat and by that time you fall into bed about 9:00 or so and maybe get up again the next morning at 2:45 again. We usually get fried eggs for breakfast on the day of a raid.

The fullness of the day of a mission is routinely explained by Fred and lacks the staggering details that he, his crew and scores of others experienced day after day after day. Besides the gruelling nature of the flight itself, which on missions of deep penetration into the Continent could last as long as ten to twelve hours, there were mission briefings before the flight, and equipment and technical checks that would ensure as good a chance as possible of mission completion. Following the mission, Fred mentions interrogation – in reality it was a serious debriefing by intelligence officers that seemed like the second showing of the feature-length film at an all-day cinema. It was an in-depth reliving of the past hours of combat, survival and loss.

After being rousted out of bed at 2.45 a.m. and eating breakfast, crewmembers went by groups to separate briefings – the flying officers, pilots, co-pilots, navigators and bombardiers had meetings as a group, while the enlisted men, the gunners, had other responsibilities. The pre-mission briefing:

… was held in a large room with a stage at one end with a large black curtain drawn across the back. When the briefing began, the curtain was opened, and the day's target was identified on a large map (often accompanied by audible moans from those assembled, or 'if it was going to be a milk run you'd hear a great sigh of relief'[12]). There was also a picture of the target. This was important because the bombardier had to see what it was he was aiming for. We were told

'At 22,000 feet you will leave dense and persistent contrails.' (Courtesy of Wilbur Richardson)

where to expect flak (flimsies/flak maps were handed out) and where we could expect to engage enemy fighters – this information wasn't very accurate. Next, the 'weather guesser' would give his briefing: 'At 22,000 feet you will leave dense and persistent contrails.'[13]

When this part of the briefing had been completed and time hacks set, the pilots, navigators, bombardiers and radio operators went to other separate briefings. Here they learned radio call-letters, codes and recognition signals for the day; times and locations for radio transmissions of mission progress; rally points, routes, IPs and other pertinent information specific to each person's onboard responsibilities.

In the meantime, the:

… gunners went in trucks to the armorer to collect the machine guns and install them – the cheek guns for the navigator and then the twin guns for the bombardier.[14]

The flight engineer, who also served as the top turret gunner:

… performed a walk-around pre flight of the B-17, checked the engine oil, turbo oil tanks and gas tanks for servicing; made sure the tank servicing caps were secure to prevent siphoning; checked the aircraft forms for any known problems that the aircraft could have and could still be sent on a mission, but that did not in any way jeopardize the mission … I was usually just finishing my inspection when the officers and radio operator arrived at the aircraft.[15]

On the way to our plane, we would stop to pick up our flight gear and a flight surgeon and chaplain would also be at the stop. The flight surgeon would spray an antihistamine up our noses so we would have an easier time breathing and to avoid sinus infections. The chaplain would assist with any of those who wanted to pray; it seemed to help those who wanted to take the chaplain up on his offer. He was a non-denominational chaplain, but if there were Catholics in the group he would say some 'Catholic things' for them so that they would feel more comfortable with those blessings. [16]

When the crew had assembled at the ship, lunches arrived, usually K-rations. Crewmembers selected from whatever was available or took something for trading with someone else.

Missions were the *raison-d'être* of the B-17; it is at that time that the truth of the axiom:

'The bomber exists for the bombardier' (was realised). The whole purpose of the mission was to get the bombardier to the target. The bombardier had to go to work as soon as the mission got rolling. The propeller fuses of the bombs were protected on the ground by a common cotter pin. Our bombardier never pulled the pin until after we left the coast of England. He didn't want to have live bombs over England. By the time the propeller spins 100 times, it is free of the plane. While the bombs are on the ground with the pins in they're virtually harmless. [17]

Then there was the duration of the bomb run, which could seem, on the one hand, to flash by, and on the other, seem like an eternity, an ever-lasting struggle with the unseen enemy below as it lofted its deadly flak from massed anti-aircraft batteries to bring them down. Before and after the flak zones, the GAF fighters took their turn at swatting them out of the sky, actions that too often caused tragic consequences for the bombers.

Finally they arrived back at the base and parked at the hardstand. Sometimes, they would gather round the ship and count the holes from flak and machine-gun fire.

The wings had so many holes in them, they looked like they had been shot up close with a shotgun. [18]

A truck would come by and take them back to the base compound where debriefing occurred and was comprised of two parts: outside and inside. Outside, they got doughnuts and coffee from the Red Cross ladies, a welcome sight because they hadn't eaten for hours. Sometimes the doughnuts were fresher than others:

but mostly we were just thankful to be back alive and didn't complain about whether or not the donuts were stale. [19]

At other times:

… because the adrenalin rush of the mission persisted for a long time, the coffee and donuts didn't sit well in your stomach, and they would be vomited right back up.[20]

Debriefing was held in a room with a table and chairs for eleven people – one for each of the crew and one for the intelligence officer. Unlike the pre-briefing, all of the crew was debriefed together. If we had returned from a really rough mission (they knew at the base whether or not this was a rough mission because they knew how far into Germany we flew and how much flak and how many fighters we had encountered), the flight surgeon would be at the door of the building with a bottle of Scotch and would pour a 'little hooker' into canteen cups. On one occasion, when the Scotch was poured, two or three of the guys didn't want theirs, and I told them to take it anyway and pour their allotment into my cup – three shots in one cup on an empty stomach, and my tongue got so thick I could hardly make myself understood to the intelligence officer. I was really embarrassed and that only happened once.[21]

He was not the only one to have an added measure to his cup.

I was always scared, usually lucky, and only fell apart after the mission was over. The medicinal booze before the debriefing helped greatly and I, at times, drank more than my share. We all did! What the heck, we were only 20 years old and had to go again the next day.[22]

The details of the mission were what the intelligence officer wanted. He waited patiently to hear about the weather ('Were we close in our estimates?'), flak, where they found it and how much there was – mild, moderate or heavy.

How many enemy planes were there and what type? The intelligence officer wanted to know about any aircraft shot down. Could crewmembers identify the plane? Did they see any parachutes coming out of the plane? How was the plane downed – fighter fire or flak? He:

… wanted to know where we were according to the navigator's log so that they could compare our position with other reported positions. Our navigator often didn't have a clue where we were. He just followed the plane ahead of him.[23]

Finally, the intelligence officer wanted to learn about the unexpected, whatever it was that was not covered in the pre-briefing. Was there flak at unexpected places? Were there more GAF fighters than anticipated? These and other questions and their answers became:

The unknown quantity, the uncertain element in every aerial combat episode (and) was summed up afterwards, 'not as briefed' …[24]

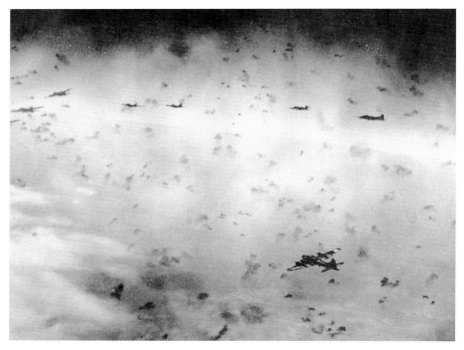

'Was the flak mild, moderate or heavy?' (Courtesy of Roy Test, source unknown)

… and maybe get up again the next morning at 2:45 again.

Had a letter from Chuck yesterday. I know where he is now and will try and get there. Still no mail from you yet. The only letter I've received from home was sent to Dyersburg by one of my friends who is an instructor at Carlsbad, N. Mex. It went from Dyersburg to Kearney, Nebr., and then here. It sure is funny how mail moves. Should have some from you any day now as some of the other boys' mail has just started to arrive. They live in New York.

So you had some snow in L.A.! Just saw this picture in 'Yank' this morning. They have a traveling P.X. (Post Exchange) here for 3 days and I bought a new pair of pink pants, long underwear, and a pair of shoes.

Pink pants (pinks): Army officers' clothing, especially trousers, of a pinkish hue.[25]

My radio is working swell now.

We had one day here the other day that reminded me of Calif. You could tell it was a nice day as a bunch of the boys started to play football.

All I have to do today is go to school for 1 hour to take a test. Some of the other fellows have to fly around here. Boy what a break not to have to fly.

Yesterday, no it was the day before, we went into town just to look it over. Quite a large place but still nothing to do there. They even have a Woolworth's 5 & 10; but they call it a 3P and 6P. 3 pence means 5 cents and 6 pence means 10 cents.

The thing I hate most is wearing an oxygen mask for about 7 hours. I still can't think of very much to write until I start getting your letters.

Your <u>little</u> boy,
Fred

P.S. tell everyone hello for me please!!

After the first mission:

> I was sitting enthroned in the nose trying to see land through the clouds when suddenly several puffs of dirty black smoke appeared just in front of us ... Flak burst broke all over. In front, above and to both sides. The ship was bouncing around like a cork in a maelstrom. We got our bombs away, turned and headed back toward England. But the flak did everything but abate. It became much worse and it seemed hardly possible that we could get out of there. I must admit that it scared the living daylights out of me. Anybody who claims not to be frightened under this sort of fire is a damned liar.[26]

Operational Mission 3: 20 March 1944 – Frankfurt, Germany

All but 146 of the 353 B-17s sent on this mission return to base because of clouds over the target zone. One B-17 from the 94th drops its bombs. Industrial areas and transportation targets in Frankfurt and other targets of opportunity are bombed. Losses include five B-17s.

Bury St Edmunds – 'we went into town just to look it over'. (Courtesy of Wilbur Richardson)

Operational Mission 4: 22 March 1944 – Berlin, Germany

Six hundred and fifty-seven Eighth Air Force bombers, including twenty-one from the 94th, divert to attack Berlin because of bad weather over the primary target. Bombs dropped total 1,471 tons and twelve heavy bombers are lost.

Coming back from Berlin, four 109s attacked a group of B-24s and took out one with a direct hit into the cockpit. The P-38s attacked, and they got involved in the fight. We got hit in the #3 engine by a 109. #4 engine was feathered by mistake. Two engines out at the same time. Here comes four 109s just taking their time to attack us when two P-38s came out of nowhere and attacked the 109s. They were a beautiful sight. When the 109s were driven off, the P-38s flew up next to us in formation and gave us the thumbs up and stayed with us as long as they could. We had to do a belly landing. With our landing in a small airfield, the Brits sent a little fire engine after us – it looked like the Toonerville Trolley.[27]

Operational Mission 5: 23 March 1944 – Brunswick, Germany

Due to bad weather only 205 of the 707 Eighth Air Force heavy bombers participating in this mission bomb their primary target of aircraft factories in Brunswick. Twenty-one B-17s from the 94th reach the primary target; two are lost. The remainder of the mission bombers attack secondary targets and targets of opportunity. Twenty-two B-17s are lost.

March 26, 1944
Sunday Eve.
Bury St Edmunds

Dear Mom,
Gosh, I just don't understand why I haven't heard from you yet. Had my first letter from the States today. It was a letter from Smitty, but he said he's sent another letter and also a birthday card. Boy this mail is rough getting started.
    The reason I haven't written for several days is that I've been to visit Charles. Really enjoyed myself. Had a swell visit with him. He looks darn good. I'm going to drop Aunt Frances a line and tell her how well he looks and feels. I know she will feel better.
    There's nothing more mixed up than this English train system. I was really in a quandary trying to get from place to place. The rest of my crew went to London. I'll go there next time. I met Chuck's friends and his Capt. who he works for. All swell fellows. Chuck really rates with them. The Capt. likes him very much. He's going to visit me here when he gets his first 48-hour pass. Saw a lot of the English countryside on the trip. It's very pretty. I also visited Cambridge.
    Heard Jack Benny tonight. He was pretty good.

Oh, before I forget, I didn't know Uncle Don died. Charles told me. You can see how far behind I am with what's going on at home. He also said Pauline was in the WACS along with Evelyn.

Well I've got five raids in now. Everyone has been to Germany. Been over Holland and Belgium in addition to being over France. I've seen Berlin before seeing London.

I'm going to end this letter short as I've given you the latest from here.

Love,
Fred

Operational Mission 6: 27 March 1944 – Cazaux, France

Seven hundred and one Eighth Air Force B-17s and B-24s, including twenty-seven from the 94th BG, attack eleven German air force airfields in France, including Cazaux, with 1,853 tons of bombs. Three B-17s are lost.

Operational Mission 7: 28 March 1944 – Chartres, France

Three hundred and sixty-four B-17s drop 937 tons of bombs on German air force airfields in France, including the one at Chartres, the target of the 94th's twenty planes. Two B-17s are lost.

28 March 1944
Tuesday night
Bury St Edmunds

Dear Mom,

Pretty tired tonight but want to let you know how happy I feel. Received 5 letters from you today. They were airmail letters and the first one was postmarked March 6th and the 5th one was dated 15 March. Guess airmail is the only way. I know you've written a lot more letters to my temporary A.P.O.# They'll probably arrive sometime, but the important thing is that now I've started to receive your wonderful letters. Also received a V-letter from Smitty.

I've got 7 raids now. The last two have been pretty easy. I've also seen Paris from a distance. You spoke of how much there was in the paper about the Berlin raid. Believe me it was really rough. I never saw so many bombs fall in all my life!!!

Despite Reichsmarshall Göring's assurance to Hitler that 'no enemy plane will enter Germany', the cities of the Third Reich were being reduced to rubble. The hammering of Berlin began on 4 March, although bad weather forced all but thirty of a strike force of 502 B-17s to turn back or to bomb other targets. But, the impossible had happened. Not only had the homeland been violated by Allied air forces, it was now readily apparent that Berlin was neither inviolate nor impregnable.

Nasty weather and poor visibility over the target zone continued until finally, on 6 March, the long-anticipated first large USAAF daylight bomber assault on Berlin was launched. It was a costly mission. They were first met by German fighters:

They were everywhere – 'Bandits at 12 o'clock high … My God … there must be a million of them.'[28]

Next came the assault of the anti-aircraft guns throwing up their massive explosive clouds of flak. Five hundred thousand Germans were assigned to anti-aircraft gun positions from the Continental coast to Berlin with the capital surrounded by:

… the most powerful flak defenses in the world, an angry cordon of 750 light and heavy guns.[29]

Sixty-nine bombers of the 474 that reached the target area were shot down, and 347 planes were damaged. The human toll was more staggering – 17 were killed, 686 were reported as missing and 31 were wounded. Fifteen of the B-17s that were lost were from the 3rd Bombardment Division's 100th Heavy Bombardment Group, the highest one-day loss by a single bomber group.[30]

Two days later, another 470 bombers attacked the Berlin area, so by the time Fred and his crew entered the fray, nearly 1,000 US bombers had been sent on missions to destroy the heart of the German Reich. He had every reason to be awed by the bombing of Berlin. His ship was part of an air armada of 657 bombers that dropped a total of 1,471 tons of bombs on this 'rough' raid. Berlin was being savaged. However, for the USAAF, the cost was high in this 'rough' mission – twelve bombers were lost and 347 were damaged.

A 'rough mission'. What is a rough mission? Crewmen tell different stories about what constituted a rough mission or a good mission – not all of which are likely to be greeted by any consensus by those who flew through those skies of hell, but all are, nonetheless, breathtaking.

A rough mission:

Three out of seven planes were shot down. Half of the squadron you're in gets shot down. That is a tough (rough) mission. This happened to me on December 1st, 1943.[31]

A good mission:

If you were on a mission where you didn't encounter any fighters (and) if you came back alive, that was a good mission.[32]

The perfect mission:

You hit your target, demolished it, and suffered no losses. Sometimes you hit a target and got more than you expected – if we hit a train or marshalling yards you might also hit an ammunition storage area or train.[33]

Then, there was the 'milk run'. Although usually associated with the same ease as a milkman making his early morning deliveries, one B-17 pilot was much more pragmatic:

A milk run is when all aircraft come back with very few casualties.[34]

Sure hope you can get your phone now. It's nice of Dr. Randel to write a letter, but don't let 'em get away with kidding you about being a mental case. They're darn nice people, he and Mrs. McNerney.

You also spoke of them bombing London. They're not doing a darn thing. Just a very few planes drop a few bombs. When we had our pass my crew was there one night that the Germans raided London. They said everyone was inside but them. They wanted to see how it looked to receive bombs instead of delivering them. We screwy Americans!

London continued on her way, ignoring the sky as best she could, but not for-getting the war. Her streets, her hotels and restaurants, her stations and her stores, her factories and her libraries, her schools and her churches and her theatres were all crowded. So were her air-raid shelters.[35]

Well, I'm going to sign off for now. Pretty tired and sleepy.

Love,
Fred

A short letter from Fred's cousin, Chuck, to Aunt Lulu:

3/26/44
England

Dear Aunt Lulu:
It finally happened. Fred walked in on me yesterday. He sure looks fine. He stayed overnight and we talked about everything. Both of us are out to win this war quick. I sure never expected to see him. A snappy Lewie.

We had our picture taken and just as soon as I get a print I'll send you one. He is stationed about a hundred miles from me. Just as soon as I can I am going to try to get up to visit him. How are you getting along? Someday us guys will all be back so don't worry.

Today the sun is out for some reason. 'Tis usually cloudy and raining etc.

Write when you can and be good and take it easy.

Love,
Charles

Don't worry Aunt Lulu. Don't worry Aunt Lulu.

GENERAL ORDERS
NO. 223
EXTRACT
29 March 1944

Under the provisions of Army Regulations 600-45, 22 September
1943, and pursuant to authority contained in Restricted TT
Message #2139, Hq USSAFE, 11 January 1944, the AIR MEDAL is
awarded to the following-named officer.

Citation: For exceptionally meritorious achievement, while
participating separate bomber combat missions over enemy
occupied Continental Europe. The courage, coolness and skill
displayed by this officer upon these occasions reflect great
credit upon himself and the Armed Forces of the United States.

FRED S. LULL, O-752877, 2nd Lt, 94th Bomb Group (H). Home
address: Los Angeles, California.

By command of Lieutenant General DOOLITTLE

Air Medal – A decoration awarded to any person serving in any capacity with
the Air Force who distinguishes himself by meritorious achievement while participating in aerial flight.[36]

Friday March 31, 1944
Bury St Edmunds

Dear Mom,
Don't have anything to write about today. We haven't done a thing for a couple of days
now so just wanted to get this letter started. Will finish it tomorrow night.
Wrote to Aunt Frances today. Told her about seeing Chuck and how well he looked and felt.
Received 2 birthday cards today. They were mailed March 6 to the temporary APO
I've got 2 rolls of film I'm going to send in to be developed. Hope they turn out o.k. It'll
probably take some time.
My crew had a swell time in London. They saw them change the guard at Buckingham
Palace, visited all the old historic places such as the Tower of London, Westminster Abbey, etc.
I'm going to visit them for myself on my next pass.
We're still trying to find a name for our ship. Due to the fact that on every mission
so far we've flown 'tail-end Charlie' or the 'purple heart section,' we think 'Prop-Wash'
might make a good name. Do you get it? I'll explain. Due to the fact that we're in the
tail end (of the formation) we get everyone else's prop wash. Simple eh! Do you know
you've got a mighty smart <u>little</u> boy! Do you think I'm a wee bit conceited? Don't answer
as you're biased.

What Fred didn't tell his mother about being 'tail-end Charlie' is characteristic of all his letters home. Being at the end of the formation of planes on a bombing mission meant that you didn't have the protection of other bombers around you, you were the last in the formation over the target and the last to drop your bombs, giving the enemy the chance to fix your range for their anti-aircraft artillery, making you more vulnerable to be hit by flak. If you survived all of this, you were the last ones home, the tail-end, the hindmost. Fred had decided that she didn't need to know these details. Being victim of the prop-wash from others' planes was far less innocuous than being the perfect target for artillery and sitting unprotected by your brothers as enemy fighters bore in on you.[37]

Don't worry Mom. Don't worry Mom.

Got paid today. Get paid in English money. Made out an application for a money order. Will pick it up tomorrow. It's for $80.00. Boy we're going to have quite a bank roll when I get home! That makes $280.00 this month including the allotment. Of course it can't all go into the bank.

Are you still going to see Dr. Randel? Be sure to keep going. Also keep getting your hair fixed. You know how well I like having your hair fixed.

On second thought think I'll mail this tonight. Will write again tomorrow night and enclose the money order.

> *Goodnight,*
> *Fred*

So ended the month of March, a month that saw missions deep into Germany with the loss or 3.5 per cent of the aircraft that arrived at their assigned target. A few months earlier, October 1943, the loss rate was 9.1 per cent.[38]

Operational Mission 8: 1 April 1944 – Ludwigshafen, Germany

Heavy cloud cover over France force abandonment of the mission by all B-17s assigned to the mission.

> *Sunday April 2, 1944*
> *Bury St Edmunds*

Dear Mom,

Still haven't done very much for a few days.

Just writing this to say goodnight and also to send this money order. Have the other money orders ever arrived home? I think there were 3 of them. One for $100.00 one for $35.00, one for $96.00 and now this one for $80.00.

So far I've received 6 letters from you. Five of them arrived on the same day and the 6th one came a day or so later. None have arrived since. We don't get mail on Sunday. Hope some comes tomorrow.

I'm just at a loss trying to think of something to write about.

Every chance they give us to sleep we sure take advantage of it! Last night I had 13 hours of sleep, but day before yesterday they woke us up before 2:00 in the morning so you can see why we sleep every chance possible.

Up to this date I've got credit for <u>eight</u> missions.

Well dear, this is all for now. Will try and write tomorrow night if I receive some mail from you. Take care of yourself because when I come home we're really going to kick it around!!!

Love,
Fred

★★★

4/4/44
Tuesday night
Bury St Edmunds

Here I am again. Still haven't done anything but go to ground school a couple hours today. There was a good crack in 'Stars and Stripes' the other day. It said spring came to England one day and was washed out the same day.

Received 2 letters from you today. Mail sure is mixed up. Also one from Smitty.

Tuned in on a German broadcast today coming from France. It was in English. It was a news program. According to it we're really beaten and the British didn't even hit the Tirpitz. It was quite funny.

If, as it has been said, that the first casualty of war is truth, then propaganda is the handmaiden of the loss of truth and its sibling, innocence. Also, if the pen is mightier than the sword, is it reasonable to postulate that the broadcast of words through the airwaves of radio is also an armament that outstrips the truth of massive bomb drops? Surely both combatant sides would have their populace think so. In the context of the German propaganda radio broadcast that Fred heard, both bombs and truth are on holiday, and innocence is shattered.

The German battleship *Tirpitz*, assigned to the far northern waters of Norway, ventured in and out of its protective fjord moorings to threaten Allied shipping bringing supplies and war materiel to Russia, an Allied partner that was being hammered in the south by the Wehrmacht and the German air force. Attempts by British forces, including attacks by mini-submarines, had failed to sink the dreadnought, and, hence, relieve ships of the Royal Navy from escort duty – ships that were badly needed elsewhere around the globe.

However, on 4 April 1944, it happened. British planes came in over the mountains that ringed the fjords and let loose a devastating rain of bombs on the *Tirpitz*. She was hit with fifteen bombs, 500- and 1,000-pounders, some that inflicted little damage, others that burst through decks with death and destruction at every level save one. In the attack that lasted less than a minute, none penetrated the 8in, armour-clad lower deck. So incredibly, although the ship was badly damaged and had more than 300 dead crewmen, it was still afloat.[39]

Yet, like an ocean-dwelling phoenix, the *Tirpitz* rose again, after months of repairs, once more to become a threat to the Allied convoy route through the frigid waters of the Arctic Ocean of the Murmansk run. She finally was sunk months later, 12 November, after Britain developed bombs that could, at last, penetrate the massive armoured deck.

Duffy's Tavern is on tonight at 10:00. Like it very much. Village Store with Joan Davis and Jack Haley is also very good.

Sure glad you were over to see Mrs. Morton and her family. They're really swell people!! You couldn't find any better. In four more days Jack will have his wings. I know how happy and proud he'll feel, but I sure hope he gets to be an instructor or something.

Boy, Jack must be a darn good bombardier. That night bombing score doesn't mean a darn thing because we never bomb at night. It's that day bombing that counts.

Oh, before I forget, how do you like us bombing Swiss towns. It wasn't B-17s. It was B-24s.

B-24 bombers that were assigned to participate as a part of Fred's eighth mission became widely scattered and '… 26 bomb (ed) Schaffhausen, Switzerland, and Strasbourg, France, mistaking them for German towns'.[40]

Switzerland is the place we all want to head for if anything ever happens. They really treat American airmen swell. Of course they keep them until the war is over which is very nice.

Landing in this neutral country, which Fred offers as a bit of reassurance 'if anything ever happens', offered something more than the land of Swiss Alps, Swiss chocolates, Swiss banking, Swiss chalets, Swiss watches, skiing and quaint villages. For American fliers, it was a nationwide internment camp under the supervision of Swiss army guards. Being apprehended in escape attempts from Switzerland resulted in imprisonment in a '… high-security punishment camp … (a) closely packed compound of mud-splattered barracks surrounded by a high barbed wire fence and patrolled by guards with machine guns and attack dogs'.[41]

In Switzerland during the war, 1,740 American airmen were interned; 947 tried to escape.

The Rule of Stupid

I'm sure there were official documents about conduct as a POW, but I never saw them. The same goes for 'detainees' in neutral countries such as Sweden or Switzerland. The military had handbooks, training manuals, reference manuals and tech orders covering every conceivable subject.

Upon arrival at an air base in England, you were given a series of 'orientation' lectures. As I recall, the lecture on bailing out or crash landing in enemy territory went something like this:

- Try to evade capture if possible – but don't do anything stupid.
- When captured and interrogated, give only name, rank and serial number.
- During captivity, look for opportunities to escape – but don't do anything stupid.
- If you divert to neutral Switzerland or Sweden because you can't make it back to England, you better be damn sure of what you are doing. The USAAF have Boeing tech reps stationed in both countries to evaluate and report on the condition of any B-17s that land in these countries. Don't do anything stupid.[42]

Don't worry Mom. Don't worry Mom.

Glad you liked the picture 'True to Life' with Dick Powell and Victor Moore. I never laughed so much in a picture in all my life.

I'm not sure yet, but think we have a name for our ship. Several names have been considered but think 'Belle of the Brawl' will be the one selected.

A nice name, Fred, but hardly original. There were eight B-17s with the name, *Belle of the Brawl* and one with the name, *Belle of the Brawl II*. There was a *Belle of the Brawl* in the 94th BG, Fred's, one in the 34th, 306th, 388th, 389th BGs, two in the 390th BG and *Belle of the Brawl II* was also in the 94th.

In addition, there were two other aircraft with similar names – both in the 401st Bomb Group: *Bell of the Brawl* and *Belle O' the Brawl*.[43]

Gosh, I'm sorry you haven't heard from me in five days. The mail probably comes in bunches when it comes doesn't it? I try and write every other day.

Well kid this just about finishes me up for tonight except to say our radio operator and engineer got promoted to T/Sgts (Tech Sgts) and the rest of our crew made S/Sgts (Staff Sgts).

Wish it was 85 degrees over here!!

Goodnight dear,
Fred

Operational Mission 9: 8 April 1944 – Handorf-Hesepe, Germany

Sixty-five 3rd Bombardment Division B-17s, with twenty-seven from the 94th BG, attack airfields and various targets of opportunity. Four B-17s are lost, including one from the 94th.

Sunday April 9, 1944
Bury St Edmunds

Dear Mom,
Here it is Easter Sunday. Happy Easter dear!!

First of all got back to work again. The total stands at 9 now. Only 21 more to go.

Haven't had any mail for several days so consequently can't write very much. Our 48 hour pass should be coming up again any day now. It's been almost 3 weeks since our last one. Going to London this time and take in all the sights.

What do you think of old rabble rouser Wilkie withdrawing from the political scene? Guess his goose is cooked! Looks as if Dewey will be the Republican man, but whoever they run he will never beat President Roosevelt.

Do you like the name we gave our ship, 'The Belle of the Brawl'? After our last raid it earned the name.

The *Belle of the Brawl* must have been very much in the thick of aerial combat as escort fighters were credited with shooting down an amazing eighty-eight German air force fighters that attacked the bomber formations of which Fred's newly named ship was a part.[44]

GAF fighter attacks were a different breed of air warfare from what bomber crews experienced when they entered the flak zones of anti-aircraft batteries. These attacks became much more personal. With closing speeds between bomber and fighter at 600mph the opportunity to locate, aim and fire machine guns was minimal, a few seconds at best. One of the best protective elements for the bombers was the massed firepower the group achieved by flying in tight formations. LeMay's dictum of flying formations of 25ft distance, wingtip to wingtip, required a firm grip on the wheel and a delicate sense of place in space. Enemy fighter plane pilots needed unusual skill at manoeuvring toward and through the massed bombers. Often, they lacked the requisite skill, and the results were disastrous.

Me-109s attacked us head on, firing and rolling as they flew through the formation. One Me-109 struck the right wing of a B-17 knocking nine feet off. The 109 rolled up in a ball of metal. The crew brought the B-17 safely home.[45]

Hope by this time the rain has stopped and the sun is shining in all its old California glory. Well dear this will have to do for this time. So 'Dear John' until next time.

Your loving son,

Fred

P.S. Bet you got all dolled up today! I can just see you slick as a queen. Dear, I can't send you anything for your birthday so I'm just going to send you all my love. I know you'll be satisfied!! This will probably get to you before your birthday, but I want to be sure you get it. I always forget if your birthday is the 14th or 15th of April. Think yours is April 14th and Mrs. Eberts the 15th.

Happy Birthday Mom!!!

Fred! How could you forget the date of your mother's birthday? Worse yet, how could you admit it to her?

'… firing and rolling through the formation.' (Photograph by the author and used with the permission of the 390th Memorial Museum, Tucson, Arizona)

Operational Mission 10: 10 April 1944 – Diest-Schaffen, Germany

One hundred and forty-three 3rd Bombardment Division B-17s, twenty-five from the 94th, are unable to locate their assigned targets in France but bomb airfields in France and Diest-Schaffen.

Friday April 14, 1944
Bury St Edmunds

Dear Mom,
Just had to write again tonight. Received 42 letters today. 23 of them were from you. Gosh it took me almost 2½ hours to read them. Some of them were addressed to Dyersburg and Kearney.

Sure glad to hear you finally got a phone put in! It will be a lot of company for you.

It's too bad Mike strayed away from home. Boy I hope they find him soon!! I know how they love him.

You know I like the brown ink best. It's a lot easier to read. Did you run out of it?

Boy, I'd sure have liked to have been at that dinner Esther gave for Pauline. Sounds as if you all had a swell time. Can just imagine how much effort Esther went to. After the dinner you were a night owl eh? Bacon and eggs at 3:00 in the morning! Can just see you the next day. Dead tired!!

Before you buy anymore bonds let's build up a little balance first, eh what? For all I know we may have a pretty good balance. By the way what is the balance in the bank, and how many bonds do we have now? Give the balance as of some date and a breakdown of our bonds. I'm just curious! Nosey me!!

Will you please send those rolls of film!

Well, I'll quit for tonight and finish it up tomorrow night.

Goodnight!

P.S. The name is painted on the ship now. Am going to take a picture of it. This check also came today. Big stockholder in the 'B of A'.

Well, no letter today so guess I'll end this prattle. How could one expect a letter today after so many yesterday.

Love,
Fred

Some of the nose art was good, some of it lacked in quality. Some displayed scantily clad pin-up models, others cartoon characters and yet others were painted only with the name settled on by the crew, often the name of the pilot's wife or girlfriend.[46]

However, painting the name of the plane on its nose was not for every crew:

We never painted the name on our Fort, because the Forts with names seemed to get shot up more than the ones without.[47]

One plane's nose art wasn't painted simply because:

… there wasn't enough time or anyone in the group with enough talent to do the paint job.[48]

Tuesday April 18
Bury St Edmunds

Dear Mom,
Haven't written for several days as we've been on pass. Gildersleeve is on the radio now. Thinks he's going to die.

'The name is painted on the ship now.' (Courtesy of Frank Barnyak)

Boy what a town London is! We didn't get there until late at night and the 'Underground' (subway) was closed so we had quite a walk from the depot to our hotel. We stayed at the Regent Palace. It's in Piccadilly Circus. You never saw so many taxi cabs in all your life. They're the cheapest way to get around. The Regent Palace is one of the best hotels in London.

Dear, I never believed it when I heard people slept in the subways. Well I saw it for myself. It's mostly the older people. It's quite a ways under the ground.

It was not until I went down seventy feet into the bowels of the Liverpool Street tube and saw humanity sprawled there in childlike helplessness that my heart first jumped and my throat caught. I know I must have stopped suddenly and drawn back. I know I must have said to myself, 'Oh my God!'[49]

The first day I went on a sightseeing tour. It was really worth every minute. All the things we've read and heard about in school books, etc. It was hard to believe we were standing on the spot where all those historical events happened.

Some areas in London have really been levelled. It's all pretty well cleaned up now.

On the bad nights, when there were many fires, London's fire fighters had to establish immediate priorities in salvation, on the basis of the general danger or wartime importance of the building threatened or blazing. This night there was a crowd in the street. A fire chief drove up in a car and quickly appraised the situation. Then he drove on to another fire a few blocks away, a fire more menacing to the war effort. The look of resolution on the faces of those Britishers in this crowd as they accepted this decision and watched London burn was something Hitler should have seen.[50]

Westminster Abbey is really a beautiful place. We went through it. Saw where the kings and queens are crowned. Also saw Number 10 Downing Street where Churchill lives, also Buckingham Palace. The flag was up showing that the King was in.

Went to the show and saw 'Buffalo Bill' that night. Pretty good picture.

Our second day was spent going through the Tower of London.

Didn't have a picture of the 'Tower Bridge'. I think it's the prettiest one of the bunch.

It felt good to sleep in a real soft bed in a good hotel!!

Haven't had any mail from you since I received all those letters.

Oh, before I forget I've got my Air Medal with one Oak Leaf Cluster now.

Goodnight Mom,

Fred

Succeeding achievement and meritorious service judged appropriate for the awarding of the Air Medal may again be recognised by the addition of a bronze oak leaf cluster.[51]

Trafalgar Square.

Admiralty Arch.

English bobby in foggy
London town.

Operational Mission 11: 19 April 1944 – Werl, Germany

Two hundred and forty-five 3rd Bombardment Division B-17s, twenty from the 94th, attack airfields at Lippstadt and Werl, Germany.

Operational Mission 12: 20 April 1944 – Mission No 115

As part of 'Operation Crossbow', 566 heavy bombers of the Eighth Air Force, including fourteen from the 94th BG, attack V-weapon installations in the Pas-de-Calais and Cherbourg areas. One plane from the 94th is lost.

Operational Mission 13: 22 April 1944 – Hamm, Germany

Three hundred and ninety-eight Eighth Air Force B-17s, including twenty-one from the 94th, attack the railroad marshalling yards in Hamm.

Fred flew Mission 13 to Hamm, but others took a more circuitous route to Mission 14:

We never flew Mission #13. We flew Mission #12 and Mission #12B, but never Mission #13. It's not that we were superstitious or anything like that, we just weren't going to fly Mission #13. If you weren't scared, you weren't very smart.[52]

GENERAL ORDERS
NO. 76
EXTRACT
22 April 1944

Under the provisions of Army Regulations 600-45, 22 September 1943, and pursuant to authority contained in Restricted TT Message #2139, Hq USSAFE, 11 January 1944, an OAK LEAF CLUSTER is awarded, for wear with the Air Medal previously awarded, to the following-named Officer, organization as indicated, Army Air Forces, United States Army.

Citation: For exceptionally meritorious achievement, while participating in heavy bombardment missions over enemy occupied Continental Europe. The courage, coolness and skill displayed by this Officer upon these occasions reflect great credit upon himself and the Armed Forces of the United States.

FRED S. LULL, O-752877, 2nd Lt, 94th Bomb Group (H). Home
address: Los Angeles, California.

By command of Major General LEMAY

Operational Mission 14: 24 April 1944 – Friedrichshafen, Germany

Two hundred and eleven 3rd Bombardment Division B-17s, including seventeen
from the 94th BG, attack aircraft industry targets in and around Friedrichshafen.
Four 3rd Division bombers are lost, two from the 94th.

Operational Mission 15: 27 April 1944 – Thionville, France

Four hundred and fifty Eighth Air Force B-17s and B-24s bomb airfields, targets
of opportunity and railroad marshalling yards, which were known to be specific
targets in Thionville.

A second mission on 27 April 1944, consisting of more than 400 planes,
attacked V-weapon sites at Abbeville in the Pas-de-Calais area and twenty-five
briefed and five unbriefed V-weapon sites were targeted in the Cherbourg and
Pas-de-Calais areas.[53]

> After the mission on April 27, we counted 120 holes from flak. Nothing critical
> was hit and we had no casualties, and we were still air-worthy. But, we had to
> fall out of formation because we were being tracked by the antiaircraft gunners
> by sight, and we thought we were sure to be hit and brought down. It scared the
> hell out of me.[54]

Friday 28 April
Bury St Edmunds

Dear Mom,
*Again I've gone 3 days without writing, but I just haven't had much of a chance. Just
dropping these few lines before going on pass. Don't know where I'll go this time. May go
to Norwich and see Hal.*

My total stands at 15 now. Half-finished.
Don't worry we don't go on every one you read about in the papers.
So you had some T-bone steaks! Swell! We'll have some real good ones when I get home.
Sure glad someone has moved in next door. Now you won't worry about being alone.
*That sure was nice of the Davidsons to give you that quilt for your birthday. Bet it's
pretty.*
*No we haven't flown in the tail end for quite a long while now. Think they're going to
make a squadron lead out of our crew.*

The pilot of the B-17, Miss Purdy, when told that his plane and crew had been selected to be the lead crew for his squadron on bombing missions, stated that he was honoured to be designated as the lead plane for his squadron and this sense of honour is implicit in Fred's letter to his mother. What he doesn't tell her is that the mission's lead plane was also the most vulnerable. German artillery men knew that the lead plane carried the radar guidance system used in directing the navigation for bombing the target and if they could knock it out of action, they would break up the groups' formation and its destructive effectiveness.[55]

I just don't have any more to say until we get back from pass. Dropped these few lines so you wouldn't worry, remember <u>no news is good news</u>. You know how the mails get tied up.

I'll tell you now I spent 3 restful days in the hospital. Had the grip (can't spell it). Just like F.D.R. had. Two great people. Feel good now. It really felt good to relax and rest. You know how I like attention. Dinner in bed and stuff.

Love,
Fred

Fred, once again, protects his mother from news that she would have worried about. At 4 a.m. on the 19th, the date of his eleventh mission:

> … the maintenance men had just completed their pre-flights and were awaiting the arrival of the aircrews when the Luftwaffe strafed Rougham Air Base. It was

"TAXI!"

This cartoon accompanied the letter of 28 April. 'Don't worry Mom. Don't worry Mom.'

sudden and, as if in cadence, there was an instant of stunned immobility by every man on the base. On what might have been the next count, everyone arrived in their slit trenches or bomb shelters. By the time the enemy aircraft made a second pass, everyone was under cover except the anti-aircraft gunners.[56]

Sunday 30 April 1944
Bury St Edmunds

Hello Mom,
Not very much dope to write tonight.
Went into London. Only stayed overnight. Just been resting the rest of my pass. Had a tooth filled today. The cavity was between 2 teeth.

Was this a filling because of a bicycle accident?

Saw the changing of the guard at Buckingham Palace while in London. They really go in for tradition and stuff.
Wrote a few letters last night. Heard Jack Benny tonight. Wasn't bad.
Got paid today. Bought an $88.00 money order. Get it tomorrow. Will send it day after tomorrow. That will make $288.00 this month.
I'm getting to be a poor foreign correspondent lately. There's just not much doing. Hope you'll forgive your little boy!!
Well my dear I'll quit for tonight.

Your loving son,
Fred

Operational Mission 16: 1 May 1944 – Mission No 124

Twenty-one aircraft from the 94th BG cross the English Channel to bomb targets at Behen, France. All return without dropping their bombs because of cloud cover at the IP (Initial Point – the point at which formations turn to head toward the target).

Operational Mission 17: 11 May 1944 – Brussels, Belgium

Twenty-nine B-17s of the 94th BG attack railroad marshalling yards in Brussels.

Operational Mission 18: 12 May 1944 – Brux, Czechoslovakia

Eight hundred and fourteen B-17s and B-24s escorted by USAAF and RAF fighters drop nearly 1,700 tons of bombs on the German oil plants at Bohlen, Brux (Czechoslovakia), Lutzkendorf, Merseburg, Zeitz and Zwickau, as well as several targets of opportunity.

Air war as such is almost over in Europe: the Allied infantryman is preparing now to march across a continent, battling along a 'road' already cut wide and long by bombers and fighters four miles upward.[57]

Operational Mission 19: 13 May 1944 – Osnabruck, Germany

One hundred and seventy-eight 3rd Bombardment Division B-17s, including twenty from the 94th BG, attack a railroad marshalling yard in Osnabruck. One B-17 is lost.

A flight surgeon's recommendation:

With respect to heavy bombardment, never allow a crew to fly more than three consecutive days. The combination of physical and mental weariness is definitely pronounced, and unless conditions make it imperative that an individual fly, he should be allowed to remain on the ground for at least one day.[58]

Sat 13 May 1944
Bury St Edmunds

Dear Mom,
   Missed writing for several days again, but we've been on the go again.

This is the first and only time during Fred's tour of duty in England that he has flown three missions in three days. These were not milk-run missions. These were missions that were devastating to the bomber crews and to the German war machine. This demand on machines and men was not unusual, though, as the surge toward the invasion of Festung Europa built to a thunderous daily occurrence.

The crew flew 32 missions in 77 days, but never flew more than three days in a row without a break. We flew to Munich three days in a row.[59]

I might add here our ship and crew (especially our ball gunner) is going to get quite a write up and maybe a picture in the papers. If we do I'll mail it home for you. Possibly it may appear in some papers at home. Look for the date of May 12th. No, that's the day it happened, but look about the 14th or 15th or any day after that. Our ball turret gunner, Roy Wander, shot down 6 German fighters and a possible 2 more. Also our left waist gunner got one and so did our right waist gunner. It was on our trip to Czechoslovakia.

In fact, none of the 814 bombers that participated on May 12 were officially recognized for knocking down an enemy although American fighters confirmed sixty-six shot-down defenders.[60]

No, I'm sorry to say Smitty is wrong. We have to do 30 missions. They used to do 25 missions.

The topic of twenty-five or thirty missions needed to complete a tour of duty was a sore point to those who had to fly the extra missions. In a mere two months, there would be yet another increase in the required number of missions – this time to thirty-five. The news was a morale buster and meant that not only were crews facing additional chances of danger and destruction, there was a psychological wall that for many was too brick-like to overcome. 'A young pilot commenting on the subject was heard to say, "I wish they would either quit changing the rules or tell us we were here for the duration."'[61]

That's a pretty good idea of yours to join the Red Cross. It'll give you something to occupy your mind.
   Dear, I'm dead tired tonight so I'm going to end abruptly.
   Five of our crew have 23 missions now, and the rest are only 1 or 2 behind them. I'm 4 behind. That's what I get for being in the hospital. I've got 19 now.
                                        Your <u>little</u> boy,
                                              Fred

Fred breaks down. For the first time, and the last, he tells his mother about a mission – a few sparse glimpses of a mission's details. He has to. He somehow has to remove the weight of the experience from his shoulders, his mind.
   When something happens to a little boy that is bad, really really bad, what does he do? Who does he tell? Perhaps he tells no one. But, in some cases, he may tell his mother. Fred tells his mother.
   He offers only hints at the whole truth of what he has witnessed and even participated in – something that almost defies description. But how does he tell her without breaking the resolve not to worry her about what he is doing? He finds a way. Fred tells her by relating the success, in part, of the ball turret gunner and the other members of the crew.
   What doesn't he tell her? If the ball turret gunner is solely responsible for shooting down six German aircraft, with the possibility of having shot down two more, and the waist gunners shoot down two additional aircraft, it takes little to realise that this sum of enemy attacks and repulses with authority and finality must somehow be connected to a larger picture.
   The sky was filled with a mad scramble of airplanes all bent on destruction – of one another and/or of something on the ground largely unseen. Nine hundred sixty fighters escorted 814 B-17 and B-24 bombers on this mission.

We missed our fighter escort at the rally point and only six were with us at the beginning. We lost #1 engine on the way in with what was later found to be a 50-caliber machine gun bullet hole (U.S. bombers used 50-caliber machine guns.) Brux was a nasty raid for fighters – the worst for fighters. We landed with

'We skidded off the runway, but everyone was okay.' (Courtesy of Wilbur Richardson)

only two engines – we shut down the #3 engine over the Channel to conserve gas and so made it back on two engines. When we landed we skidded off the runway, but everyone was okay.[62]

German fighter aircraft during the Brux raid numbered in the hundreds. Third Division B-17 formations suffered the greatest blow from the German fighter aircraft with forty-one of forty-three B-17s lost, including two from the 94th BG. The *Belle of the Brawl* was a part of the 3rd Bombardment Division and in the midst of this metal- and body-rendering violence.

Is he cleansed by this revelation? Not likely. Will he remember this day? Perhaps. Perhaps not the details. Perhaps not at all – it may be safer to put it away forever.

On the night of May 12th there were new and wild war stories embedded in the minds of the men participating on this mission.[63]

Does Mom read between the lines of this letter and wonder about what Fred hasn't told her? Does she ever find the story of this raid in the newspapers? Questions left unanswered and unanswerable.

Don't worry Mom. Don't worry Mom.

In his post-war memoirs, Nazi leader and Hitler confidant, Albert Speer, noted that the success of the daylight raid on 12 May of 935 Eighth Air Force bombers on fuel plants in central and eastern German, including the Brux area, signalled the end of the technological war and the collapse of armaments production.[64]

Monday May 15, 1944
Bury St Edmunds

Dear Mom,
Received 2 letters from you today.
   Don't have a darn thing to say tonight, but wanted to drop you a few lines before we go on pass tonight.
   Think we'll go to the rest home this week or next. Boy will it be a pleasure to just loaf.
   Oh, by the way, our crew is a squadron lead crew now. That means our crew leads our squadron. There are 3 squadrons in a group.

As bombardier in the lead crew, Fred now had the role and responsibility for the tactic of 'bombing on the leader'.

When the bombardier opened his bomb-bay doors, then the other planes in the group would do the same, and when the others saw the first bombs leave the plane of the lead bombardier, then they would release theirs.[65]

Another thing before I forget, Mike, Dick, and I are in for 1st Lts. now. Probably take a month before we get it though.
   I really feel swell now. Better than I have for a long time.
   Yes, your stomach will be better when I get home and you start cooking our dinner again. What a pleasure and wonderful thing that will be.
   Don't know where we'll go or what we'll do on this pass. There just isn't anything to do in these English towns.
   Isn't this a poor attempt at a letter, but if I didn't get one off to you at least every 2 or 3 days I know how you'd worry but as I said before no news is good news.
   Goodnight.

Your loving son,
Fred

GENERAL ORDERS
NO. 122
EXTRACT
16 May 1944

Under the provisions of Army Regulations 600-45, 22 September 1943, and pursuant to authority contained in ltr 200.6, Hq. Eighth Air Force, 2 April 1944, subject: 'Awards and Decorations,' an OAK LEAF CLUSTER is awarded for wear with the Air Medal previously awarded, to the following-named Officer, organization as indicated, Army Air Forces, United States Army.

Citation: For exceptionally meritorious achievement, while participating in heavy bombardment missions over enemy

```
occupied Continental Europe. The courage, coolness and
skill displayed by this Officer upon these occasions reflect
great credit upon himself and the Armed Forces of the United
States.

FRED S. LULL, O-752877, 2nd Lt., 94th Bomb Group (H). Home
address: Los Angeles, California.

          By command of Major General LEMAY
```

Wed. May 17, 1944
Bury St Edmunds

My Dear Louise,
Here I am back from pass. Went up to see Hal Hoerner. Boy it was swell seeing him again.
We talked over old times and laughed our heads off about things that happened at the bank
and mostly about things Dan Kraus used to say. Hal looks and talks just the same. I also
was in Norwich when on pass. Dick and Al went to Cambridge, the boys went to London
and Mike went to some other place. This time we were all spread to the four winds. We
usually all go together.

What's a guy to do when he has a three-day pass?

Hank Hall remembers 'there weren't a lot of the typical tourist attractions
in London that were open. The Tower was closed. St. Paul's was closed for a
time. Westminster Abbey was open, though.' So, the boys may have gone to the
American Red Cross Rainbow Corner or, like others of their brethren, they may
have '… got drunk; got into a lot of trouble'.[66]

One crewman from the 94th and a friend from another crew went to London
to get a souvenir for his girlfriend back home. On the way to Selfridges department store a V-2 bomb exploded just ahead.

'… the boys went to London.'
(Courtesy of Wilbur Richardson)

'I decided right then I wanted one of the figurines.'

We couldn't go through the front door of the store because it was damaged so we walked in through the front showcase window watching out for glass shards still hanging from the window frames. Inside the store we were in the section where porcelain figurines were sold and an older gentleman in a suit and bow tie came up to us, brushing the dust from the bombing from the shoulders of his suit, and said, 'May I help you Yank?' I decided right then I wanted one of the figurines.[67]

Traveling here is worse than at home. Their trains and buses don't know what the word speed means. They stop every couple of miles, etc.

Oh, before I go on, had a letter from Gene Larson today. He's in Italy in the 15th Air Force. He had 22 missions in when he wrote the letter. Think they have to do 50 missions down there.

Combat crews of the Fifteenth Air Force had to complete fifty missions before they could be relieved from combat. The missions that the Fifteenth flew were considered to be less dangerous than those of the Eighth – there were fewer anti-aircraft guns and fighters in combat zones assigned to the Fifteenth Air Force. That may have been difficult for crews of the Fifteenth Air Force to understand, considering that it has been estimated that the flak zone around the Ploesti oil fields, a target of the Fifteenth on multiple occasions, was said to have been surrounded with a ring of 700 anti-aircraft batteries.

There were three rings of AA guns around Ploesti. A ring of 88 mm batteries, a ring of 105 mm batteries, a ring of 128 mm batteries plus 15 individual 88 mm batteries. There was always fighter plane protection on raids to Ploesti. I thought the P-51s were the best.[68]

I'll wait until this evening before finishing up this letter because I may get some mail this afternoon.

The last few days have been like winter again. Cold as heck!

No mail today so I'll say goodnight.

Your <u>little</u> boy,

Fred

Operational Mission 20: 19 May 1944 – Berlin, Germany

Four hundred and ninety-five 1st and 3rd Bombardment Division B-17s, including seventeen from the 94th BG, using a radar guidance system, bomb Berlin through very heavy cloud cover. Sixteen B-17s are lost, including one from the 94th struck by bombs dropped from a sister ship above.

> We went to Berlin twice. I remember one-time GAF fighters came at us head on. We knew they had to be German fighters because they came at us from the front, but they passed us so fast that we couldn't identify what kind they were. A landing gear and other debris from a B-17 flew past our plane.[69]

Don't worry Mom. Don't worry Mom.

Sat May 20, 1944

Bury St Edmunds

Dear Mom,

Have to hurry so we can catch the train for the rest home. We'll be gone for a week so if my letters are kinda scarce you'll know why.

Boy, it's going to be swell just resting, riding horses etc. I'll tell you all about it.

Well I've got 20 missions now. Have been over Big 'B' twice.

By the time Fred had been over Big 'B' twice, he was well experienced with the most deadly force of the German defences, flak. By the end of the war, flak would account for more planes being shot down, about 5,400, than the 4,300 lost to GAF fighter planes.

> There was horrendous, horrendous flak. It was miserable. It seemed like it was constant and started long before we got on our five-minute bomb run. It looked and felt like we were the only plane they were shooting at. When we got back from the mission, we counted more than 400 flak holes in the plane – mostly in the left wing.[70]

By all who encountered it, it became the Flak Pervasive. They feared it. It was coming. It was there in the ever-diminishing distance. They could see the explosive black smoke blooms and knew that they were puking out finger-size iron shards

Date: 5/19/1944
Target: Berlin
A/C: Miss Donna Mae
    94th BG 331 BS [A]
The bomb about to hit the elevator
missed us by inches.
  Notice the street and cloud pattern
between the wing and tail.

Notice Elevator Trim Tab
down to raise the nose,
elevator still down.
  Crew should have bailed
out by now.

'They were way out of position.' (Miss Donna Mae photographs, courtesy of Wilbur
Richardson)

Finger-size iron shards.

that could bring them down or make them prisoners in a flying sieve. Sometimes the black smoke blossoms were so numerous and so thick they couldn't see the plane in front of them.

Soon they would feel it as it capriciously ripped into the ship, puncturing and shredding wings, engines, fuselage, cockpit, tail, gas tanks, oxygen lines, and they could see it hit other ships in the near and far distance.

> I thought that if we ever got through that wall of flak it would be a god-damned miracle.[71]

They could only watch and wait for the metal fragments from the 88mm anti-aircraft cannon shell bursts to tear into that especially vulnerable component of their aircraft, themselves. Sometimes they were just lucky; other times, not.

> An 88mm shell hit the bottom of our plane, went straight up through the body behind pilot's seat and out the roof of the ship without hurting anyone or anything vital. I about wet my pants.[72]

They hated it. They hated it because of the overwhelming feeling of helplessness that it created in each of them. They hated it because they couldn't fight it like an enemy fighter, on equal terms – 'You're trying to kill me, and I'm trying to kill you.' It was a one-way battle of death and destruction from an unseen enemy. There was no give and take. With flak, it was all take.

The ship would be buffeted and shoved around like a rude intruder into a queue. There was no evasion. The mission to bomb the target was primary, so the pilot flew the ship onward in as straight and level a course as possible, perhaps struggling with effort to do so because of their flight into the flak barrage.

B-17 bombardier's position. Sometimes they were just lucky; other times, not. (Courtesy of Wilbur Richardson)

After the automatic pilot and bombardier took control of the flight of the ship and when 'bombs away' was finally heard, they got the hell out of there, making the turn to return home, through more flak and to the enemy fighters that were sure to be waiting for them, especially those bombers limping back with flak wounds. Then there was the worry about having enough gas to reach the Continental coast, the Channel and finally the base, the possible need for the field ambulance, post-mission interrogation, the hut and the sack. And tomorrow another trip to …

Don't worry Mom. Don't worry Mom.

After we get back from our vacation it won't take long to finish up and then we all can take a big, big deep breath!!!

I'm not quite sure yet, but the only way I'll get home after this tour is to take pilot training, otherwise I'd have to stay here as an instructor or be a 'ground gripper' in S-2 (Intelligence).

Ground gripper – a non-flying individual.[73]

Pilot training would be a good deal, as it would take a year and then I could be in the Ferry Command or Air Transport Command. The big thing about it is you could be with me!!!

'… straight and level into a flak barrage.' (Courtesy of the 390th Memorial Museum, Tucson, Arizona)

Had a letter from Chuck yesterday. The reason I haven't heard from him is my letter went to N.Y. before it went to him.

So Mr. Reynolds told you never to stand in line. Well listen to me my dear, you get in line and wait your turn. Anything Dan and I used to hate was having Reynolds come back with checks and deposits when we were waiting on customers. Do you feel told off!!!

Well, I'll quit for now and try and drop a few lines in a couple of days from the balmy shores of southern England (I use the word balmy, loosely).

Love,
Fred

★★★

Monday May 22, 1944

Dear Mom,
Boy am I living the 'Life of Riley' right now. We're at the rest home. You'd never believe it could happen in England. It is located way out in the country. It is an old English country estate taken over by the U.S. Government.

In August 1942, Colonel Grow got permission to operate AAF rest homes for patients with flying fatigue.[74]

First thing they did when we arrived was to give us civilian clothes. You ought to see the Esquire fit I have on my clothes. A pair of brown pants (very short), a snappy shirt and a gray sweater, but believe me it feels good to wear them anyway. We had steak for dinner last night and chicken for lunch. Guess for breakfast we're having fried ham and eggs. This

Roke Mannor – 'Flak House'.

morning at 9:00 the butler came around and woke us up and then brought a glass of fruit
juice. Breakfast is at 10:00.
  We can play tennis, shoot skeet, fish, ride horseback, etc. (or just rest).
  This is the best thing the Army has done. It gives airmen a chance to forget, relax and
gain back some of their expended energies. (Hey that's a pretty good line!!)

They were tired, they were drained of the physical and emotional strength needed
to complete a mission with a reasonable chance of success. You could tell just by
looking at them; it was their posture, the looks on their faces.

> About the only qualification for admittance to a rest home is a set of tight lines
> that begin to grow around a man's eyes when his string of ops has stretched too
> long, or one haul in particular has been vicious and narrowly completed.[75]

The only time you wear your Army clothes is for dinner. (Dinner is at 7:30.) It looks nice
to see everyone all dressed up at night after being dirty all day. I'm taking some pictures.
  Well, I'll drop a few more lines in a couple of days if I don't get too fat to move around.
You haven't said lately how your new glasses are and how your eyes feel.
  Here's Mrs. Whelan's address: her boy's name is Bob Whelan (our Radio operator).
Your 'loafing' son,
Fred
P.S. They also serve tea at 5:00 in the afternoon. Eh what!! Anywhere you want to go they
drive you in a jeep.

★★★

Wed May 24, 1944
Roke Manor

My Dear Louise,

Just a few more quick lines from my hacienda of rest (haven of rest to you kid).

Think I've gained some weight. At least I feel better than I have since entering cadets. Haven't had so much exercise in months. Played tennis, croquet, shot skeet, and also some archery yesterday and today. Tomorrow we're going horseback riding. We usually play Hearts in the evenings. Last night they had a movie here. It was very good. Ann Southern in a 'Maisy picture'.

My face has gotten tan. Gosh, just about like California sunshine would do! (Wish it was Calif. sunshine!!)

There will be a lot of mail when we get back to the base. Will have to spend an evening answering it all.

Please excuse this chicken scratching as I'm using a straight pen with a lousy point.

Have taken some pictures and have one more roll left to take before we leave here Saturday. Gosh it's going to be tough to leave.

Well, I just wanted you to know what the latest dope was so I'll end for now and write in a day or so again.

Love,
Fred

★★★

'Boy am I living the "Life of Riley" right now.'

Sunday May 28, 1944
Bury St Edmunds

Dear Mom,
Well, we're back on the dear old base. The vacation is over. Now we can get to work again so we can get home pretty soon!

Never had such a hectic day travelling. Train was so crowded; had to stand up all the way. The queue (line) was so long waiting for the train.

When we got back we found out our ball turret gunner bailed out over France. We told him before we left he ought to go with us to the rest home and not tempt fate. He wanted to catch up to the crew. He'll be a prisoner of war if they catch him, but you have a good chance of getting out of France. The French people help you.

> And it is valuable among men who have to face danger to have one or two who really do not seem to care about it, and who go on believing against all reason that whatever happens they themselves will come to no harm.[76]

While Fred and the crew of the *Belle of the Brawl* were relaxing, shooting skeet, horseback riding and 'dressing for dinner', Roy Wander was killed in action on 25 May. Another crewmember of the plane in which he was making this extra mission was reported as 'missing in action'. Nine others evaded capture and were 'returned to duty' (RTD). So, Roy indeed tempted fate, a challenge he probably should not have undertaken, especially because the name of the plane in which he was shot down was *Friday the 13th.*[77]

Don't need any tooth powder or shaving cream. Thanks anyway.

Glad you like your Mother's Day gift! Couldn't do as much for you as I wanted dear.

Have you heard where Smitty is yet?

Glad to see you're back to brown ink. It's a lot easier to read.

I'm sure glad the Parkers are next door to you. They sound like very nice people. What a change for that apt.

Wrote Charles a letter from the rest home (flak house).

No, dear I won't get tired of you hanging around me as I'm going to be hanging around you pretty much myself.

I gained weight and got a tan at the rest home. They even had vitamin pills for us to take.

Jack Benny will be on in a few minutes.

Should have my promotion any day now. It just has to come back from Division Hq. We had to tell them what we wanted to do when we finished our tour so they can get to work on it. They aren't taking instructors as schools are closing so I put in for pilot training. That will take a year or more.

Well Mom I'll quit for now. I'll try and write tomorrow night.

All my love,
Fred

Operational Mission 21: 30 May 1944 – Watten, France

Twenty-six B-17s from the 94th BG bomb V-weapon sites at Watten and Siracourt. A 'milk run' with only three planes receiving minor flak damage.

Tuesday May 30, 1944
Bury St Edmunds

Dear Mom,

Not much news to report tonight. Got back to work today. Makes 21 in now. Most of the crew have 25 in. They've only got 5 more to go.

Believe it or not the weather here has been so hot it makes one sweat. In fact it's too hot.

Yes, that's a good idea for you to wear the ring until I get home.

Yes, Harry is a co-pilot.

Do you know who got that clipping about me in the paper?

Gosh there just isn't anymore to write about tonight. Hope you'll excuse the brevity of this note.

Love,
Fred

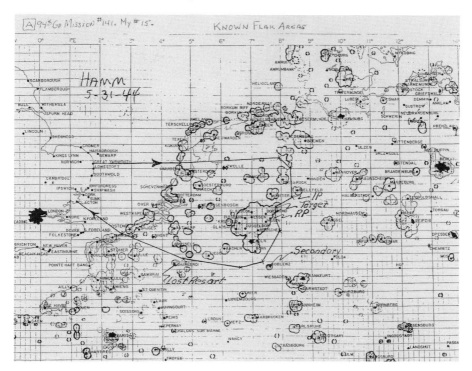

Flimsy/Flak map of 31 May 1944, mission to Hamm. (Courtesy of Wilbur Richardson)

Operational Mission 22: 31 May 1944 – Hamm, Germany

The 53rd Bombardment Division B-17s, including six from the 94th BG, attack railroad marshalling yards at Hamm.

> In April and May 1944, while continuing attacks on Germany often enough to force concentration of enemy air strength in that area, the heavy bombers entered on a phase of operations directly related to the impending assault (D-Day). This was a series of heavy attacks on marshalling yards and airfields in France, the Low Countries, and western Germany, over an area large enough to preclude any indication of the precise invasion area. The attack on marshalling yards was designed to paralyze repair and maintenance facilities, thus wearing down the capacity of railways for movement of troops and supplies and forcing the enemy to maximize use of road transport.[78]

Operational Mission 23: 2 June 1944 – Calais, France

Eight hundred and five Eighth Air Force B-17s and B-24s, including twenty-one from the 94th, attack V-weapon sites. No planes are lost. Eighth Air Force heavy bombers concentrate attacks from 2 June through 5 June on transportation and airfield targets in northern France and begin bombing coastal defence areas around the Pas-de-Calais in an effort to deceive the Germans regarding the sector of northern France to be invaded on D-Day.

```
SPECIAL ORDERS 157
RESTRICTED
H.Q. ETOUSA
5 JUNE 1944


EXTRACT


O, AC, Eighth AF, listed below, is temporarily promoted to the
   gr indicated in AUS w/rank fr date of this order


2nd Lt to 1st Lt


FRED S. LULL, O752877


By command of General EISENHOWER
```

Chapter Eleven

D-Day – The Invasion: 'It's on'

June 6, 1944
Orders of the Day
SUPREME HEADQUARTERS
ALLIED EXPEDITIONARY FORCE

Soldiers, Sailors and Airmen of the Allied Expeditionary Force!

You are about to embark upon the Great Crusade, toward which we have striven these months. The eyes of the world are upon you. The hopes and prayers of liberty-loving people everywhere march with you. In company with our brave Allies and brothers-in-arms on other Fronts, you will bring about the destruction of the German war machine, the elimination of Nazi tyranny over the oppressed peoples of Europe, and security for ourselves in a free world.

Your task will not be an easy one. Your enemy is well trained, well equipped and battle hardened. He will fight savagely.

But this is the year 1944! Much has happened since the Nazi triumphs of 1940-41. The United Nations have inflicted upon the Germans great defeats, in open battle, man-to-man. Our air offensive has seriously reduced their strength in the air and their capacity to wage war on the ground. Our Home Fronts have given us overwhelming superiority in weapons and munitions of war and placed at our disposal great reserves of trained fighting men. The tide has turned! The free men of the world are marching together to Victory!

I have full confidence in your courage, devotion to duty and skill in battle. We will accept nothing less than full victory!

Good Luck! And let us all beseech the blessing of Almighty God upon this great and noble undertaking.

/s/ Dwight D. Eisenhower[1]

Operational Mission 24: 6 June 1944 – Caen Area, France

Thirty-nine aircraft from the 94th BG, all marked with a white stripe on the wing and fuselage to identify them as invasion aircraft, are assigned to bomb coastal defences, including pillboxes, machine-gun and anti-tank emplacements in Caen. Other Eighth Air Force heavy bombers bomb transportation chokepoints. In all 1,729 bombers dropped more than 3,596 tons of bombs on D-Day.[2]

> Unfortunately … the strikes on Caen resulted in numerous 'collateral' casualties to French civilians.[3]

Tuesday June 6, 1944
D–Day
Bury St Edmunds

Dear Mom,
Well it finally happened didn't it! Were you surprised to hear it? Where were you and how did you first hear it? Bet the whole country was in a state of excitement!

American radio audiences upon hearing his sign-on greeting, 'This, is London', knew that his reports were eye-witness accounts of the war. On this day, Edward R. Murrow's recounting of the thunderous roar of the motors of the hundreds and hundreds of planes in the great D-Day air armada that passed his vantage point was sensed in the bones of his listeners and felt in their hearts. That was the effect his voice, his reporting had on those who crowded around the kitchen table Motorola.

> Early this morning we heard the bombers going out. It was the sound of a giant factory in the sky. It seemed to shake the old gray stone buildings in this bruised and battered city beside the Thames. The sound was heavier, more triumphant than ever before. Those who knew what was coming could imagine that they heard great guns and strains of the 'Battle Hymn of the Republic' well above the roar of the motors.[4]

I had an idea it would happen today. I mean we thought so last night.

> … At the 94th Bomb Group in Bury St Edmunds, on May 25, something occurred that made everybody really start talking about this invasion that should be coming soon. All crew members had to carry their sidearms, .45s, at all times on the base. The ground crews were given various kinds of shoulder weapons to carry with them as they worked on the airplanes.[5]

Right now we're listening to a German propaganda broadcast. It actually makes one laugh.

Special bulletins were spread across the front pages of the country's newspapers, making the folks at home aware of new place names, new battles, new denials from the German propaganda machine. Paratroop landings, beaches stormed, Omaha, Juno, Sword on the Normandy coast of France, Le Havre, Cherbourg, Caen, Sainte Mère-Église, Pointe du Hoc, and news of victories with a high price paid in Allied casualties.

Gildersleeve will be on in a few minutes.
The crew has 28 now. I've got 24.
Didn't get to see very much today. Guess they really gave our boys the support today. The radio said we had 12,000 planes over the Channel today. Boy, why don't the Germans give up.

… then a new sound gradually droned into our ears, a sound deep and all encompassing with no notes in it – just a gigantic faraway surge of doom-like sound. The heavies.

They came from directly behind us. You see clots of them against the far heavens, too tiny to count individually. They came on with a terrible slowness.

In flights of 12, three flights to a group – stretched out across the sky. They came in 'families' of about 70 planes each.

Maybe these gigantic waves were two miles apart, maybe they were 10 miles. I don't know. But I do know they came in a constant procession I thought would never end …

Their march across the sky was slow and studied. I've never known a storm, or a machine or any resolve of man that had about it the aura of such a ghastly relentlessness …

And then the bombs came. They began ahead of us as the crackle of popcorn and almost instantly swelled into a monstrous fury of noise that seemed surely to destroy all the world ahead of us …

Nothing deviated them. They stalked on, slowly with a dreadful pall of sound, as though they were seeing only something at a great distance and nothing existed in between. God, how you admired those men up there and sickened for the ones who fell.

And then we could see a flare come out of the belly of one plane in each flight, just after they had passed over our heads.

The flare shot forward, leaving smoke behind it in a vivid line, and then began a graceful, downward curve that was one of the most beautiful things I've ever seen.

It was like an invisible crayon drawing a rapid line across the canvas of the sky saying in a gesture for all to see: 'Here! Here is where to drop. Follow me.'

And each succeeding flight of oncoming bombers obeyed, and in turn dropped its own hurtling marker across the illimitable heaven to guide those behind.

Long before now the German ack-ack guns had gone out of existence. We had counted three of our big planes down in spectacular flames, and I believe that was all. The German ack-ack gunners either took to their holes or were annihilated.

How many waves of heavy bombers we put over I have no idea. I had counted well beyond 400 planes when my personal distraction obliterated any capacity or desire to count.

I only know that 400 was just the beginning. There were supposed to be 1800 planes that day, and I believe it was announced later that there were more than 3000.[6]

Glad you had a good time out at Kennells! Bet you really ate chicken. I know you.
Well, no news I can write about so I'll quit for tonight.
I love you so much dear!
What's that nerve medicine for? Let's don't have that kind of stuff.
                                        Your little boy,
                                               Fred

On the day of the greatest armed invasion ever conducted, with thousands of ships, thousands of aircraft and tens of thousands of men in the air and on the ground engaged in armed conflict, Fred's letter home is restrained; one of those 'no-news-I-can-write-about' letters – and so he says almost nothing at all.

It is left to others to convey the enormity of this event, the news for which the folks back home, indeed the entire world, had been waiting. Whether Fred's statement of 12,000 planes, or Ernie Pyle's report of 3,000 planes, or the lesser count of 1,729 planes aloft during the invasion is more accurate is of speculative interest – one is more massive in number, the other more descriptive in its effect.

What Fred saw from the air was very little. The skies were almost totally overcast at the target zone. What he saw in the air around him one can only guess. They flew in support of 'our boys' in the invasion, and they returned to England. He listened to *Gildersleeve*.

However, that this was not an ordinary mission is clear from his citation orders:

```
GENERAL ORDERS
    NO. 179
   EXTRACT
 6 JUNE 1944
```

Under the provisions of Army Regulations 600-45, 22 September 1943, and pursuant to authority contained in ltr 200.6, Hq. Eighth Air Force, 2 April 1944, subject: 'Awards and Decorations,' an OAK LEAF CLUSTER is awarded for wear with the Air Medal previously awarded, to the following-named Officer, organization as indicated, Army Air Forces, United States Army.

Citation: For exceptionally meritorious achievement, while participating in heavy bombardment missions over enemy occupied Continental Europe. The courage, coolness and skill

The 94th Bomb Group B-17 at the French coast on D-Day – 'Guess they really gave our boys the support today'. (Courtesy of Wilbur Richardson)

displayed by this Officer upon these occasions reflect great
credit upon himself and the Armed Forces of the United States.

FRED S. LULL, O-752877, 2nd Lt., 94th Bomb Group (H). Home
address: Los Angeles, California.

By command of Major General LEMAY

For the folks on the home front there were affirmations of patriotism in evidence
from every medium, with *Life* magazine offering the epitome of declarations 'on
the eve of the invasion':

D-Day – the day of darkness and of death

Day of decision and deliverance,
Day when the whole world waits and holds its breath:
Guerrilla Greeks, the Underground in France,
The hate in Belgium hoarded for this hour,
The hate in Holland straining at her dikes,
Norway's long hate, whose hunger will devour
The vile invader when his death-knell strikes.

There are so many to set free, dear Lord,
So many lands and lives to liberate;
For strength to wield the clean avenging sword
Oh, free me first from fear of what may wait!
Once, Lord, he feared it even as I fear it:
'Into Thy hands I now commend my spirit.'[7]

Chapter Twelve

Six to Go

Dear Mom,

Listening to Fred Allen right now. Falstaff is pretty good.

Oh, before I forget, I'm a 1st Lt. now. It finally came through today. It means about $25.00 more a month. Didn't have any silver bars so had to borrow a couple from one of the boys.

So Smitty's in Porterville. Isn't that near San Francisco?

We've got big maps of the invasion up on the walls. They're real good ones; we can follow the advance as it continues.

I haven't done a thing since my last letter to you and think that was 'D-Day'.

Wonder if Chuck is over there yet. He'll be o.k. wherever he is.

Someone said our mail was very slow in leaving here lately. Hope it doesn't hold up my letters to you.

We all got very domestic today and cleaned our stuff up. I put maps on top of the table affair I've got my radio rigged up on. The backs of the maps make a very nice scarf effect. Dusted our picture off also.

Could you believe that there are some fellows over here that their families don't know that they're flying in this mess!! That's hiding the truth and I think it would be more of a strain on home folks when they find out. What do you think?

I wrote to my mom every day. It is difficult to understand how hard it must have been for that dear woman to be so concerned about my safety every day.[1]

Lately there just isn't very much to write about. Am anxious to hear your reactions to the invasion.

Goodnight dear.

Your loving son,
Fred

'We've got big maps of
the invasion up on the
walls.'

'Dusted our picture
off also.'

Operational Mission 25: 12 June 1944 – Montdidier, France

Bad weather over Germany cancels planned attacks there but 1,277 Eighth Air Force B-17s and B-24s, including thirty-five from the 94th BG, attack sixteen German air force airfields in northern France. Six rail bridges also are bombed.

Monday June 12, 1944
Bury St Edmunds

Dear Mom,

I've been a bad boy and haven't written for several days. Have been kinda busy, but haven't been flying as often as before. Being a lead crew we don't fly every mission; we just fly every few days.

Didn't get to bed at all last night. Dick and I went to the show and saw 'Du Barry Was a Lady'. After we got out of the show at 11:00 came back to the hut and started to go to bed, but they had us come down to the pre-briefing so we didn't get to bed at all.

So after we got back from the mission today we all went to bed and slept until dinner time. So am kinda tired tonight. There just isn't any news to write about.

The weather sorta held us up for a couple of days. Too bad we couldn't have had those days to help our boys on the ground. The paper said the weather was bad so I'm not giving away any military information.

Sounds as if our boys are doing o.k., but bet it's really hell.

Allied and German troops were reported locked in savage street fighting in the battered strategic city of Caen, 15 miles to the east of Bayeux. And the United Press said in a dispatch from Supreme Headquarters, Allied Expeditionary Force, that at least one junction had been effected between amphibious and airborne Allied troops on the north side of the peninsula about 12 miles east of Cherbourg. Allied planes were said to be giving strong tactical support to the ground troops as they streamed toward the port.[2]

Fred's concern about 'our boys on the ground' is both paternal and caring. Although sometimes the boys on the ground may have wondered about the boys in the air, an understanding, though unspoken, between the two different brothers of war was fostered by the common experience of combat.

… [T]he more seasoned doggie just sort of wonders why he doesn't get to go home after a certain number of 'missions.' He laughs about the youthfulness of the Air Corps officers and he wishes somebody looked after him as well as somebody looks after the Air Corps. But he doesn't bitch when he sees a formation of planes going through heavy flak and he feels pretty awful when he sees one go down and thinks of the guys in it.

As the war goes on, a sort on undeclared fraternity develops. It might be called 'The Benevolent and Protective Brotherhood of Them What Has Been Shot At'.[3]

'… a nice souvenir.'
(Courtesy of Gary
Hammerstrom)

*Mom, will you send me my Parker '51' and a bottle of Parker '51' ink. Make it black or
blue ink. That pen you sent won't work so I'd rather have my good pen. Also can you send
some writing paper similar to this I'm writing on.*

*Oh, before I forget, I bought you a cigarette lighter from one of the boys on the field. It's
made out of a 50 caliber machine-gun bullet. You just have to pull the lighter out and pour
in the fluid. It may be too big for you to carry around, but it will make a nice souvenir.*

*Hey, before I forget, will you also please send me a bottle of vitamin pills. Don't get
enough calcium over here for your teeth.*

*Well, will end for now. Hope you'll forgive me for my letters of the last weeks. They
haven't been very interesting or very newsy; there just isn't very much I can tell.*

Goodnight dear.

Your loving son,
Fred

P.S. Thought you'd enjoy this copy of 'Stars and Stripes.'

Giant Blows Are Struck by Plane Fleets – The greatest single blow since D-Day
in support of Allied ground troops on the continent was struck yesterday by a
force of up to 2,000 American warplanes in a savage assault on a wide variety of
enemy military installations in France.

About 1,000 Eighth Air Force Fortresses and Liberators, escorted by a like
number of P-47s, P-38s, and P-51s, bombed German coastal batteries, bridges
and viaducts as other Allied aircraft covered advancing ground forces and lashed
Nazi supply and communication lines.

The weather deteriorated slightly yesterday after the heavies roared forth on
their morning mission, but so adequate was the umbrella thrown over every
inch of the 50-mile battlefront that it was called the closest air support ever
given ground operations.[4]

'There's nothing cuter than Boston Bull puppies.'

Tues. June 13, 1944
Bury St Edmunds

Dear Mom,
Just wanted to say goodnight to you. Still nothing doing. The mail is kinda slow and mixed up now. Haven't had a letter for 2 days. You've got me spoiled Mom.

I sent my Air Medal and the cigarette lighter home today. Also received 2 more Oak Leaf Clusters today. They still owe me one more.

Had another letter from Gene Larson today. He's got 29 missions in now. He says they get sent home after about 35 missions. From there they fly up to Austria and Rumania.

Will finish tomorrow after the mail comes. Goodnight dear.

Wednesday:
Here I go again. Had 5 letters from you today dated the 1st, 2nd, 5th, 6th, and 7th.

Those pictures of the dogs were swell. You know how much I love them!!

I'm sure sorry you worried so much about not hearing from me, but guess it saved a lot lives though. (That's what counts!)

Fred has received his first mail from his mother since D-Day. Her concern about Fred's safety is specifically amplified for the first time, and Fred's response is what has come to be expected: 'Don't worry Mom. Don't worry Mom.' Fred allows a glimpse of his sense of the importance of the missions he has flown to break through finally. By putting his life in danger, he and his crew, and thousands of others like him, are trying to ensure that the lives of others will be saved. No matter how little he ever says about what he does, she still will worry. That's what mothers do.

Be safe my son. Be safe my son.

Today our crew finished their 30 missions. That is 5 of them did. The co-pilot, navigator and radio operator have 29 in. Just one more to go. I have 26. Four more to go. Due to the invasion we may have to do a couple of more missions. I don't think it will bother us. Even if it did they won't be rough missions. I feel very optimistic about the whole thing.

Well, I'll say goodnight for now. Will write tomorrow if anything new happens.

Love,

Fred

P.S. Still didn't get to bed last night. Slept this afternoon after we landed. The radio said we had 1500 bombers out today. The sky was filled wherever you looked. Wish those damn 'square-heads' would quit.

Operational Mission 26: 14 June 1944 — Florennes, Belgium

(There is some discrepancy here regarding the date of the completion of this mission. His note to his mother in the letter of 13 June states that he had completed his 26th. Fred's official flight records show that the mission was completed on 14 June.)

Nine hundred and eighty-three Eighth Air Force B-17s and B-24s, including thirty-five from the 94th BG, attack GAF airfields, supply dumps and targets of opportunity.

Sat. June 17, 1944

Bury St Edmunds

Dear Louise,

How do you like the greeting kid?

Joan Davis and Jack Haley are on now. Very good.

Gosh, there's still no news to write. Just want you to know everything is o.k. Hope by now they've released the mail. I know how you are about it. We may go on pass in a day or so. Will probably go to London.

Got another new crew in our hut tonight. They're wondering what it's all about.

The commanding officer of the field … made it plain that this is a combat field and this was what we spent our many months of training for. He told us that we would fly 25 missions (later increased to 30 and again to 35). He also mentioned that the field's losses to date averaged about 4% per mission. This didn't go over too well since it didn't take much math to figure that 4% times 25 equals 100%. In other words, we each would be due to be shot down during the 25 missions.[5]

I haven't done any flying for it seems like ages now.

So you stayed up all night on Invasion night. These British radio announcers are so reserved you'd never know there was a big invasion on. They just say things are going according to plan on the Normandy beaches.

The other crew in our hut just got back from London today and they said they saw some of those pilotless planes down south of England. They're the so-called German secret weapons.

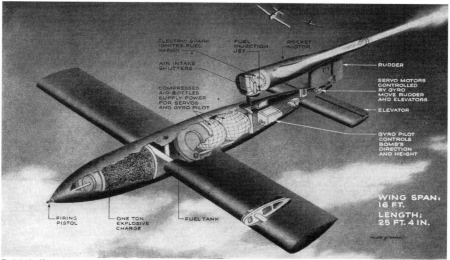

The "robot bomb" is really an aerial torpedo. The engine (*upper right*) works merely by exploding with a spark a mixture of gasoline and air, the jet issuing out at the rear. Rudder is set before launching for direction and drift and is controlled by a cheap gyro. Mass-produced, it might cost $1,000, a little more than its explosive equivalent of a one-ton bomb.

The V-1 ' buzz bomb', as shown in a magazine clipping in Fred's wartime scrapbook, '… had wings and a ram jet engine and were launched out of France'.[6] '… You'd hear a put-put-put noise like a washing machine, then nothing until it hit with a whomp'.[7]

The V-2s were liquid propulsion missiles that the Germans launched from the continent against England.[8]

Did I tell you my crew has 30 missions now. Bob Whelan (radio operator) and Dick Webb (navigator) have 29 missions. I've still only got 26. Poor little me. Think I said we may do a couple extra. I doubt it very much though. The reason for adding any if they do is because all these new crews have quite a few missions in, in such a short time and also they have had just short ones across the Channel. Therefore it wouldn't be fair to we older crews to let them finish with 30 missions while we did 30. By this I mean in our 30 missions we averaged about 240 operational hours while in their 30 missions they may fall way short of our hours so that's why they may raise it a few to make them do as many hours as we have. Do I make this clear or is it muddled? Tried to give you the whole picture.

Last night I was lying on my bed listening to the radio (Fred Allen) and thinking of the things we'd do when I get home. Won't it be wonderful!!! I really don't think it will be too much longer before I get to come home. Things change around here day-to-day.

Goodnight dear,

Fred

Operational Mission 27: 18 June 1944 – Misburg, Germany

One thousand, three hundred and seventy-eight Eighth Air Force B-17s and B-24s, including twenty-six from the 94th BG, attack oil refineries around Hamburg and Misburg, as well as two GAF control centres.

Wed. June 21, 1944
Bury St Edmunds

Dear Mom,
Just starting this letter while we're waiting for the train to leave. Notice the stationary; from the Savoy Hotel. It's the best hotel in London. You've heard of it haven't you dear? We just stayed there one night. It's too rich for our blood!! Had a cup of coffee this morning. It was 3 shillings or 60 cents in our money.

The room was luxurious, but particularly eye opening was the bathroom. The bathtub was the largest I had ever seen and the walls and ceilings were covered with mirrors etched in art deco motif.[9]

Haven't had a chance to check my mail for several days so hope I have some when we get back to the base. Then will have some more things to write you.
Bought a new pair of gloves and 2 pairs of pajamas while here this time at the Officers' P.X. The pajamas have red stripes and the other pair have blue stripes. Dick also bought 2 pairs. The boys will sure make fun of us when we get back to the hut and wear them. We also ordered Battle jackets while here. They cost about 11 Pounds complete with embroidered wings, bars, and ribbons on them. They really look sharp. You wear them in place of a blouse. 11 pounds comes to $44.00 so won't send so much home next month in the money order, however my extra dough from the promotion will make up a little for it. The jacket will take 3 or 4 weeks to make and by that time I hope we're finished with flying!!

Mr fastidious dresser will look snappy now both in and out of uniform. Who cares whether or not the boys make fun of striped pajamas when you have a tailor-made battle jacket to wear!

Have 27 missions in now.
Last night saw Ginger Rogers in 'Lady in the Dark.' Liked it very much. Her song about the 'Saga of Jenny' took her back to the days when she and Fred Astaire were dancing.
Excuse this pencil as it's the only thing available.
This will floor you. I had a manicure at the Savoy's barbershop. You know how my nails are, so this did them some good. Mike and Dick made fun of me, but they got worked on also.
They say last night was one of the worst nights for the pilot-less aircraft, but I didn't hear a thing. Don't know what the Germans hope to gain by them as they aren't doing any good.
A lot people still spend their nights in the tube (underground, subway). It looks awful uncomfortable to me.
Yesterday we went to the wax museum. It's wonderful. Have all the famous people, past and present, and historic scenes in wax. Can't see how they make them look so real. The Savoy Hotel is almost next to the Thames River.
Will quit for now and finish after getting my mail.

Later:

Got back and found a letter from you dated June 9th

No, my dear we're still in England. I don't think heavy bombers will ever move to France.

Guess poor ole Louise is really working now at the dear 'B of A'. She shouldn't work too hard though.

So you're listening to all the soap operas now. Gosh you shouldn't miss 'John's Other Wife.'

Here I am at the end of my thoughts again. Take care of yourself for the old boss and I'll write again soon. Hope the mail is going through now.

Love,
Fred

Operational Mission 28: 22 June 1944 – North-west France

Thirty-six planes from the 94th BG bomb a V-1 central supply site. Thirty-four aircraft are damaged by intense flak.

Friday June 23, 1944
Bury St Edmunds

Dear Mom,

No news since I wrote you day before yesterday after getting back from pass.

Had 2 letters from you today.

So Helen Trent is still looking for romance! Gosh, wonder if she'll ever find it.

Smitty didn't have very much to say in the letter you forwarded. Told of his promotion and hard work, but said he enjoyed it. That's a beautiful ring you sent a picture of.

Oh, by the way, I've let my hair grow back now. It was a lot more comfortable the short way.

Did you give any of those colored pictures of me to anyone?

Those pictures of you were swell!! You look wonderful!! Also I can see you're taking care of yourself which pleases me the most. Yes, your slack suit is very nice. I like it better when you wear a blouse and then sort of a sleeveless jacket with it. That also is a new blouse isn't it!

Had my best look at the invasion beaches yesterday. We flew almost right over them. Never saw so many boats in my life. Have 28 in now.

Well dear will quit for now. This is your foreign correspondent signing off for now.

Love,
Fred

P.S. Thanks again for the pictures Mom. I really appreciated them!

Operational Mission 29: 24 June 1944 – Wesermunde, Germany

Eighteen 94th BG B-17s attack an aircraft industry site at Wesermunde.

'It was supposed to be a rough mission. We went to Germany.' (Courtesy of Wilbur Richardson)

Saturday June 24, 1944
Bury St Edmunds

Dear Mom,

Hold onto your hat kid; get the smelling salts; and get Dr. Randel handy; because your little boy will be home very soon!! Can't tell you when or how I'm coming home, but we're leaving very soon. The whole crew is coming home. Don't know if we'll fly or come by boat. Hope it's by boat.

They woke me up early this morning to go on a mission. It was my 29th mission. Went with another crew. Boy I hate flying without my own crew. It was supposed to be a rough mission. We went to Germany.

The twenty-ninth mission … and all I thought about on that run was 'One more, one more, one more.'[10]

As we were coming in to land this afternoon, I saw my crew standing alongside the runway sweating me in.

How did they sweat him in? They watched the airspace where ships returning from their missions would first appear. They listened for the first sound of the Wright engines that would finally become a roar as they neared the base for landing. They counted to see if all had returned. They looked for flares that would indicate dead or wounded crewmen on board. They paced. They worried. They drank too much coffee and smoked too many cigarettes. They may have even sweated a little. Finally, they lined up 'alongside the runway' and at last let out a sigh of relief as the wheels touched down.

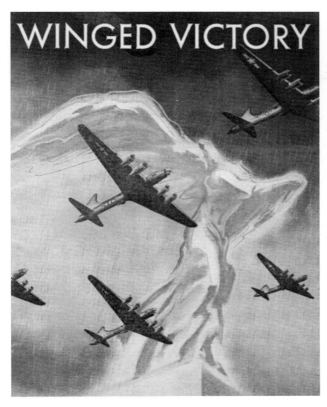

'… sweating me in.' From the pages of the playbill for *Winged Victory*. For his crew 'sweating me in' would have been 'waiting expectantly' for him to return.

Well anyway they came over to the parking strip and told me we were going home. I didn't believe them at first, but they were serious so I finally believed them.

Don't send me any more mail or packages. Hope you haven't sent my pen yet. Well, if you have they'll send it back home for me.

Also have my summer uniform cleaned and pressed.

I'm so happy!

Am going to send you a cablegram tomorrow. Don't know if this letter will get there before the cable or not.

Will probably arrive in New York. May have to wire for some money when I get to New York. Hope not though.

Well, I'll quit for now.

Just remember I don't know when we'll get home, but I'll be there. So don't expect me too soon. In other words dear I don't want you to get too excited.

All my love,

Fred

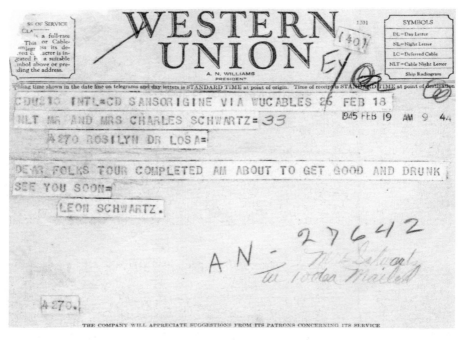

While Fred stated how 'happy' he was to have completed his tour, another notified his folks about what action he was taking to celebrate: 'am about to get good and drunk'. (Telegram reprinted with permission of Leon Schwartz)

Operational Mission 30: 25 June 1944 – Supply Drop to French Partisans

One hundred and seventy-six B-17s of the Eighth Air Force, including thirty-four from the 94th BG, drop parachute canisters filled with supplies to French interior forces.

Resupply drops to the Free French Forces deep in the interior of France were a rare occurrence. On the ground a reception committee came out of their hiding places, signalled for the supply drop, emptied the canisters and took the much-needed supplies to the assigned distribution points.[11]

We flew across all of France to near the Swiss-Italian border at the normal 25,000-foot altitude. Near our zone, we made a fast descent to about 300 feet, which was very unusual and dangerous for us. We were in a mountainous area and would drop the canisters in a valley. We passed low over red-roofed French villages, and sometimes it seemed the wingtips almost scraped the jagged edges of the mountains as we headed for the Rendezvous Point.

We split into threes, and from my ball turret, I had an excellent view, a grand-stand seat in my Plexiglas-aluminum globe as we swooped low through the valley. The resistance fighters would dash out quickly to pick up canisters.

Supply canister convoy. (Courtesy of Wilbur Richardson)

Supply canister preparations. (Courtesy of Wilbur Richardson)

Sometimes, a cart would be used. Then they rushed back to the woods. Some would wave or make a large Vee sign with their arms to show thankfulness.[12]

After the final mission: 'I can say that I've done my job as well as I know how and that I never screwed up anything in the air. I did what might be expected of an average American, and I may add that I am proud as hell of that distinction, and proud that I hit my target when the going got rough.'[13]

A wheels-down, low and slow approach to the drop zone. (Courtesy of Wilbur Richardson)

'… I had an excellent view, a grandstand seat in my Plexiglas-aluminum globe as we swooped low through the valley.' (Courtesy of Wilbur Richardson)

Monday June 26, 1944
Bury St Edmunds

Dear Mom,
Just a few more lines dear to let you know the latest. I said I was going to send you a cable, but found out these airmail letters probably get there quicker so I didn't send one.

Still don't know when we're leaving, but they're doing the paper work on it now. Also want to tell you not to expect to receive many letters if any from now until the time I get home. Will probably send you a wire or will phone from New York or wherever we arrive.

Right now Joan Davis and Jack Haley are on. Jack Benny wasn't bad last night.

When I wrote you the letter saying I was coming home I only had 29 missions. They said I could quit then, but I wanted to do 30 so I could get my D.F.C. (Distinguished Flying Cross) and 'Lucky Bastard Certificate.' You'll get a kick out of it. It's a club for those that have finished a tour. Well anyway, I did my 30th mission yesterday. It was quite a long one and boy did I sweat it out. Guess you can imagine how one feels on his last one, especially when I didn't have to do it.

Anybody who goes when he doesn't have to is a plain damned fool.[14]

Fred was no fool, but he was courageous and, most of all, he was conscientious. Yes, he could have called it quits after finishing his twenty-ninth mission and returned home with his crew, but he chose not to.

You're ... imbued with a firm determination to carry through the job you've started.[15]

Although he insists that he flew his thirtieth mission to become eligible for the Distinguished Flying Cross and membership in the 'Lucky Bastard' club, Fred simply could not have gone home having completed only twenty-nine missions. His crew flew their thirtieth mission without him, when he was in the hospital with infected sinuses. However, Fred would fly thirty missions, not one less. The pilot of the *Belle of the Brawl* had said, 'We came over together and we'll go home

'I did my 30th mission yesterday. It was quite a long one and boy did I sweat it out.' Now, they could go home together.

together', and as far as Fred was concerned, each will have done his complete duty of thirty missions.

The thirtieth was the toughest, and boy did he 'sweat it out'! They went in without bombs to reduce weight of the loaded aircraft because they were flying supplies to French resistance fighters. Some of the bombers had fighter escort; Fred's did not. They dropped their bundles of munitions, food, medicine and other supplies and headed back home – 'We were sitting ducks.'

The 94th and 100th Bomb Groups received the French *Croix de Guerre avec Palme* for their participation in this mission.

I'll leave it to you to tell Mrs. Paddock that I'm coming home so she can tell Smitty. Hope he can come home while I'm there!

Well I cawn't think of anymore to say tonight so will quit for now. Good night dear.

Love,

Fred

P.S. Again I say don't expect any more letters and if you do get one consider yourself lucky.

GENERAL ORDERS
NO. 243
EXTRACT
28 JUNE 1944

Under the provisions of Army Regulations 600-45, 22 September 1943, and pursuant to authority contained in letter, 200.6, Hq. Eighth Air Force, 21 June 1944 Subject: 'Awards and Decorations,' the <u>DISTINGUISHED FLYING CROSS</u> is awarded to the following named OFFICER for extraordinary achievement, as set forth in citation.

FRED S. LULL, O-752877, 1st Lieutenant, 94th Bombardment Group (H), Army Air Forces, United States Army. For extraordinary achievement while serving as bombardier of a B-17 airplane on many heavy bombardment missions over enemy occupied continental Europe. Through the courageous applications of his bombing technique on sustained operations in aerial combat, Lieutenant Lull has directly aided in the destruction of important military installations on each of these missions, among which were the operations over Augsberg, Germany, 16 March 1944; Berlin, Germany, 22 March 1944; and Brux, Czechoslovakia, 12 May 1944. The courage, coolness, and skill displayed by Lieutenant Lull on all these occasions reflect the highest credit upon himself and the Armed Forces of the United States.

By command of Major General PARTRIDGE

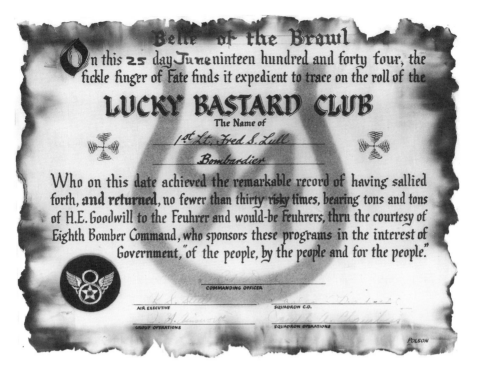

'… a cherished possession and a symbol of luck, skill and courage.'[16]

'Distinguished Flying Cross – For heroism or extraordinary achievement while participating in aerial flight.'[17]

For 'courage, coolness, and skill' in missions that included:

- his first – Augsburg, Germany, 16 March 1944:
  a terrifying experience, where it was duly noted that he lived up to criteria of 'courage, coolness, and skill.'
- his fourth – Berlin, Germany, 22 March 1944:
  more than 600 B-17s flew on this mission after which Fred casually mentions, 'I've seen Berlin before seeing London.'
- his eighteenth – the horrific air battle over Brux, Czechoslovakia, 12 May 1944:
  Forty-one of forty-three 3rd Division planes did not return.

GENERAL ORDERS
NO. 244
EXTRACT

28 JUNE 1944

Under the provisions of Army Regulations 600-45, 22 September 1943, and pursuant to authority contained in letter 200.6, Headquarters Eighth Air Force, 21 June 1944, Subject: 'Awards

and Decorations,' an <u>OAK LEAF CLUSTER</u> is awarded for wear
with the Air Medal previously awarded, to the following-named
Officers and Enlisted Men, organizations as indicated, Army Air
Forces, United States Army

  <u>Citation</u>: For exceptionally meritorious achievement, while
participating in heavy bombardment missions over enemy
occupied Continental Europe. The courage, coolness and
skill displayed by these Officers and Enlisted Men upon these
occasions reflect great credit upon themselves and the Armed
Forces of the United States.

<u>94th BOMBARDMENT GROUP (H)</u>
(331st Bombardment Squadron)

FRED S. LULL O-752877   1st Lt

By command of Major General PARTRIDGE

Chapter Thirteen

Homeward Bound

V-Mail
July 1, 1944

Dear Mom,

We're not at the base now. Don't know when I'll get home. Just have to be patient. My leave will start from where you said you stayed during the first war. Remember how you said they had band concerts and community singing with the soldiers. Changed my English money into American money today. Imagine it will be pretty hot traveling from the East Coast home, but who cares anyway!!! Sure hope Smitty or Jack Morton get to come home while I'm there. Well as usual _cawn't_ find very much to say so will sign off until I see you in person. This is my last letter.

Love,
Fred

'On our way home, June 30, 1944.'

MOVEMENT ORDER FOR GP E-14 - 14 TD (Combat Crew)
HEADQUARTERS
12TH REPLACEMENT-CONTROL DEPOT (avn)
APO 635

LETTER ORDER NO. 7-29
EXTRACT
5 JULY 1944

Pursuant to directives contained in Sec V, Par 1, WD Cir 127, 29 May 1943, WAR-19023, Ltr AG 210.453 (1 June 1944) OB-S-E-SPMOT-M, Subject: 'Procedure for return of Individuals for Temporary Duty' dated 3 June 1944, and provisions of Ltr Hq ASC, USSTAF, Subject: 'Return of Combat Crew to U.S. for Rest and Recuperation' dated 26 April 1944, the Air Corps Offs and EM, ETOUSE, named in Par 9, having reported to this station per competent auth, permanent station as designated will proceed by first available water transportation on TD for 21 to 30 days (exclusive of travel time) in the Continental U.S. at the discretion of the CG AAF for rest and recuperation, and will report to Reception Station in U.S. to be named by endorsement to this order by CG of the port at which debarked. This is a temporary change of station.

Upon completion of this TD, the Offs and EM concerned will return to this Theater by TOP Air Force Priority water transportation.

Per diem is not authorized.

The records required in Par 8a Ltr.210.45, subject 'Procedure for Return of Individuals for Temporary Duty' will be carried by the person in charge of TD Gp and will be delivered to the CO upon arrival at destination.

Form 24 (Service Record) Form 28 (soldier's individ pay card) Form 77 (Off Pay data card) Form 81 (Immunization register) C & E Adjustment Form (or Form 32)

Clothing and baggage to accompany any individual will not exceed 100 lbs per individual. Baggage will be marked in compliance with Par 12d of WD Publication 'Preparation for Overseas Movement' (POM 1 Aug 1943).

Gp E-14-14-TD (Combat Crew) will be under the control of the Commanding General, Army Service Forces fr overseas sta until released by proper auth in the U.S.

No information whatever concerning the War Department, Army or personal activities of a military nature within the theater will be disclosed to the public through newspapers, magazines, lectures, books, radio or any other means without clearance by Bureau of Public Relations, War Dept. or by appropriate public officers of Army installations.

The following Off and EM are reld fr TD with Casual Pool, 12th RCD AAF-591 and placed on further TD with Gp E-14-14 TD (Combat Crew) while en route to Reception Station.

RANK	NAME	ASN	PERM AAF STA
1ST LT	FRED S. LULL	O752877468	
T/Sgt	Harry C. McAteer	39400146468	
T/Sgt	Robert A. Whelan	39553275468	
S/Sgt	Morris Shapiro	39554717468	
S/Sgt	Robert E. Brown	19177164155	

1st LT FRED S. LULL, O752877, AC, is designated as CO of Gp E-14-14 TD (Combat Crew) during the entire movement fr present sta to Reception Station in U.S.

By order of Colonel GAYLE

MOVEMENT ORDERS
EXCEPT
20 JUL 44

HEADQUARTERS, ASF, NYPE, Fort Hamilton, Brooklyn 9, New York

TO: Commanding Officer, Reception Station, #14, Presidio of Monterey, California.

Group E14-14 TD (Combat Crew) and all individuals included therein, except as indicated below, arrived at the New York Port of Embarkation at 2315 19 July 44.

The following individuals included in the Movement Orders are not moving from the Port for the reasons indicated below:
  NONE

Group E14-14 TD (Combat Crew), consisting of 1 officer and 4 enlisted men, will proceed by rail to Reception Station #14, Presidio of Monterey, California, for a period of temporary duty. Immediately upon completion of temporary duty, the above group will proceed from the Reception Station to the AAF REDISTRIBUTION STATION #1, ATLANTIC CITY, NEW JERSEY, to await the Port Call from the Commanding General, New York Port of Embarkation, Brooklyn, New York, for return movement overseas.

Readiness date for the Port Call is 5 September 1944.

In accordance with AR 3-2215, the QMC will issue fourteen (14) meal tickets each to four (4) persons for four and two-thirds (4 2/3) days.

In accordance with Sec II, paragraph 6 a (4) Letter WD AGO, Washington 25, DC, dated 3 June 1944, File AG 210.453 (1 Jun 44) OB S-E-SPMOT0M, subject: 'Procedure for Return of Individuals for Temporary Duty,' PER DIEM IS NOT AUTHORIZED.

For the Commanding Officer:

/s/ Boris M. Dayyan

'The New York shoreline came into view late this morning. It was a nice sunny day … What a sight this nice old lady was this afternoon.'[1]

Fred was home on leave from the latter part of July until the end of August, when he once again began his frequent 'Dear Mom' correspondence. While he was home on leave, he visited with family, friends and his former high school where he was interviewed for the school newspaper.

The Whelan family and the Lulls had become friends, who visited each other with pictures taken, meals shared and the closeness that came with the shared experience of having two sons in the war: two sons who were airmen; two sons who flew in the same plane – crewmates, the closest kind of relationship in skies filled with uncertainty, possible death, and finally a triumphant and safe return home.

Officers Club
Presidio of Monterey, California
Wed. 8/30/44

Dear Mom,
Don't have anything to write, just wanted to say hello. Am going to call you today. We leave (from Presidio of Monterey, California to Atlantic City, New Jersey) tomorrow morning. Gosh it sure is tough we couldn't have stayed home 3 more days.

Haven't been doing very much, just having meals with the Whelan's. We drive down to Carmel. It's only 4 miles from here. The food is better there. It sure is foggy and lousy weather up here.

As far as I know now we're going on a civilian train. There are just 10 of us going from here.

'To Fred – Gook luck and better bowling next time F.S. Love Arleen Whelan.'[2]

Will drop you post cards en-route also will telegraph you from New Jersey when we find out what is cooking.

Keep your chin up dear and it won't be long before I'm home for good. The war news this morning really looks good; only 34 miles from Belgium.

Love,
Fred

Four days earlier, Paris had fallen to the French Second Armoured Division, and General Charles de Gaulle had proclaimed himself President of France. In less than a week, *Stars and Stripes* announced in large headlines: 'Yanks in Germany. The incredible onward sweep of the Allied forces deep into Nazi-held territory was so fast today that headquarters maps were changed hourly.'[3]

When Fred's leave at home ended, he was sent temporarily to the Presidio in Monterey before continuing on to Atlantic City for additional R&R and reassignment. Even in Atlantic City, though, Fred's adventures continued. The city was battered by a hurricane and, on a happier note, he and 'the boys' had dinner with Bob Whelan's sister, Arleen, one of the judges of the Miss America pageant being held in Atlantic City.

Arleen Whelan, a movie and stage actress of the 1930s and 1940s, appeared in such movies as *Kidnapped* (1938) with Warner Baxter and Freddie Bartholomew, *Gateway* (1938) with Don Ameche, *Young Mr. Lincoln* (1939) with Henry Fonda and *Charley's Aunt* (1941) with Jack Benny.

The Ritz Carlton – 'It's really hot stuff'.

9/4/44
Monday
Atlantic City

Dear Mom,
Just a few quick lines tonight to let you know the latest dope from dear 'ole Atlantic City.'
We arrived here about 10:30 this morning. We're staying at a very large hotel. It's right on
the beach. It's really hot stuff.

There was a bus, with a sergeant helping some guys get aboard. He helped officers and enlisted men indiscriminately, so we let him help us too. Then the sergeant climbed inside and said to the driver in a casual tone: The Ritz-Carlton.

Hitting Stateside, the incoming AAFer is met at a port of debarkation or at a casual reception centre by a liaison officer who informs him of the redistribution station to which he is to report. He will then be given a furlough, a 20-day delay in transit.

The first question they ask him at Atlantic City is 'Have you had your furlough?' If he's already been home, then he settles down to the almost completely unshackled and painless business of being processed for 'redistribution' and recommended for a new duty that fits his talents and his physical/mental condition.[4]

Went for a short swim this afternoon and then went to the show this evening. 'Arsenic and
Old Lace'. Had a swell train from Chicago to Phil., Penn.
Now for the news you really want. The first thing we heard after arriving here was that
the enlisted men were not going to be shipped back over to England. They don't need them
there anymore. That means Bob and the rest of our boys. As for the officers they don't know
yet what they're going to do. Mike Pedulla ('Belle of the Brawl' copilot) is being sent to

Nashville, Tenn. to a rest home for a couple of weeks and from there he's going to Florida
to be reassigned to a different job of some sort. He got sent there because they said he was
nervous, etc. I won't have my physical examination for several days yet so won't know
anything until then, but remember what I said about flying, 'No more for me!!'

A bombardier in B-17s had completed his thirty missions over Europe and had
returned to the United States at about the same time that Fred and his crew
returned. The bombardier was interviewed by a columnist for *The New Yorker*
magazine and put into perspective his feeling about flying again:

> Pilots and navigators seem to feel different about the flying end of it; they don't
> seem to get that feeling of never wanting to go up again. Maybe that's because
> they're really flying the ship. When you're only one of the hired hands, who's
> being carried along to do the dirty work, to drop the bombs and do the killing,
> you don't feel so good about it.[5]

There's nothing definite around here because of the present war situation. Gosh, can you
believe they're in Holland already! I don't think it will be long.
    I'll write in a couple of days when I know some news about the situation here.
    You can write to this address dear.

All my love,
Fred

What a change of attitude this is for Fred. Thirty combat missions in harm's way
sucked the joy of flying from him. He was drained. What he saw, what he did and
what happened to him, his plane and his crewmates were enough to change him,
perhaps forever. 'No more flying for me!'

Wed. Sept. 6, 1944
10:00 in the morning
Atlantic City

Dear Mom,
Right now I'm sitting in my room on the 11th floor writing this letter to you. Mike and I
have the same room. It's right in front looking out to sea.
    They had the 'Miss America Pageant' here yesterday so I took a roll of film of it and
of us on the beach. I may get a tan yet. Can get all the film I need right here in the hotel
for only 29 cents. Will probably take my physical tomorrow and the next day. Guess Mike
will be here for another week before leaving for Nashville, Tenn. He'll stay there for about
2 weeks to a month and then go to Florida for reassignment. It's sort of a hospital at
Nashville. Don't know how many of them there are, but they send you to the one closest to
your home if it's possible.
    This is my 3rd day here and have been spending the afternoons on the beach. Tough life
eh kid!
    Also, has 'Lassie' come home yet?

I will have this roll of film developed and send it home for you. How did your pictures turn out? You can send them here and then I'll send them back to you.

Gosh, can't think of anymore for now, but will write as soon as I find out any news.

Love,
Fred

★★★

Thursday Sept. 7
11:30 in the evening
Atlantic City

Dear One,

Well Al (Belle's pilot) and Dick (navigator) are leaving here in the morning. Don't know for sure where they're going, but it's probably back to our old base. I finished my physical exam today. I'm in perfect shape. As far as I know I'll probably catch up to Al and Dick before they board the boat. Sure hope so as long as I have to go. We're the only 3 men in our crew that are going back. It's a heck of a deal to have to go back, but you can see from the fact that the rest of the crew is staying here that Al, Dick, and I are going to do ground work over there. I'm not sure, but I'll probably call you before you receive this letter. If I don't call soon I'll call before I leave for our ocean voyage. A lot can happen before we even leave yet!!

Arleen got here yesterday. She's a judge in this 'Miss America Contest of 1944'. It's really a big thing every year. They were taking her picture, etc. after the show tonight. Boy she really looked sharp!! Saturday night the finals are held. Tonight was just preliminary.

Arleen had us all over to dinner at her hotel tonight. It was really wonderful! She's so darn nice and sweet.

Am supposed to pick up my pics Saturday so will mail them home. Also am sending a roll of exposed film home. Several of the pics may be ruined as the camera came open and let the light in.

Oh, before I forget, don't write any more letters here as it will take them so long to catch up.

Am getting anxious to know how the colored pics came out also how we look on the screen.

Mike and the boys feel kinda lost because they're not going with us. I'll sure miss them, but at the rate our armies are going it won't be so long will it!! (I mean before it's over).

I'll probably send some money home next week.

Please tell everyone hello for me.

Goodnight,
Fred

The fun of spending time in Atlantic City, enjoying the sights, relaxing and playing at the beach, spending some time with Arleen and her hosting dinner for the boys was overshadowed by the new turn of fate that threatens to send Fred and two of the other crewmembers back to England. He is disappointed, and his expression of what comes close to anger is somewhat muted, probably for his mother's sake – 'It's a heck of a deal to have to go back'. Breaking up of the crew, that interdependent team upon which the mutual reliance of ten souls was required for any chance of survival, was an unwelcome twist of the blade of 'going back'. 'I'll sure

The boys certainly enjoyed themselves as Arleen made them feel so much at home.

miss them' – but, it won't be long 'before it's over' (it was to be another eight months before the German capitulation).

Don't worry Mom. Don't worry Mom.

Friday Morning
Atlantic City

Dear Mom,
Tried to call you this morning, but there was a 2 hour delay. We really had a time here yesterday and last night. Guess you heard and have read about it by now. It's the first time I ever saw or was in a hurricane. It really wrecked this place.

I got trapped over at Bob's hotel last night and couldn't get back over here until this morning. My hotel is only about 100 yards from his. It's almost noon now and at noon they're having a meeting to decide what we're going to do. We're probably leaving this hotel as we have no water, lights, or plumbing. You never saw so many stores and cars flooded in your life! The Boardwalk is ruined. Am going to try to take some pictures of it. There's all kinds of debris along the beach this morning. I'm going to quit as I have to finish packing my stuff before the meeting so I can move or whatever they're going to have us do.

Love,
Fred

WESTERN UNION TELEGRAM

1944 SEP 16 AM 4:43
DEAR MOM WILL ARRIVE IN SPOKANE MONDAY NIGHT LOVE = FRED

Change! Another constant with which Fred has had to learn to manage. Not only does he not return to England and the war, he is sent to a rest home (in reality a

'You never saw so many stores and cars flooded in your life!'

Fred inspecting the ruined boardwalk.

convalescent centre[6]) similar to that of his co-pilot, Mike. Fred is assigned to Fort George Wright just outside Spokane, Washington, where he will spend more than a month resting and recovering from the stress of combat. He will try to regain a sense of what a normal life is like, how to, once again, sleep through the night without waking up at three in the morning, screaming and trying hard not to remember what he had just seen in his dreams.[7]

It is while Fred is in Spokane that his interview for his former high school newspaper is printed:

Lt. Lull in Europe Battle; Lt. Fred S. Lull, W'40, is home from the Battle of Europe after completing 30 missions as bombardier in a B-17. His last ten

'A doctor and nurse at Ft George Wright Convalescent Hospital.'

missions were during the invasion. He modestly disclaims credit for bravery or hazardous undertakings, although admitting that his plane collected a lot of shell holes from here and there.

For the past month, he has been in a rest camp in Spokane and now awaits reassignment.[8]

Wed. Sept. 20, 1944
Spokane, Washington

My Dear Louise,
Ah yes, it looks bad for the Nazis tonight; their gums are keeping fit with Forhan's; 4 out of 5 may be suffering from gingivitis.

Fred, post-war work as a Gabriel Heatter impersonator probably isn't a good idea.

As usual it sounded good to hear your voice over the phone!! It rained here last night and this morning, but cleared up this afternoon.
Gosh this is really a beautiful deal here. The doctor said you are here for a month at least.

Men who flew combat missions were prime targets for what became known as combat fatigue, mission fatigue, flying fatigue, battered nerves, combat stress, combat flying stress, operational stress, operational exhaustion and temporary or permanent psychiatric casualties. In their own vernacular, they became flak happy.[9]

These debilitating disorders were related to the experience of participating in bombing that resulted in death and destruction of the unseen enemy, the misses and near misses of enemy bullets, and witnessing the killing and maiming of men who were friends, crewmembers or fellow aerial combatants flying in jeopardy, falling through the air in mortally damaged ships. These were men for whom combat fatigue was more than physical exhaustion, although that was certainly a factor. These were men disabled from the cumulative and combined effects of fear, physical and mental strain, fatigue, lack of sleep, anxiety, tension and stress, and spending too many hours on pure oxygen in below-freezing temperatures in cramped battle stations.

> The sight of blood made him ill. Once he had to bandage the head of a gunner who had been hit with flak because under the circumstances no one else could do it. He nearly passed out.[10]

Debilitating, too, was the likely recurrent needling of passive stress, that feeling of helplessness crewmembers felt when they were flying into and through flak.[11] Stress-ignited feelings of helplessness might also occur or reoccur as the result of the physical and psychological preparations for a mission, only to have it scrubbed because of bad weather at the target area or because of failure of fog to lift at the base, or for reasons known at command levels but unknown, or at least not communicated, to those waiting to fly into combat.

> These factors are the psychological disturbances which arise in combat flying personnel – the 'gremlins' of the mind, in whose grip even the strongest willed man is powerless.[12]

Fred may have been wrestling with his combat memories and gremlins lingering at or just below the surface of consciousness for some time. Certainly, others were afflicted with similar consequences of battle:

> I'd wake up after I got home and the same FW would be coming after me and I'd wake up screaming.[13]

Someone, somewhere at some time, noticed in Fred the need to let the ball of twine that represented his emotional struggles unwind. He needed something other than a return to active duty and flying status. Six weeks of recuperation at the rehabilitation facility in Spokane became his road to recovery.

His letter home, written two days after his arrival, reveals that he is more than a little pleased to learn: '… this is really a beautiful deal here'.

The food is wonderful. They've got all kinds of things to do such as handicrafts, horseback riding, tennis, golf, etc. From the officer's club which is also the mess hall we get a beautiful view. It's situated right on the banks of the Spokane River.

'This is looking from the veranda of the Officer's Club. Pretty view, eh what!'

Oh, before I forget, will you go down to Silverwoods at 6th and Broadway (as if you didn't know) and buy me another <u>green shirt</u>. Size 15½ collar and 34 sleeve length. The shirt costs around $18.50. You know the kind that doesn't itch. They're getting kinda scarce so I want one more. Then you can send it to me. You get it on the 3rd floor of Silverwood's.

Can't think of very much more to say for now. Will probably hear from you tomorrow or the next day.

Went into town this afternoon and saw a show.

Think I'll take up photography here. They teach you how to develop and print your pictures.

Will probably get some money Friday so will send it home then.

Goodnight for now.

Love,
Fred

★★★

Friday Sept. 22, 1944
Spokane, Washington

Dear Mom,
Received your letter today. Those colored pics turned out pretty good didn't they! Also those other pics aren't bad. I'll mark the back of them for you.

That's a pretty good notice in the paper about me.

Let me know if you receive these 2 money orders o.k. Don't see any need for sending my letters airmail as it doesn't take very long from here.

Went horseback riding this morning for 2 hours. Had a very nice ride. We got up where we could look out and see the whole city of Spokane.

No, we weren't in the basement during the hurricane, because it was flooded. We were on the tenth floor.

It's been kinda warm today. Rained last night though.

If you think that's a good photo book for our pics get it. A cheap one isn't worth having.

A lot of people have noticed my ring.

Bankamericans In Uniform

—*News of Our Boys*

Around the World

THIS FORMER Western-Olympic staffer, Lt. Fred S. Lull, was home on leave last month wearing D.F.C. and Air Medal, earned as bombardier with 8th Air Force operating out of England.

In Walt's letter he wanted to know if Louise's apple business is booming. He said when he passed through L.A. it seemed everyone was drinking and not eating so he said you ought to change to selling orange juice and for a quarter extra put a kicker in it.

Well dear here I am out of news. Will say goodnight now.

Love,
Fred

P.S. Saw 'Bride by Mistake' last night. Very good. You'd like it I think.

★★★

Monday Oct. 16, 1944
Spokane, Washington

My Dear One,

I'm sorry about our phone conversation Sunday, but I was just about yelling. Guess you were also. Used a different phone as the other one was out of order.

We had quite a bit of excitement here Sat. night. Didn't know it when we talked. About 4:00 in the morning a guy sneaks into the nurses quarters. He went into one of their rooms. She woke up and as she sat up he let her have it with a fire axe. Thank goodness it didn't kill her. He split her head. As soon as he did it he ran out, but left his fingerprints on the door in blood so they are checking up on fingerprints. They think he's a mental case from somewhere.

In the meantime all the nurses are pretty tense. They've got several guards over at their quarters now. Isn't that a heck of a thing to happen on an army post?

On the phone I told you I'll probably get a 10 day delay in route. That means I'll be home for another ten days. Don't know if it's certain, but it's very possible.

These last two days have been awful foggy in the mornings.

Guess we'll go to Grand Coulee Dam next Monday. They've got a trip scheduled.

Will finish this letter later on today after the mail comes in. May have a few more lines to add.

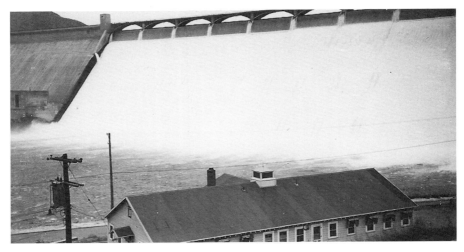

Grand Coulee Dam.

Later:
Received your letter and one from Smitty. Well it finally looks as if Smitty is going. His letter had a San Francisco APO# on it. He says he's somewhere on the west coast and is very mysterious about it. He didn't have very much to say.

Dear, you get the coat you like best! Don't get a cheap one.

Well, am going to get dressed now as we're going to see 'Porgy and Bess' tonight.

Your little boy,
Fred

★★★

Friday Oct. 20, 1944
Spokane, Washington

Dear Mom,
Am going to start this now and will finish after tomorrow's mail comes.

Had a very pleasant surprise today. Had just come out of the Link trainer when there was a phone call for me. It was Mr. Story from L.A. He is one of the customers at Western-Olympic. He's very nice. He took me to lunch in town and then we drove around. Had a very nice afternoon. It certainly was nice of him to take the trouble. His son just is back from Italy. He's a fighter pilot.

Wrote a letter to the Collector of Internal Revenue in L.A. and asked him when I last paid my income tax. Gave our home address. Am supposed to have my income tax fixed up four months after returning to the U.S. Also am having them send my paycheck to our home address as I might not be here on the end of the month.

Sat. Morning
Saw 'San Diego I Love You' last night. It was very good. Had a lot of laughs. Guess it was supposed to be a B picture, but it had Edward Everett Horton, Jon Hall, and Louise Allbritton. It's one pic that didn't have something about war in it.

Received your letter today. Am listening to football game from the Coliseum. U.C.L.A. is getting the pants kicked off them! Next Sat. U.S.C. plays Saint Mary's. They also play Wash. Monday night at the Coliseum.

Smitty will never be where she'll (his mom) have to worry about him. What they do is listen in on the Jap radio.

Well, cawn't think of anymore for now so will bid you adieu.

Love,
Fred

Chapter Fourteen

Back to Texas –
Pilot Training

WESTERN UNION TELEGRAM

1944 NOV 23 850 PM
FROM ODESSA, TEXAS
HAVE TEN MILES TO GO MISSED YOU FOLKS TODAY LOVE
= FRED

```
STATION HOSPITAL
MIDLAND ARMY AIR FIELD
MIDLAND, TEXAS
                                    24 November 1944
SUBJECT:     Clearance for Flying Duty.
TO:          Operations Officer
1. I certify that I am physically qualified for flying duty.
Fred S. Lull
2. This is to certify that Lull, Fred S., 1st Lt. ASN 0 752 877
having reported from AAFRS #3, Santa Monica, Calif. has been
cleared for flying duty this date.
                                    FLIGHT SURGEON
                                         (signed)
```

Fred has not only been cleared for 'flying duty', but also has been assigned to participate in pilot training. The constant of change occurs once again and whatever plans he may have had about his military future after leaving England have been met with yet another adjustment – return to the United States, home, no more flying, Atlantic City, return to England, Spokane instead of England, pilot training.

This is the army, Mister Jones – (Reprise).[1]

Friday Nov. 24, 1944
Midland, Texas

Hi Dear,

Arrived here last night at about 9:30. Sent you a telegram from Odessa, which is about 7 miles from here. Have been kinda busy today. Will start to school Monday morning. Don't know too much about things here yet. Think it lasts 9 weeks. The first 3 weeks are navigation and some stuff about bombsights. Will let you know all about it when I find out. They have cadets on this field.

Guess who I ran into here? Gene Larson. It sure was good to see him again! There are several guys here that graduated from Roswell with us.

Fred bought a car after he left Spokane and drove to Texas. Although gas rationing was in effect, men reporting for active duty were given exemptions for rationed goods such as gasoline.

I stayed in Phoenix the first night and Las Cruces the second night. The third night stayed at Carlsbad with Walt Lunny and his wife and baby. Had Thanksgiving dinner with them yesterday and then came down here.

Had very good weather all the way. Didn't have a bit of trouble with tires or anything. It only took the guy about 5 minutes to adjust my car before I left L.A.

Hope you all had a nice dinner yesterday (Thanksgiving)! It's surely probable we'll all be together next year!

I went through a school zone at 35 mph. The cop was very nice; just gave me a warning ticket. I did 50 mph all the way here.

It's harder each time I leave home. I get more homesick, but we're so lucky and don't have a bit of room for kicking. It can't be too much longer before this darn mess is over.

I'm going to try to write every other day by regular mail as we'll be going to school around 12 hours a day for awhile and I'll give you all the latest dope.

Please give everyone my love.

Love,
Fred

★★★

28 Nov. 44
Midland, Texas

Dear Mom,

Just a few lines tonight before jumping in bed. Feel kinda tired. This is just like being in cadets again; we're just cadets senior grade. We're just as busy and our schedule is just as bad. The only difference is we don't march to class like we did in cadets.

From all indications I'll probably get my orders to go to pilot training in Feb. or March. Some of the fellows that got here before me have received theirs and they go in Jan. and Feb.

The only thing to do around here when you have free time is to go to the local cinema. As I said, it's just across the street.

The sun shines here, but the wind blows and it's kinda cold.

Will start sending these letters by regular mail now as they will come in regular order.

Wed:
Not a darn thing more to add tonight. Got a box today so I can send you those dirty things. Don't give any away as I have to stand in line to get two packages at a time. Won't send them for a few days yet as I want to try and fill this box. They're Lucky Strikes as that's all I can get.

Fred then and for the rest of his life was anti-smoking: 'those dirty things.'

He is able to purchase them for mother at the base PX at a much lower cost than civilians could, although he did have to 'stand in line' for just two packages. Unhappy as he is about his mother's habit of smoking, he continues to supply her with government-issued cigarettes during the rest of his time in the army. The cigarette lighter, made from a 50-caliber machine-gun shell that he sent to Louise from Bury St Edmunds now becomes clearer as an appropriate gift. She smoked and wore slacks. Fred must have been beside himself at this non-traditional image of motherhood.

I certainly don't enjoy going to school again. It's too darn much work. They're really giving us a good course in navigation.

This picture doesn't give a very good picture of the bombsight, but the papers there probably have a better picture than this. The kid is looking into it from the wrong side.

Well, will probably hear from you tomorrow. Hope so!!

Boy the cockroaches are plenty thick here.

                       Goodnight dear,
                         Fred

★★★

                      Monday Dec. 18, 1944
                      Midland, Texas

Dear Mom,
Have had a very busy day. It's 9:00 in the evening. Finished flying at 6:30. Dropped 5 bombs. Seemed kinda funny to fly again.

Sure sounded good as usual to hear your voice yesterday. You still sound a wee bit weak. Just keep resting. Received 20 letters today. They were sent from overseas. Also received those pictures I sent in to be censored. They just developed 'em but didn't print them. Will have them printed and sent home. They're not the ones I thought. Guess I must be mixed up. Also received this $4.80 check from the bank on my stock. It's kinda old, but guess it will go through.

Am going on a navigation flight tomorrow. Should be sorta interesting.

Enjoyed reading your letters. Will send them with the book. Want to keep them with the rest of them I have.

Well, will sign off for now.

                         Love,
                         Fred

This is the first time that Fred mentions anything about saving letters. He is going to send back to his mother the letters she has written to him to keep with the others. That Fred is a sentimentalist is now established. Yet, keeping his letters together represents more than just building a collection of letters. They're not quite the same as a collection of 'love letters'. Well, perhaps they are indeed 'love letters'.

None of Louise's letters have ever been found.

Tues. Dec. 26, 1944
Midland, Texas

Dear Mom,

Well, Christmas has come and gone again. It'll be the most wonderful thing in this world if we're all home together again next Xmas. We passed a very quiet day. Went into Odessa to kill some of the time. Saw a show. Had a very nice dinner here on the field. My thoughts and heart were home with you dear. But poor Aunt Frances is the one to feel sorry for; she doesn't know where either Charles or Wes are.

It sure sounded good as usual to hear your voice Sunday; but you still sound a little bit weak. Got your Xmas present Sunday afternoon. You couldn't have gotten anything better. Don't know how you always pick out the right things. I was going to mention to you about a hair brush or a clothes brush. I bought a cheap hair brush several weeks ago and have been brushing my hair, but yours is really swell!! Thank you!!

I went to Midnight Mass Xmas Eve here on the post. It was very nice. The choir was wonderful. The singing was beautiful.

While Fred waxes nostalgic on spending this Christmas in Texas and looks forward to spending Christmas next year with his mother, others are even farther from home, trying to make the best out of the situation in which they find themselves. Any improvement in their lives seems worth the effort — even if it turns to awkward poetic mawkishness:

T'WAS THE NIGHT BEFORE CHRISTMAS
T'was the night before the mission and
All through the group,
The wheels and big
Wigs were grinding out the poop.

The bombers were parked on their
Hardstands with care,
Waiting for armament
Soon to be there.

The flyers were nestled all snug in
Their beds,
While visions of milk runs danced
In their heads.

When out of the darkness there came
A quick knock;
We cursed the O.D. and looked
At the clock.

'Briefing in two hours' the voice
Calmly said.
Well that meant we'd have forty
More winks in bed.

Time marches on … and then, yawning
And sighing,
We leaped from the sack
To make with the flying.

We rush to the mess hall quick as a
Flash,
To eat powdered eggs
And hideous hash.

Then the long bumpy ride to the group
Briefing room,
Where the big wigs preside to
Dish out our doom.

The target is told, the first six rows
Faint,
For lo and behold,
Vienna it ain't!!
The brain has slipped up, my poor achin'
Back,
We're bombing a place that throws up
No flak!!!

So it's back to the truck and off to the
Line;
The road is now smooth, and the
Weather is fine.

The crew is at station, the checklist
Is run,
The engines run smoothly as we
Give them the gun.

Then suddenly the pilot calls in despair;
'Look at the tower!
They just shot a flare!'

We dashed to the window with heart
Full of dread;
The pilot was right,
The darn thing was red!!

So it's back to the sack and we sweat
Out our fate,
For there's a practice formation
At quarter past eight!![2]

Other US airmen that Christmas were in much less favourable settings — they were prisoners of war. However, even in these circumstances, there was a sense of humour, crude, it might have been; it somehow seemed appropriate:

Christmas '44 — that was a difficult time because of the Battle of the Bulge. In the late summer of '44, one POW pilot had said to another, 'We'll be home for Christmas or I'll kiss your ass in the middle of the parade ground and give you 30 minutes to draw a crowd.' True to the his word, the pilot in question had both of his ass cheeks painted in Mercurochrome, and the boasting pilot ceremoniously kissed each cheek. The German guards went nuts about this and wanted to know, 'Was ist los? Was ist los?' — 'What's going on here? What's going on here?'[3]

Had a letter from Smitty today. Made good time. Only took 8 days. One of your letters also took 8 days.

It started to rain last night and has turned into ice. Everything is covered today and tonight with about ¼ inch of ice. People have been slipping and sliding around all day. No, I haven't had the car going today, so don't worry for nothing. This is very unusual here; just like in California. Wish it would snow instead, but looks as if it's going to clear up.

Gabriel Heatter is on now. I think he is best of any of them. He gives the best facts. Don't pay attention to the return address. Just was lazy and didn't write it all out. Well dear cawn't think of much more to write tonight.

Have you heard Bing Crosby on any of the Xmas programs? I think he is really the tops!!

> *Goodnight,*
> *Fred*

There were as many stars in hometown windows as on the tops of Christmas trees, and gift stores were short of almost everything, including Santa Claus … it has been one of the quietest Christmas seasons for many years. Peoples' thoughts are somewhere else; over the oceans, in the camps, in all places where millions of men were doing a mean job that took doing.[4]

Sat. Dec. 30, 1944
Midland, Texas

My Dear Louise,

Expected to hear from you today, but probably will tomorrow. Haven't heard for several days. I should talk; I've been kinda lax in writing to you, but we've been sorta busy and there just isn't much happening. We haven't flown for the last 6 days due to fog and cloudy weather. Has rained a little. We may fly tomorrow if the weather is clear. This bad weather has put us behind schedule quite a bit.

Guess we'll have to fly twice a day next week to make up for lost time. Next week we'll find out if it's our last week here or if we'll be kept here for the extra 3 weeks. I put in for the extra 3 weeks. Don't know if I'll get it or not. If I do it means I'll be in the training command. The other guys that leave here after next week will go to Louisiana for a maximum of 6 months. They'll go to more school. Don't know what they'll do with them there. Apparently there is going to be a pool. By that I mean they'll take men from there as they're needed in different jobs. Things are sorta up in the air. They don't have a definite policy as of yet.

The training command is a better deal but it's a lot harder on the individual. By that, I mean in training command you're more or less an example all the time. You have to be just so or get your fingers slapped!!

Some of the cadets graduated yesterday. They have just one more class of them on the field. They'll be finished this month.

Sounds as if you had quite a time playing cards at Frances'. Imagine playing all night!

Again I say don't pay any attention to my return address. I'm just getting lazy. Continue to use the full address.

Still haven't heard from Al. The mail is very slow. Had a Xmas card from Dick's family. His mother said his mail was very slow.

Well, I'm thinking of you tonight. The situation in Europe looks a lot better. They may have planned it that way. Our generals aren't so dumb.

Love,
Fred

Headlines from *Stars and Stripes*:

Patton Retakes 13 Towns; Hammers Nazi Bulge from South As Air Power Cuts Enemy Lifeline; 9th Hits Bridges, Roads Behind Front – In the course of this onslaught the Ninth airmen knocked down 397 enemy planes and destroyed or damaged 787 tanks and armored vehicles spearheading the offensive, almost 5,000 trucks and 1,700 railroad cars. In addition, concentrations of foot soldiers were strafed incessantly and supply lines battered.[5]

Wed. Jan. 3, 1945
Midland, Texas

Dear Mom,

Got both of your letters today; the bank statement, also the pictures. Your second one sure made good time it was mailed Jan. 2 and I got it Jan. 3rd.

Boy, am I tired tonight! We reported to the flight line at 1:00 yesterday afternoon and we didn't finish down there until 11:00 at night. We flew a navigation mission then landed, grabbed a bite to eat, then took off again and dropped bombs. Yes, indeed, all and all we had a pretty full day! The topper is that we had to get up at 6:00 this morning for school. The reason for so much flying is that the bad weather put us so far behind. Didn't fly today but will fly a lot again tomorrow. Am not saying for sure, but think I'll be kept here for the additional 3 weeks of training so that means staying in the training command.

Received this check the other day. Big stock holder!! Wrote a check for $12.00 today for a bill here. Knew you would want to take it off your book.

Sure is lucky for Don Lehman he's getting out of the Army. The infantry needs men and they're taking them from other branches to be put into the infantry. I never thought he was troubled with sinus. Oh well, guess we can't all be lucky. Bet it doesn't hurt his feelings much.

I'll say goodnight for now.

Love,
Fred

★★★

Friday Jan. 5, 1945
Midland, Texas

Dear Mom,

Will start this now and finish later. Am still waiting to see who is going to stay here. Guess we'll find out tomorrow. You ask what the deal at Monroe, Louisiana is. Think I tried to explain it to you before, but I'll try again. Well down there you go to school. It consists of 1/3 bombing; 1/3 navigation and 1/3 administrative work. From the way they tell us it's a pool and from this pool you are drawn to fill vacancies that come up in different bases and fields anywhere in the country. The training command is where the training is done for bombardiers, navigators, pilots, etc. In other words you instruct cadets or officers.

Am pretty tired tonight again. Flew from 1:00 yesterday afternoon until 10:30 last night. Didn't fly today, but will fly a little tomorrow; also will fly quite a bit Sunday.

Tomorrow marks the end of six weeks of school here. Has been pretty busy. Well, will end this short note and will write Sunday. Probably will be able to give you the dope on this school deal.

Love,
Fred

★★★

Monday Jan. 8, 1945
Midland, Texas

Dear Mom,

Well as usual you can't depend on this Army! We're just waiting now for orders to go to our new field. They really crossed us up. We were all so sure of staying here for the extra 3 weeks, but they decided otherwise. Gene is going with me. The last letter I wrote you I was so sure of staying, but still if you remember I still said <u>maybe</u> and not to count on it. We can't figure it out how they picked the ones to stay. Think it must have been out of a hat. Gene and I had over a 90% average and asked to stay, but still they kept guys that failed several of the courses. The only thing we can figure out is that they knew we're going to pilot training and decided it was best not to keep us.

The Army constant: Change, again.

The orders were supposed to be out today, but naturally they weren't, so probably they will be tomorrow or the next day.

We're not sure yet where we're going, but the best guess is Monroe, Louisiana. Rumors are flying as usual about getting leaves, etc. All I hope is that we get a leave, but who knows. Before you get this letter you'll probably have had a telegram from me telling of my latest trek. As Jack Richardson would say, 'The swamps of the South.'

Gene and I have been playing gin rummy lately.

Flew all day yesterday (Sunday). Some fun!

Well my dear, will quit now.

Love,
Fred

WESTERN UNION TELEGRAM

FROM SELMAN FIELD, LA
JANUARY 15, 1945 5:03 PM
ADDRESS IS REDEPLOYMENT TRAINING SCHOOL
(B) SELMAN FIELD MONROE LA = FRED.

Sunday Jan. 14

Dear Mom,

We left Midland yesterday at noon and stayed between Fort Worth and Dallas last night. Got up about 9:00 this morning and came on into Dallas; had breakfast at one of the best hotels (your wealthy son) and then we got a room at this hotel. Going to stay here all day and leave early in the morning as we have to report tomorrow night. It's only around 300 miles from here. Going to have a nice dinner and see the ice show here in the hotel tonight. Just gentlemen of leisure!

Has been rather an uneventful trip so far. Haven't gone over 50 mph. Good weather, etc. (I knew this would interest you).

In my last letter I told you I was going to write a check for the income tax and said it should be around $16.00. Well the gal in Santa Monica figured it wrong; instead of paying $32.00 I should pay $93.00 so the next check is for $76.69 instead of sixteen so subtract $76.69 from your check book.

Monday: (night)
Arrived here about 3:00 this afternoon. Sent you a telegram. As yet don't know what's doing for sure; the school starts next Monday. Will find out as soon as possible and let you know. Rumor has it that most of the work will be administrative; that is train for ground jobs and just get in four hours a month flying time.

Have never been on such a big Army field. Seems as if it stretches out for miles. This is better looking country than around Midland, but it's so darn far from home. Sure wish I'd hear pretty soon about my pilot training. Would give a lot to go next month when Gene goes!

They call this school here Redeployment Training. We're the first class to go through. They say the idea of it all is for us to fill the jobs that these ground grippers have filled for 3 and 4 years. Sounds good doesn't it!

We certainly had a swell dinner last night. We reserved a table for 7:30 and were so called big shots!

> *Goodnight dear,*
> *Your loving son,*
> *Fred*

My address is:
  Lt. F.S. Lull O-752877
  R.T.S. (B)
  Selman Field,
  Monroe, Louisiana

The R.T.S. (B) stands for Redeployment Training School (Bombardier)

```
             OFFICE OF THE FLIGHT SURGEON
               SELMAN FIELD, MONROE, LA.
                      CLEARANCE SLIP

                                          19 JAN. 45

MEMORANDUM TO THE COMMANDING OFFICER
SELMAN FIELD, MONROE, LA


                 1ST LT. F.S. LULL


Having reported for duty from: hospital, quarters, DNIF, sick
leave, another station, minor crash, has been cleared for
flying this date.


FOR THE SENIOR FLIGHT SURGEON
(signed)
```

Monday Jan 22, 1945
San Antonio, Texas

Dear Mom,
Just now got up out of bed. We're on our way to San Antonio. Gene is with me. It's only 76 miles from here. Got here late yesterday afternoon and decided to stay in the wonder state's capital city.

Fred! Although it is clear that you are not very fond of Texas it is really unnecessary for you not to remember that the state capital is Austin, not San Antonio.

This is going to be the part that stops you. Last Friday we're going about our business as usual when one of the fellows tells us there's a notice up on the bulletin board saying all the men that had come in from Midland could have leaves; so before you could bat an eye lash we're over to the notice. We had the applications filled out and approved. We were to have 15 days.

After turning in the approved applications we were to come back that afternoon to pick up the orders to come home, but about 2 hours later a special action telegram came to headquarters saying that 50 of us were to report to San Antonio for the tests for pilot training. We had nothing to do about it. They just sent our names to them so we had no other choice. You said in your letter you get so mad at me for hurrying the orders. Believe me my dear I have nothing to do with Uncle Sam's affairs as you've already found out many times before.

Yet once again, change!

Didn't send you a telegram as I'll send it from San Antonio with my new address.

From what we hear it's pretty hard now to get through because they have so many and the physical is much tougher on that account.

We have to go through all the tests we went through before to get into cadets. None of us are very optimistic about passing them.

Well, it's time to eat breakfast and get on the road again. Will finish this when we arrive.

Later:
Well here it is later on. It's now 9:00 in the evening. Don't know anymore. Sent you a night letter, but sent the wrong address so you can use this address on the envelope. Your letter will get to me though. Sorry my dear for sending the wrong one.

We're right next to Kelly Field. Randolph Field is about 20 miles from here. We went over this afternoon and went through a B-29. They're quite an airplane, but I've had enough of heavy bombers!!! Just heard on the radio the Russians are only 165 miles from Berlin. Good eh!

Soviets Smash 20 Miles Into Reich. Key Polish Cities Fall in Sweep.[6]

Just after we left Shreveport, La. We saw a wreck. A truck run into a car on the highway. We were the first ones on the scene. I jumped into the rear of the truck and started throwing pipe and other heavy stuff out the rear while Gene was trying to get the 2 guys out of the front seat. They were pinned in by the weight of the stuff that I was throwing out, but we got them out in good time. One guy had hit his head on the windshield and had shattered it, but fortunately he hadn't hurt himself. To top it off they were drunk and wanted to know where they were. Isn't that the way always, drunks don't get hurt and some poor sober guy would get killed.

My radio sure comes in swell!

Don't know if I explained very well, but so much happened in that one day we're just now getting straightened out. We were all packed and ready to leave when they stopped our orders and this new order came through. If I pass this test and stuff this pilot training takes over a year now.

> *Good night,*
> *Fred*

WESTERN UNION TELEGRAM

FROM SAN ANTONIO, TEXAS
22 JANUARY, 1945 2:45 PM
DEAR MOM NEW ADDRESS AAFPS CLASSIFICATION UNIT SAACC SAN ANTONIO TEXAS THIS IS FOR PILOT TRAINING LETTER FOLLOWING LOVE = FRED.

> *Wednesday Jan. 31, 1945*
> *San Antonio, Texas*

Dear Mom,
Received your letter after coming back from my physical exam this morning. Well, guess I'm in. The Dr. told me I passed all the tests and the physical and am qualified for pilot training. Don't know when we'll move over to the other side of the field and start pre-flight. Maybe in a couple of weeks. Pre-flight lasts for 5 weeks. Didn't weigh too much this morning; only 146½ lbs. The doctor asked me if I had operational fatigue. Have been traveling quite a bit. Think that's the cause of my low weight. Will probably gain now that I'm settled.

Next month Grace Moore is coming here in 'La Boheme' (can't spell it) am going to get a ticket. Should be very good. You like her voice so well.

Why didn't you tell me that you were so sick after your last flu attack? It didn't hurt your kidney did it?

Do you remember the name of the tonic that I got you before? Think it was 'Stuarts' something-or-other. I think it would do you some good.

What picture of me do you mean taken in Spokane?

How is your cig. supply? Let me know about a Ronson lighter. They just don't ever have 'em in the P.X.s here. They're really hard to get. Have tried to get you one before.

Got paid today so am sending this check for $100. Let me know how we stand.

Haven't anymore to say. Want to get this mailed tomorrow as you'll have it Sat. and won't have to go until Monday without mail.

Goodnight dear.

Love,
Fred

★★★

Thursday Feb. 15, 1945
San Antonio, Texas

Dear Mom,

Am starting this during our lunch hour. Had a Valentine card today from Mrs Whelan. She said Arleen is going to do a play pretty soon. I see where Arlene Francis is doing a play in New York now. Listened to her program the other night. Do you ever hear Falstaff's program?

From the 'Who's Who in the Cast' section of *The Playbill*, Arleen is described as having been:

Employed in a beauty parlor after she left high school, her peaches-and-cream loveliness and her dark red hair attracted the attention of a camera man who arranged for her to make a movie test. She was forthwith engaged to play in 'Kidnapped' with Warner Baxter and Freddie Bartholomew.[7]

Ever the politician and the patriot, the Mayor of New York proclaims in the same *Playbill* that:

The way that the Theatre has responded to our defense effort is a matter of pride to every citizen, for the work of the Theatre in keeping up the morale of the members of our armed forces is something which in its way is as vital to our war effort as the production of additional military equipment.[8]

I just can't believe that the war is going so well! If it just keeps up! Has Aunt Frances heard from Chas. lately?

It was hotter'n than heck yesterday, but it's cloudy today. Screwy Texas; almost like California eh!

Your little boy isn't as smart as he thinks. Took those tests yesterday to see if we could skip the subjects, but I only passed 2 of them. The only excuse I can find is that they were ambiguous questions.

This coming payday I won't be able to send any money home, or it will be darn little. As I haven't flown and gotten my 4 hours flying time in for the month I won't receive my flying pay, $88.00. May not get it next month either but will probably get 3 months all at once in April and then I'll be able to send quite a sum home.

Remember that I said I had lost a few pounds and only weighed 146 lbs. Well have gained a few pounds back now and am feeling in good shape. This regular schedule and athletics is what puts you in good condition.

THE DOUGHGIRLS

THE PLAYBILL
FOR THE LYCEUM THEATRE

A 1945 *Playbill* cover showing the Doughgirls, with Arleen second from the left, behind Arlene Francis.

May go into town for a while tonight. Don't know why though.
Don't see why you ever to go Western-Olympic when you can just go up to Pico Heights and do your business. Just send it inter-branch.

Time Out:
Just got back from town. Was so darn hot we came right home after dinner. It's not the heat here it's the humidity. The clouds were down low holding heat close to the ground.

Gene and I signed up for dancing lessons today. The course consists of 6 lessons. We will start next week. No harm in learning how to dance properly.

Dancing? Fred, dancing? He must be talking about some other Fred.

Well my dear will sign-off for now. Wrote to Smitty, and Mr. and Mrs. Whelan tonight.
                                        All my love,
                                                Fred

★★★

                                        Tuesday Feb. 20, 1945
                                        San Antonio, Texas

My Dear Louise,
Will just start this now. Had our first dance lesson last night. Have 5 more left. They start right from the beginning.
    By all means see 'Thunderhead, Son of Flicka.' The color is beautiful and I know you'll like it very much. I enjoy horses. Think they are beautiful! Now I'll tell you one not to see. The name of it is 'The Fighting Lady.' It's a Navy full-length film about aircraft carriers and their planes. It's in color. Know you wouldn't like it as it's all about aerial combat and show planes being shot down, etc. It's all true, actual happenings.
    Heard Grace Moore on the radio last night. She was being interviewed by one of the local radio stations. This is going to be quite an event for San Antonio having the Metropolitan Opera Co. here. Will bring in a little culture to Texas. (They can use it). There just isn't anything to do here. They only have a couple shows. Besides, the shows they get are older than what we get here on the field.
    The weather is still lousy, just like it was in England, misty and just lousy in general.
    Am glad you didn't lend that pillow. People will continue to take advantage as long as they can. If you had lent it they'd just keep asking for it and then they'd be borrowing your blankets; beside I don't want some stranger sleeping on my pillow. (aren't we mean!)
    Yes, we read about the dog killing that baby. Too bad, but the parents should have known better. Dogs are jealous of babies and they probably noticed that it was and should have gotten rid of it.
    Did Mike tell you what he was doing at Pecos? As far I know it's a primary and basic flying school.
    Took a math test yesterday. We're half way through the math course. Didn't do too hot. Got 80%. Oh well the main thing is to pass 'em. Have gotten so I can take 10 words a minute in code. However that's nowhere near what Smitty and Bob have to take as radio operators. They do 20 or more words per minute.
    Will quit for a while until the afternoon mail comes in; may have some mail and can add a few more lines.

Later: Wed. night
No mail yesterday or today so will send this as it should be there by Sat.
                                        Good night,
                                                Fred

★★★

Tuesday March 7
San Antonio, Texas

Dear Mom,
Not very much to report, just want to get a few lines off to you. Had several more cards
today. Received your birthday present today. That's the nicest wallet I've ever had! You sure
know what and how to pick things out for me!!

Will give you the latest on our move from here. By all the rumors on the grapevine we're
going to leave here Friday or Sat. It's not for sure, but it's very probable. Still don't know
where yet. Can hope though!!

If you haven't sent my summer stuff don't do so until I get to the new field. However, if
you've sent 'em already it's o.k. Can't remember if my pants were a 33 waist, but they must be
mine. Please send the swimming trunks and overseas cap when you send the shirts and pants.

Am sorry to hear you had a cold again dear. Gosh, I just don't see why you get them so often.

About the cigarettes. Sending so many won't they get stale on you? If you think they
will you'd better not try to keep them all. After this I'll only send a carton at a time.

Think I'll have my hair cut short again. It's a lot more comfortable. Never gets in your eyes.

Just heard the news a minute ago. Boy, they're really moving. Just can't see how the darn
Germans can hold out much longer. If they do they won't have a darn thing left in Germany.

Cologne Falls — First Army Takes City 24 Hours After Entry: The Reich's fourth
largest city fell to Yank doughboys a little more than 24 hours after the Third Div.
entered the Rhine capital from the northwest, to be joined by the 104th Inf. Div.
Elements of the divisions worked side by side within Cologne and by nightfall
had pushed to the Rhine River.[9]

Mrs. Whelan said Bob had a letter from Webb and he expected to come home pretty soon.
Think he ought to stay there if he had any kind of a deal as they just don't know what to
do with 'em here in the States.

Well this is another poor excuse for a letter, but you know how it is. My next letter will
probably give you all the dope on the next move. Won't mail it until Friday or Sat.

Love,
Fred

★★★

WESTERN UNION TELEGRAM

FROM SAN ANTONIO, TEXAS
MARCH 9, 1945; 11:07AM
DEAR MOM AM GOING TO TAKE PRIMARY AT LANCASTER CALIF
AM LEAVING HERE FRIDAY WILL BE HOME SOMETIME SUNDAY
WILL TRY TO STAY HOME FOR A DAY LOVE = FRED

PERSONNEL ORDERS
NO. 15
HEADQUARTERS
ARMY AIR FORCES WESTERN FLYING TRAINING COMMAND
1104 West 8th Street, Santa Ana, California
14 March 1945

EXTRACT

Pursuant to authority contained in Paragraph 2, sub-Paragraph
5, Army Regulations 35-1480, 10 October 1942, and letter,
Commanding General, AAF, dated 8 October 1942, file 210.4,
the following named Officer Students, who presently hold
the aeronautical rating, or ratings, indicated and who have
been duly assigned to a course of instruction leading to an
additional aeronautical rating of Pilot at an Army Air Forces
Special Service School, are hereby required to participate
in regular and frequent aerial flights, while undergoing such
instruction, effective 14 March 1945.

1st Lt Fred S Lull O-752877, AC-AUS, Bmbdr
(and others)

All orders in conflict with this order are revoked.

By command of Major General COUSINS

After travelling from Texas and a leave at home, Fred writes his first letter from
Lancaster, California, a town in the high desert approximately 70 miles from his
home in Los Angeles.

Wed. April 4, 1945
Lancaster, California

Hi Dear,
*Just a couple of lines as there isn't much to say and besides I'm tired and almost ready to go
to bed.*

*Did it rain after I left Sunday night? Started to rain when we left Lockheed. Didn't last
long though.*

*Wrote a check yesterday for $34.43. Was for our room and board for 17 days. Will be glad
to get back on an Army post where they don't charge me rent.*

Oh, before I forget, we're invited out to dinner at Gene's house Sunday.

*Still don't know when we get off this weekend. Rumor has it we may be off Sat., but
you know how it goes. At any rate I'll be home for dinner Sat. night. Could possibly be
home Friday night sometime, but don't count on it.*

'Beginning of Pilot Training. War Eagle Field, Lancaster, Calif. March, 1945.'

'My primary instructor, Mr Gunn. Doesn't he look happy? Must of [sic] had a good ride!'

Well, will say goodnight.

Love,
Fred

P.S. I really enjoyed myself last weekend. It was nice having such a fine dinner and to have you and Aunt Rosie for dinner partners!

Fred writes just one letter from Lancaster. He was close enough to home to be able to visit frequently and call often.

Germany had introduced jet–fighter planes into aerial combat, and the USAAF had dominated the skies of Europe with the B–17 and B–24. Yet, primary pilot training in the spring of 1945 began with fabric–covered biplanes.

It was during this time that Fred's hero and commander-in-chief died. On 12 April, the news, unexpected, plunged the country into a state of mourning, anxiety and uncertainty.

One of the most poignant reports of the president's death appeared in *Yank* magazine. It was direct. It was short. It was 'G.I. Joe' at his finest: 'So Long, Sir.'[10]

V-E DAY
So they've given up.
They're finally done in, and the rat is dead in an alley back of the Wilhelmstrasse.
Take a bow, G.I.,
Take a bow, little guy.
The superman of tomorrow lies at the feet of you common men of this afternoon.
This is it, kid, this is The Day, all the way from Newburyport to Vladivostok.
You had what it took and you gave it, and each of you has a hunk of rainbow round your helmet.
Seems like free men have done it again.[11]

VE Day: 8 May 1945. Although the war in the Pacific would continue for several more months, the war was over in Europe. For bomber crews in the ETO it meant that no more would they smell the pungent exhaust fumes of the engines as they started up for another mission, nor would they again smell the smoke from dreaded on-board fires or recognise and dismiss the odour of cordite from firing machine guns. No more would they hear the sounds of flak and bullets ripping the metallic fuselage of their Flying Fortress. There would be no more yelling in order to be heard over the sounds of battle; no more oxygen masks and mind-numbing cold of high-altitude flying; no more blood; no more gore; no more witnessing the shredding and disintegration of sister ships; no more searching the skies for parachutes deployed; no more fear of battle; no more waiting for 'bombs away'.

Now, 'Let's go home' could really mean, 'Let's go home'. Now, there would only be memories, unless they were transferred to the Pacific for more.

Friday May 25, 1945
Merced, California

Hi Dear,
Arrived here yesterday. Quite a change to get back on an Army field again. Seems funny to be on a place again where they have a show, P.X., etc. As far as we can see so far it's a pretty nice place however it appears as if they're going to keep us going from dawn to dusk. We're 6 miles out from town and 151 miles from San Francisco; 332 miles from L.A. The only time we'll get off is Sunday. From what we saw of Merced it doesn't look too bad.

Had a fair train ride. Came up on the San Joaquin Daylight (The Streamliner). It leaves L.A. at 8:00 in the morning and gets here at 5:00 in the evening.

I could have come home Wed, but had no way of traveling and besides I'd of no sooner arrived home and I would have had to turn around and go back. Sent you a carton of cigs.

Did you get them? Better use'm up as they are not wrapped in cellophane. Starting June 1st we in the Army will get only 6 packs a week and no more. That's so civilians will get more. Guess you'll be able to get a few then.

Don't forget to send a list of our bonds.

Will be able to send $100.00 home besides your allotment.

Well, there's no more for now. Will write in a couple of days to give the latest news. Tomorrow and Sunday we've got to be processed and scheduled, etc.

Love,
Fred

★★★

Tuesday May 29th
Merced, California

Dear Mom,

Looks as if my letters aren't going to be so numerous. By golly on this schedule we just aren't going to have any spare time.

Believe it or not it started to rain this evening about 5:13. Raining like the dickens now. First bad weather we've had. Very unusual! (California you know).

Had my first ride today before the weather got bad. We're flying in AT 6s. They've got 650 horsepower. Boy, what a lot of airplane. All these darn gauges, switches, levers, etc. This is a lot different than the PTs we learned in Lancaster.

So far over 30 guys have quit that came up here in our bunch. Guess some more will quit also. Guess they can't take it any longer. This is training you can't buy. I'll stick with it as long as they'll let me. Could be washed out at any time as you well know.

This is a remarkable change in attitude about flying for Fred. His earlier comments to Louise about not wanting to fly any longer have floated away. Finally being in a position of flying from the pilot's seat, to be responsible for the flight, even in a basic trainer, Fred has tasted the thrill once again of flying and has been transformed by it.

Flew for an hour today. Here we have Army pilots for instructors. Think I'll like that a lot better. Had a swell fellow today. Would like to stay with him! They may change us around as they expect some more instructors in a day or so.

Will try and take some pictures pretty soon.

Was lucky and bought a box of Kleenex today also another carton of cigs. Both cartons don't have cellophane wrappers so better use them first. Will send 'em as soon as I can find time to get to the post office.

Well, will finish this tomorrow so you'll get it Saturday.

Wednesday:

Received your letter today. Boy it was all patched up. Had been damaged by the canceling machine.

Didn't fly today. Still cloudy.

So you think you're pretty sharp being able to remember back. Shows one's intelligence eh! (just kidding)

The best news of all in your letter is about Charles coming home! Can just imagine how Aunt Frances feels.

Thank you for the list of our bonds. Will keep track of 'em now.

Should get paid pretty soon. Am going to send the whole check home and then will write several checks. Will give you the amounts when I write 'em.

Well, will say thirty for now.

Love,
Fred

★★★

Wed. June 6, 1945
Merced, California

Dear Mom,

Today, just a year ago the invasion of France was begun. We've come a long way since then. Let's hope before (I know it will) next June 6 the Jap war is over!

Am really tired tonight; flew for 2½ hours today. Soloed also. Flew with the squadron commander instead of my own instructor today. We went up and did some air work and then came down and shot some landings. Thought he'd be gray haired after some of my landings. Believe me they were terrible! Could hear him cuss several times, but he didn't do it over the interphone at me, he just said it out-loud to himself. However I could hear some of it. Finally after another landing he said do you think you can take it around? I said, 'I think I can.' So I did and did a lot better by myself. So far I've got 9 hours and 10 minutes in. Guess Gene will solo in a day or so. Gosh, there are a million things to do while you're landing this thing!

Had a letter from Aunt Frances today. It was really a very lovely letter. She said Charles was in the hospital in Germany. Didn't know why though. Said the draft board put him in limited service.

It's 8:00 now. Just got back from dinner. When we fly in the afternoon it makes us late. Fly tomorrow morning so will go to the show tomorrow night and see 'Son of Lassie.' Should be pretty colors.

Well, will say goodnight now and be sure and take care of yourself!

Love,
Fred

P.S. Heard from Smitty also. He's having a big time in Australia. Sounds pretty good.

★★★

Sunday June 10, 1945
Merced, California

My Dear Lou,

Good morning to you on this bright, clear Sunday morning. However it is just a wee bit windy.

They let us off yesterday afternoon. Didn't do a darn thing, just went out the back door to the swimming pool and went for a dip and got some sunshine. Guess we'll do the same thing today.

As of yesterday I've gotten 16 hours and 5 minutes. Flew 3 hours yesterday.

The biggest news to report today is that this field is being moved to Minter field in Bakersfield, California by the end of this month. That means I'll be able to get home on several weekends. This is going to be a B-29 base I think.

Who's been talking to you again? This stuff about going to combat after I finish here, etc. This phase of pilot training won't be finished until sometime in Aug. and from basic (which we will finish in Bakersfield) we go to advanced flying school until around November. When we finish there we get our pilot wings. This last part of the training will probably be at Phoenix or Douglas, Arizona. After completing pilot training they don't know what to do with the pilots. They've got thousands (I mean thousands) just sitting around not doing a darn thing. There's just no place for them. What we've been told so far is that they'll do one of two things upon graduation with us ex-combat men that are taking pilot training and complete it. One is put us in the A.T.C. (Air Transport Command) or discharge us from the Army. The reason for training us they say is to build up a big reserve of pilots.

Don't worry Mom. Don't worry Mom. And this, for the last time during the war.

Almost forgot to tell you the other big news. Gene quit the other day. He's got 90 points and he's going to try and get out. He doesn't care very much about flying. Hate to see him leave! He'll probably be around here for several weeks waiting for orders. In the meantime he'll probably go home for a few days. As I said before quite a few fellows have quit, but I don't think it will look so good on their records.

See by this morning's paper L.A. had a big reception for Generals Patton and Doolittle. Heard some of it over the radio last night.

Where did you hear that baloney about missions in England under 25 not counting in the Pacific? All missions count. Someone is just talking that doesn't know what he's talking about. Don't know how those kind of rumors get started. We haven't heard anything about it yet.

No, I don't miss the car a bit. It's really a relief to have it off my hands until I can be home again and have a new one. Never used it enough to pay for having it. Think I was lucky getting out from under it so well!

Start flying instruments next week. Instead of riding in the front seat I'll ride in the back with a hood over me so I can't see out at all. The instructor will fly from the front seat. He'll take it off and land and I'll fly it around by the instruments. It's really wonderful practice.

Haven't had a chance to pick up my cigarette ration card yet. Will try this coming week. It allows us 6 packs a week.

Well, will say good bye for now.

Love,
Fred

★★★

Tuesday June 19, 1945
Merced, California

My Dear Lou,
Have kinda neglected you so far this week by not writing, but talked to you Sunday. You
sounded as if you felt pretty well. I'm glad of that, but whatever Dr. Randel tells you to do,
you be sure and do it!!!

As for the situation here believe me it's been hot. Today it was a little over a 100 degrees. Has
been that way for a week. Bakersfield usually is about 10 degrees hotter than here. Oh boy!

Will send a carton of cigs in a day or so. Better use 'em as they don't have cellophane and
may dry out.

The latest dope about moving is that we will leave for Bakersfield, Monday and that we
will fly down.

There are four of us living in my room and 3 of 'em have quit pilot training. I'm the only
one left. Pretty soon there won't hardly be any left.

Tomorrow we're taking a X-country (cross-country) trip. Will only take 2 ½ hours. Will
fly up just a few miles south of Sacramento and then down to Coalinga and back to here.

Have been getting treatment on my back. They seem to help, but apparently there must
be something wrong as this has been going on for a year now. Makes it hard for me to
concentrate on this darn training. The gal in the physiotherapy dept. said the right side was
pretty tight and there was a lump there. She advised me to see the Col. here. He's the head-
man in the hospital. The regular doctors don't know enough about this kind of trouble.

The details of this physical problem are scanty, except that his back is tight and
there is a lump, but the fact that the problem has been there for a year takes the
beginning of this ailment back to his combat missions in Europe. The mystery of
the origin of Fred's back problems was probably never resolved, but it was a problem that was to stay with him for the rest of his life, eventually leading to a spinal
laminectomy in the 1970s.

Am getting pretty tan. Lie around the swimming pool every Sunday.
Sorry you had a little trouble with your next door neighbors.
Gosh, there's not much more to say so will say thirty for now.
Good night dear,
Fred

Fred was transferred to Minter Field in Bakersfield, California, and was again able to
travel home frequently. Correspondence to Louise doesn't begin again until late July.

Monday July 30
Bakersfield, California

Dear Mom,
No news, just a few lines to relate my experiences aboard that streamlined comfort, the
'Santa Fe bus'. It didn't leave L.A. until 8:15 and we had several delays en-route. It was
just after we left Gorman that traffic tied us up. The reason, a trailer of a big gasoline truck

had turned over spilling gas all down the road. They stopped everyone and told 'em no smoking. Well after passing that someone came alongside and said the bus was on fire, just about that time you could smell smoke and in another couple of minutes the smoke was so thick you could hardly see two feet in front of you. I took the woman's baby next to me and made it forward to get out. Some of the people in the back were getting a little bit tense in fact they almost got panicky. Anyhow no serious damage was done and we got under way in a few minutes.

A hero, once again.

Missed the 12:00 bus so had to wait for the 1:00 bus, but it was 45 minutes late so I finally got to bed at about 3:00 in the morning and had to get up at 6:00. Three hours sleep. Some fun!! Am kinda sleepy tonight. Guess I'll go to bed early.

Haven't heard anything for sure yet, just rumors. So won't repeat 'em. Just expect me when I get there.

Oh yes, before I forget Bill gave you a nice compliment. He hadn't seen you look better in a long time. In fact I think you looked pretty sharp myself!

Goodnight,
Fred

Chapter Fifteen

Texas, Again? — It's Over!

August 8, 1945 ... this Atomic Bomb (Nagasaki) changed all orders.[1]

Sunday Aug. 12, 1945
Pampa, Texas

Hi Dear,
Guess you're waiting just like the rest of us for the official word that Japan has quit. It may come later on today. According to the radio President Truman and his staff were in the White House early this morning and the place is full of newsmen and radio reporters. Old Gabriel was predicting this for several days before it happened. He's been saying the war was on an hourly basis. 'Ah yes! It looks good tonight!'

Have no idea how Japan's surrender will effect our status in this pilot training, but my personal guess is that they'll have us finish our training and graduate as long as we've gone this far. Also don't think we'll get out before 6 months. They just can't release millions of men all at once. Anyhow if you remember we signed up for the duration plus six months.

The main thing is that it'll just be a matter of time before we get home. Can just imagine how happy Mrs. Morton is that Jack will never get over there in B-29s now. However, might I add I know one person who will be the happiest one of all; MRS. LOUISE A. LULL!!!! Her dear boy will be home again to start bossing.

Yesterday had my first ride in the B-25. We flew for 4 hr. 40 mins. And out of that time I just got 1 hr. 40 mins. of pilot time. Three students go up with an instructor and split the time. It's really a darn nice airplane. Made 2 landings and just generally felt the airplane out. We have to get 12 hrs before we can solo. When you do solo you and another student fly together and take turns being first pilot. When you are not 1st pilot, you sit in the right hand seat and act as co-pilot. This plane cruises at 200 mph. Don't even notice it. Also it lands at 120 mph. Sure seems like an awful lot of airplane compared to the AT-6. Think I really like it.

Today is very nice and sunny, however it hasn't been half as hot as Bakersfield. Rained the other night. Is it still hot there? (Silly boy).

Next weekend they're having a rodeo in town, guess I'll take it in. That's about the only attraction that would get me into town. Just isn't anything to do. As for around here the show is all we have, but most of the time we won't have time even for that.

'Yesterday had my first ride in the B-25 … It's really a darn nice airplane.'

Guess I'll go to the show this afternoon so will finish this letter afterwards.

Later:
It's 5:15 in the evening and no further word about the war has come so will finish now.
Well dear goodnight.
                    Love,
                    Fred

★★★

                    Tuesday Aug. 14, 1945
                    Pampa, Texas

Dear Mom,
Well dear this is the day we and the whole world have been waiting for. Just finished having dinner at the Club when the news came over the radio. It's hard to find words to describe our feelings. Chiefly my thoughts are with Mrs. Richardson and Mrs. Morton. It's just like a reprieve at the last minute for Jack Morton. Now he'll never have to leave this country.
    Listening to the radio it sounds as if every city in the country has gone wild. Can just imagine how it is in L.A.

VJ DAY

Banner headlines half a page high in Los Angeles, Seattle, Denver, Dallas, Boston and in every city and town across the nation proclaimed:

PEACE! VICTORY! WAR ENDS!

The words prominently featured were read and reread – unconditional surrender; capitulation; and again and again, PEACE. Massive crowds poured out into every street, kissing and hugging, often with strangers, sharing their joy with roaring whistles, bells, horns, sirens, confetti, ticker tape and car rides, because gas rationing would soon be over, wouldn't it? It was Bedlam, and why not. The war was over!

The newspapers of 15 August 1945 filled with news of the end of the war proclaimed victory and freedom through paid advertisements with nearly as much newsprint space as reportorial columns:

'The moving finger writes; and having writ moves on.'
Let this Day be an Eternal Warning to all evil men who deny human Rights and outrage human Decency.

RING OUT BELLS OF VICTORY!
This is Victory ... Hark! To the joyous bells of freedom, pealing
    forth the glad song of peoples delivered from oppression.
This is Victory ... Hark! To the stern bells of avenging justice,
    Relentlessly sounding the overthrow of the oppressor.
This is Victory ... Hark! To the solemn bells of memory...
    sorrowfully tolling their tribute to the legions of the fallen.
This is Victory ... Hark! To the eager bells of welcome, sending
    their notes far over the sea, calling the warriors home.
This is Victory ... Hark! To the mighty bells proclaiming Right
    Triumphant, calling us to press on to the goal for which we
    Strive, to everlasting peace ... good will among men.

With firmness in the right
as God gives us to see the right,
let us finish the work we are in,
to bind up the nation's wounds,
to care for him who shall have
borne the battle, and for his widow
and his orphans, to do all which
may achieve and cherish a just and a lasting peace among ourselves
and with all nations.[2]

Received a letter I mailed the 28th of June to Mike Pedulla. It's really been around. It was returned to me. Can't make out all the places it's been. It's been to Hobbs, New Mexico also has Washington on it. Still don't know where he is.

This morning before any of us knew the news I went over to the School Secretary and told him I was quitting pilot training. He did his best to change my mind. Finally he asked me why I was quitting. So I told him. Told him how the flight surgeon at Bakersfield wanted to ground me and how I talked him out of it. I've tried, but my back has been bothering me too much to allow me to concentrate on pilot training. He had me go up to the hospital to see the flight surgeon. He won't be back until Friday so the assistant grounded me until the flight surgeon gets back.

Well my dear can't think of any more to say tonight. Just wanted you to know my thoughts were with you tonight.

All my love,
Fred

★★★

Friday Aug. 17, 1945
Pampa, Texas

Hi Dear,

Just a few lines to give the latest facts and news. There was no need in my quitting training as they called everyone together today and told us what the set up was. Here it is: all flying training is suspended. The only ones that will continue training are the ones that want to stay in the post-war air forces now that the war is over. They had us sign a form saying whether we wanted to continue or not. Naturally your number one son signed that statement saying no to post-war air forces. Have no idea how long they'll keep us waiting here. Don't imagine it will be long. Who knows maybe I'll be a civilian sooner than we all expected.

Say, not that I'm in a hurry, but don't you think it wouldn't be a bad idea if you could find several shirts for me at Silverwood's or Desmond's. A couple of white shirts and a couple of prints. You always did pick out my shirts. Get Arrow shirts size neck 14½ inches and sleeve 34 inches.

The reason is that I hear shirts are scarce especially if everyone will be getting out now. Don't get anything that is or looks cheap!! Try and get ones that you got for me for Christmas the last time.

Can just hear what you're saying to yourself. 'That kid, just can't wait, has to hurry up and do something.'

Have no idea what I'm going to do . Whether to go to college or work. If I go to college we'll have to go back to our high school days finances. We'll only get $75.00 a month. If we have to stay in 'Catalina Gulch' for a while we can put up new wallpaper, paint the woodwork, and the bathroom, and I can clean up the yard and throw devil grass seed and start some kind of a lawn.

From the tone of this letter it sounds as if I'd be getting home tomorrow, but it doesn't hurt to look ahead a little bit does it!!

Seeing as today is Friday airmail wouldn't get there before Monday so will just send it by regular mail.

From now on my letters will be kinda lax as there just isn't any news happening. However, will write as soon as we hear any news.

About half of the guys signed to stay with the training. The reason is that most of 'em are afraid to face the world. Some have never held a job before. They've been getting too much money. Anyhow we never had very much, but we didn't want for anything. As for me

I'm getting tired of some 'shoe clerk' telling me what to do, especially when he doesn't know as much as we do.

Well my dear you can relax now and I'll be home as soon as dear old Uncle Sam will release me!!

> Love,
> Fred

This is the day! I have waited so long for this and now we are on our way back to the good old 'U.S.A.' I can hardly wait.[3]

> *Wed. Aug. 22, 1945*
> *Pampa, Texas*

Dear Lou,
Well a lot has happened as we expected it would. Heard rumors yesterday, but today we were called for a meeting and told that we were getting ready to go to the separation center. They wanted to know how we wanted to travel and to be sure of our correct address. Have no idea yet when we'll leave as they have to wire the separation center to find out when they can take us. My guess is that it'll be about a week. I'm going to ride out with a fellow that lives in Long Beach. Will send you a wire when we know when we're leaving here so don't depend on what I said about that, it may be a week. (You know the Army!!)

Am going to send a box of stuff home. Open it as there will be 2 boxes of Kleenex and 6 packs of cigarettes. The other things are dirty clothes and shoes, etc.

By the way was your dad bald headed? Let me know!

Fred, what a strange enquiry? He had a full head of hair as a young man and kept most of it throughout his life – although it did become quite grey. Among his professional colleagues, he became known as the Grey Fox.

Are you finding it easier to get cigs now?
Boy, was it cold here last night and today. Has been raining also. Bet you'd like some of the rain. Took several pictures today.
There just isn't a thing more to say. The only thing for sure is that we don't know when we'll leave here. Just think I'll soon be out of this Army!!

> Love,
> Fred

★★★

> *Friday Aug. 24*
> *Pampa, Texas*

Dear Mom,
This will be my last letter from here. Said I would wire you, but there's no use in doing that. Will call you when I arrive at Ft. MacArthur [Los Angeles]. Don't know when we're leaving here, but it shouldn't be long. Most of the separation centers want the guys from

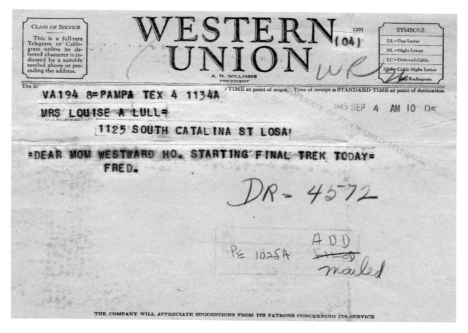

here between the 1st and 5th of Sept. They haven't heard from Ft. MacArthur yet, but it'll probably be around the same time. Will have to leave here a few days before reporting date so as you can see by now you can just expect me when I get there. Oh yes, there's no use for you to send anymore mail to me.

   Am having a hard time killing time. It drives me nuts to just sit around as you well know!

   Well my dear will bid you adieu from the great (?) state of Texas. Hope it's the last time I'm ever in it!!!

Will be seeing you soon (for good),

Fred

ARMY
SEPARATION QUALIFICATION RECORD
MILITARY SPECIALTIES
28 Oct. 45
EXCERPT

BOMBARDIER: Located, identified and accurately bombed assigned targets from B17 aircraft on 30 combat missions in the European Theater of Operation. Adjusted bombsight for specific conditions in accordance with mathematical tables. Able to navigate by pilotage and dead reckoning. Proficient in gunnery and map reading & calibration of navigation instruments. Officer has 900 flying hours. And 231 combat hrs.

SEPARATION CENTER, FORT MACARTHUR, CALIFORNIA.

Certificate of honorable service in the Army of the United
States, given at Separation Center, Fort MacArthur,
California, 28th day of October, 1945.

Epilogue

We were so young.[1]

Fortitude. Faith. Fear. Structural mechanical integrity. Blood and gore. Awe. Stress. Survival. Anxiety. Trauma. Resiliency. Humour. These personal and mechanical traits hardly seem appropriately linked. But, in the case of the B-17 and the men who flew them, they miraculously coalesce:

> There was a legend in the 8th Air Force about a Flying Fortress with the call sign George 309.
>
> After a raid deep into Germany, cut off from the rest of its formation, slashed and battered, the lone straggling Fortress crawled through the air back to England. Approaching its home base the pilot radioed the control tower:
>
> 'Hello, Lazy Fox, hello, Lazy Fox. This is G for George, 309, G for George, 309, calling Lazy Fox. Will you give me landing instructions, please? Pilot and copilot dead, two engines feathered, fire in the radio room, vertical stabilizer gone, no flaps, no hydraulics, no brakes, control cables shot away, crew bailed out, bombardier wounded and flying the ship. Give me landing instructions.'
>
> After a brief pause the tower replied:
>
> 'I hear you G, for George. Hello, G, for George. Here are your landing instructions. Repeat slowly, please, repeat slowly. Our Father who art in heaven ...'[2]

His high school newspaper called him a hero. German civilians affixed the label of '*terrorflieger*' or air-gangster to Fred and his kind. He probably would not have acknowledged that he was either one although his intonement of 'bombs away' may have seemed gangster-like to the Reich's citizens and filled them with untold terror.

He was bombardier and crewmate, and was referred to as lieutenant, sir and friend. His mother called him son.

It was not in his nature to either embrace the war and killing, as did John Hersey's *War Lover*,[3] or become obsessed with the ruination of the Germanic white whale as a twentieth-century Captain Ahab. The country was at war. He was young, he was patriotic, he answered the call, he trained, flew his missions and experienced hideous destruction and the death of others. He knew about chance and luck intimately. He grew old, he came home.

The collective voices of the past that once flew B-17s into harm's way have reflected on how that past, as defined by their participation in the war, affected them. 'Did the war change you?'

Yes it did. I was much more mature afterwards. I was just 21 when I came home, but I felt like I was thirty. I wasn't a youth anymore. I got old fast.

No, I don't think so. The training changed me though. It enabled me to mature quicker, and I think better, probably.

Oh, yah. It was the best experience in my life. I was a kid, 22 years old, living at home. It gave me the opportunity to be responsible for someone/something else. Being 'out there' and being shot at – that was something else!

No, it didn't change me at all.

Darned if I know. I'm fatalistic – not religious. One of the crews that I trained with in the States was lost in combat; the pilot was a close personal friend. I was sad at their loss, but was too busy or tired to dwell on their loss.

No. I was 20 going on 60.

I had been beaten by the partisans who picked me up after I had parachuted. They had beat me up pretty good, especially around the head and shoulders. At the end of the war, I went to the flight surgeon to get something for headaches that wouldn't go away. X-rays revealed a tumor above my right eye, and I was told that if it wasn't removed, I'd go blind or insane.

Definitely. I was from a Depression-era family. I'd never been to a hotel, eaten at a restaurant or been on a train or on a plane. I was young and invincible. It was a great adventure and I enjoyed it right up 'til they got earnest in trying to kill me. Then I put my flak helmet right on.

Yes. I was a farm kid from Nebraska and always wanted to fly. You grew up in a hurry – I grew from a kid of 18 to an adult in about a year and a half. When I returned, someone said, 'My how you've matured.'

It was ironic – I came out whole. It was a cause I believed in so I wasn't conflicted by what I had done. I thought the Germans had it coming after what they had done in Spain, England, Holland, Poland, Russia, etc. I felt that I had been sent over there to do a job. I did the job and was proud of the job I did. It

Dyersburg, 1943.

Summer, 1944.

was a sense of having met a test. It did not have a negative psychological effect on me.

It's hard to know if the war changed me or not because I don't know if I would have turned out any different if I hadn't been in the war. I do know that it makes you think differently – you learn the hard way about life and quickly learn that nothing will ever be the same again. You learn to get along and adjust to whatever comes your way. You learn to live with what's happening around you and how to adjust to what's happening.[4]

Was Fred changed by the war? It would be speculative at best to try to answer that. However, like his colleagues have stated, there was a maturity factor that would be difficult to deny. The loss of youth and the ageing to manhood is evident in the comparison of photos of Fred taken near the beginning of his war journey and after the completion of his combat missions. It's the eyes, they say it all – the spar-

kle of youth, the sense of wonderment are absent in the older Fred. The stiffener of his hat has been removed, the sign of the combat veteran, the side edges drooping at a tired angle. The corollary of Fred's face is remarkable.

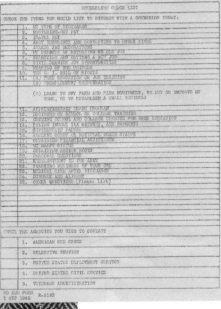

Fred came home to 'Catalina Gulch' and, like millions of others, needed to find a place for himself in a world as strange to him at the end of the war as the military experience was at the beginning. Questions loomed, and answers had to be found. The government tried to help by giving each who mustered out a booklet, 'Going Back to Civilian Life', that described what the returning serviceman could

going back to

civilian life

In typical army fashion there was a form to take to a counsellor for those who chose to go.

expect and what he should be aware of: 'What about a job; Your G.I. Bill of Rights; Benefits for Dependents; Additional Facts for Your Future'.[5]

When you went into the army, you were taught how to be a soldier, how to fight, how to survive. When you came out, you were on your own. This time there were no drill sergeants to teach you, you were on your own. You had to learn to fit back into a world where you weren't shooting at someone and no one was shooting at you.[6]

Civilians learned to become soldiers, airmen, sailors and marines. Now, as veterans, they had to learn to become civilians again. They became employed, they went to school, started families and time passed. The war began to slip away into the past, further into the past for some than others, but into the past it slipped, nevertheless.

Fred returned to work at the bank and, within months of his discharge, began a new journey – fulfilment of his ambition of becoming a teacher. He graduated from Los Angeles City College in 1949 and from the University of Southern California with a Bachelor of Science degree in 1951. Armed with a degree and teaching credentials, he began to teach in Los Angeles at a school for children with physical disabilities.

Graduate work at USC earned him a Master of Science degree in Education and a school administrative credential from the State of California. His continued teaching experience, advanced degree and credentials provided him the opportunity to assume leadership roles within Los Angeles Unified School District, which included principalships at several schools.

Fred retired from teaching and school administration in 1984 to continue a post-war love affair with travel – African safaris, rafting down the Colorado of the Grand Canyon, horse riding in the Colorado Rockies, Antarctica, Tahiti, China, Japan, leisurely cruises and tours. He returned to Europe once in 1956, but always returned to California.

Fred's legacy? It was not as a family man – he remained a bachelor; 'The war passed me by'. Yet, there is a legacy of the man as an educator. No one knew that there might also be a legacy of the man as a wartime hero. That was his choice.

Three years after his retirement and three years before his death in 1990, the Los Angeles Unified School District passed a resolution that resulted in the renaming of a school in Fred's honour. At the dedication ceremonies, he was honoured for his 'dedicated service to the field of special education, enabling children, parents, and teachers to achieve the highest realization of their hopes and dreams, guiding teachers to fulfil their finest teaching goals, and believing that a disability should never deter a child from reaching his or her highest potential'.[7]

It also was announced at the school dedication that an endowed scholarship, in Fred's name, had been established at California State University, Los Angeles, for the purpose of financially assisting young men and women who were training to become teachers of children with physical disabilities. This is Fred's legacy – the kind he wanted.

Louise died in 1953. Her legacy, the bombardier who wrote 150 letters home.

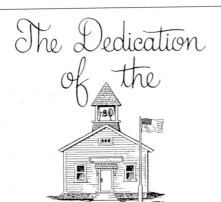

The Dedication of the

FRED S. LULL

SPECIAL EDUCATION CENTER

June 4, 1987

A Final Word – Bravery in the Plexiglas Nose

Bombardier Medal of Honor Recipients During Second World War

Fred was in the company of heroes who served above and beyond the call of duty. Two bombardiers were recipients of the Medal of Honor during the Second World War. They were courageous. They were brave. They were selfless. The Medal of Honor was awarded to both posthumously. The citations are listed in chronological order.

1st Lieutenant Jack Warren Mathis
Rank and organization: First Lieutenant, U.S. Army Air Corps, 359th Bomber Squadron, 303rd Bomber Group. Place and date: Over Vegesack, Germany, 18 March 1943. Entered service at: San Angelo, Texas. Born: 25 September 1921. G.O. No. 38: 12 July 1943.
Citation: For conspicuous gallantry and intrepidity above and beyond the call of duty in action with the enemy over Vegesack, Germany, on 18 March 1943. 1st Lt. Mathis, as leading bombardier of his squadron, flying through intense and accurate antiaircraft fire, was just starting his bomb run, upon which the entire squadron depended for accurate bombing, when he was hit by the enemy antiaircraft fire. His right arm was shattered above the elbow, a large wound was torn in his side and abdomen, and he was knocked from his bombsight to the rear of the bombardier's compartment. Realizing that the success of the mission depended upon him, 1st Lt. Mathis, by sheer determination and willpower, though mortally wounded, dragged himself back to his sights, released his bombs, then died at his post of duty. As the result of this action the airplanes of his bombardment squadron placed their bombs directly upon the assigned target for a perfect attack against the enemy. 1st Lt. Mathis' undaunted bravery has been a great inspiration to the officers and men of his unit.

2nd Lieutenant David Richard Kingsley

Rank and organization: Second Lieutenant, U. S. Army Air Corps, 87th Bombardment Group, 15th Air Force. Place and date: Ploesti Raid, Rumania, 23 June 1944. Entered service at Portland, Oregon. G.O. No. 26: 9 April 1945.

Citation: For conspicuous gallantry and intrepidity in action at the risk of life above and beyond the call of duty. 23 June 1944 near Ploesti, Rumania, while flying as bombardier of a B-17 type aircraft. On the bomb run 2nd Lt. Kingsley's aircraft was severely damaged by intense flak and forced to drop out of formation but the pilot proceeded over the target and 2nd Lt. Kingsley successfully dropped his bombs, causing severe damage to vital installations. The damaged aircraft, forced to lose altitude and lag behind the formation, was aggressively attacked by 3 ME-109 aircraft, causing more damage to the aircraft and severely wounding the tail gunner in the upper arm. The radio operator and engineer notified 2nd Lt. Kingsley that the tail gunner had been wounded and that assistance was needed to check the bleeding. 2nd Lt. Kingsley made his way back to the radio room, skilfully applied first aid to the wound, and succeeded in checking the bleeding. The tail gunner's parachute harness and heavy clothes were removed and he was covered with blankets, making him as comfortable as possible. Eight ME-109 aircraft again aggressively attacked 2nd Lt. Kingsley's aircraft and the ball turret gunner was wounded by 20mm. shell fragments. He went forward to the radio room to have 2nd Lt. Kingsley administer first aid. A few minutes later when the pilot gave the order to prepare to bail out, 2nd Lt. Kingsley immediately began to assist the wounded gunners in putting on their parachute harness. In the confusion the tail gunner's harness, believed to have been damaged, could not be located in the bundle of blankets and flying clothes which had been removed from the wounded men. With utter disregard for his own means of escape, 2nd Lt. Kingsley unhesitatingly removed his parachute harness and adjusted it to the wounded tail gunner. Due to the extensive damage caused the by the accurate and concentrated 20mm. fire by the enemy aircraft the pilot gave the order to bail out, as it appeared that the aircraft would disintegrate at any moment. 2nd Lt. Kingsley aided the wounded men in bailing out and when last seen by the crewmembers he was standing on the bomb-bay catwalk. The aircraft continued to fly on automatic pilot for a short distance, then crashed and burned. His body was later found in the wreckage. 2nd Lt. Kingsley by his gallant heroic action was directly responsible for saving the life of the wounded gunner.[1]

Notes

Epigraph

'I judge when the tale is all in': Gill Robb Wilson, Newspaper clipping from Fred Lull memorabilia/scrapbook; in the author's possession. Newspaper name unknown, n.d.

Prologue

1. *'Tom Brokaw has proclaimed'*: Tom Brokaw, *The Greatest Generation* (NY: Random House, 1998).
2. *'These men do not proclaim'*: Harry Slater, *Lingering Contrails of The Big Square A; A History of the 94th Bomb Group (H), 1942–1945* (privately printed, 1980), x.
3. *'Apparently some things warriors'*: Evalyn Dearmin (Professor Emeritus, California State University, Los Angeles), personal communication, 27 March 2007.
4. *'Accounts such as these'*: Robert Morgan, *The Man Who Flew the Memphis Belle* (NY: Dutton, 2001).
5. *'Don't worry Mom'*: Harry Duncan and Paul William, *Don't Worry Mom* (NY: Ford Music, 1944), 2.
6. *'I noticed some movement'*: Roy Test in discussion with the author, 15 February 2007.

Chapter One, The Beginning

1. *'highest honor attainable'*: *Poly High Optimist* John H. Frances Polytechnic High School (Los Angeles, December 1939), 3.
2. *'seemed unable to find words'*: ibid., 4.
3. *'A new order is coming'*: *Poly High Optimist* (Los Angeles, n.d.).
4. *'all eager to serve'*: photograph caption of newspaper clipping from Fred Lull memorabilia/ scrapbook; in author's possession. Newspaper name unknown, n.d.
5. *'The war was fought by civilians'*: Hank Hall in discussion with the author, 22 November 2006.
6. *'It was $21.00 a month to start off'*: Harold Schuchardt in discussion with the author, 22 November 2006.
7. *'We all sweated out'*: Frank Halm, personal communication, 25 September 2007.
8. *'Who would be dumb enough'*: Dewayne Bennett, *Stories of a B-17 Bomber Pilot* (privately printed, n.d.), 13, 14.

Chapter Two, Classification Center

1. '*What's this Classification Center, anyway?*': John Hibbits, *Take 'er Up Alone, Mister!* As told to F.E. Rechnitzer (NY: Whittlesey House, 1943), 18.
2. '*The rationing point system*': Robert Heide and John Gilman, *Home Front America; Popular Culture of the World War II Era* (San Francisco: Chronicle Books, 1995), 55.
3. '*It was a sacrifice for those*': Robert (Bob) Brown in discussion with author, 18 January 2007.
4. '*Regulations for Operation of Aircraft*': Gratis information sheet, Planes of Fame Museum, Chino, California.
5. '*This is the army, Mister. Jones*': Irving Berlin, *This Is The Army* (NY: 'This Is The Army' Inc., 1942), 3.
6. '*At the start of the (Sneider)*': Hibbits, *Take 'er Up Alone, Mister,* 27/28.
7. '*This is the Army, Mr. Green*': Berlin, *This Is The Army* (NY: 'This Is the Army' Inc., 1942), 3.
8. '*Texans thought*': Brown discussion.
9. '*What did you get*': Hibbits, *Take 'er Up Alone, Mister!* 19.
10. '*There are ten men*': Commanding General, Army Air Forces, *Combat Crew* (NY: n.d.), 17.

Chapter Three, Bombardier Training

1. '*We can only afford*': Moss Hart, *Winged Victory*; The Army Air Forces Play (NY: Random House, 1943), 40.
2. '*Circular error*': Bob Dickson, personal communication, 24 September 2007.
3. '*The USAAF*': Robin Neillands, *The Bomber War; The Allied Air Offensive Against Nazi Germany* (Woodstock, NY: Overlook), 74.
4. '*Mindful of the secret trust*': US Centennial of Flight Commission. http://www.centennialofflight.gov/essay/Dictionary/NORDEN_BOMBSIGHT/DI145.htm. The Bombardier's Oath was more than an article of trust and honour for bombardiers. It was also a part of the wartime propaganda directed to young men in the book *Bombardier; Tom Dixon Wins His Wings With The Bomber Command* by Henry Lent (NY: Macmillan, 1943), 34. The oath that Tom Dixon took, however, was slightly different from the one bombardiers in training recited: 'Mindful of the sacred trust …'
5. '*Bombsight does all*': George D. Drissey, Chicago, '*Bombsight Does All But Think*', Dec. 13 – (UP). Newspaper clipping from Fred Lull memorabilia/scrapbook, in the author's possession; newspaper name, unknown.
6. '*A feat made*': Albert L. Pardini, *The Legendary Norden Bombsight* (Atglen, PA: Schiffer, 1999).
7. '*The folks at home*': Hibbits, *Take 'er Up Alone, Mister!* 53.
8. '*Accurate and effective bombing*': Headquarters, AAF, Office of Assistant Chief of Air Staff, Training, Office of Flying Safety, *Pilot Training Manual for the Flying Fortress B-17* (Washington DC [?]: n.d.), 18, 19.
9. '*This is the Army, Mister Green*': Berlin, *This Is The Army* (NY: 'This Is the Army' Inc., 1942), 3.
10. '*If it means*': Bill Mauldin, *Up Front* (NY: Henry Holt, 1945), 8.
11. '*In 1944, the price tag*': Jeffrey L. Ethell, *Bomber Command; American Bombers in Original World War II Color* (St Paul, MN: Motorbooks International, 2003).
12. '*In the air or*': William F. Somers, *Fortress Fighters; An autobiography of a B-17 Aerial Gunner* (privately printed, 2000), 22.
13. '*A total of*': Martin W. Bowman, *Combat Legend; B-17 Flying Fortress* (Shrewsbury, England: Airlife Publishing, 2002).
14. '*the infantry is*': Mauldin, 5.
15. '*That night, with the pilot*': Ernie Pyle, *Here Is Your War* (Chicago: Consolidated, 1944), 129.
16. '*Less than a year*': Daniel Epstein, *Sister Aimee; The Life of Aimee Semple McPherson* (NY: Harcourt Brace Jovanovich, 1993).
17. '*The bombardier's kit*': War Department, Bombardiers' Information File (Washington DC [?]: War Department, 1944), 1-3-1.

18. '*The Norden bombsight*': Robert (Bob) Dickson discussion with the author, 22 November 2006.
19. '*Needless to say*': Mollie Panter-Downes, 'Letter From London; July 26 (By Cable)', *The New Yorker*, 31 July 1943, 34.
20. '*This was not sport*': John Steinbeck, *Bombs Away; The Story of a Bomber Team* (NY: Paragon House, 1990).

Chapter Four, Officer, Gentleman, Bombardier

1. '*Off we go*': Robert Crawford, *The Army Air Corps* (NY: Carl Fischer, 1939), 1.
2. '*The Army Air Corps*': James H. Straubel, 'The Army Air Corps; The Official Song of the United States Army Air Forces', *Winged Victory*, play programme notes (n.p., n.d.), 33.

Chapter Five, Advanced Flight Training

1. '*Over 29,350 heavy bomber crews*': Ethell, 7.
2. '*This is the Army*': Kathleen E.R. Smith, *God Bless America; Tin Pan Alley Goes to War* (Lexington, KY: University Press of Kentucky, 2003), 95.
3. '*I left my heart at*': Irving Berlin, *I Left My Heart at the Stage Door Canteen* (NY: This Is The Army, Inc., 1942), 2.
4. '*We don't take our training*': Hart, *Winged Victory*, 15.

Chapter Six, Rattlesnake Bomber Base and Beyond

1. '*BEWARE RATTLESNAKES*': Thomas E. Alexander, *Rattlesnake Bomber Base; Pyote Army Airfield in World War II* (Abilene, TX: State House Press, 2005), 66.
2. '*When the dust cleared*': ibid., 68.
3. '*One veteran of the base building*': ibid., 65.
4. '*A sign on a bulletin board*': Dickson discussion.
5. '*While it is a truism*': Rehm, 'Fifty Missions Over Europe; Psychological Study of An Average Combat Tour', in *Observations of Combat Flying Personnel*, ed. David G. Wright (NY: M.C. Josiah Macy Jr. Foundation, 1945), 4–12.

Chapter Seven, They Become a Crew

1. '*The crew will live*': Steinbeck, *Bombs Away*.
2. '*White Christmas … (was) a nostalgic*': Smith, 23.
3. '*I'm dreaming of a white Christmas*': Irving Berlin, *White Christmas* (NY: Irving Berlin Inc., 1942), 2.
4. '*You can always tell*': Hall discussion, 22 November 2006.
5. '*I'm dreaming of a white Christmas*': Berlin, 2.
6. '*But on Christmas eve*': Franklin Delano Roosevelt, *Fireside Chat, December 24, 1943* (Franklin Delano Roosevelt Presidential Library, Digital Archives).
7. '*Slacks on Campus*': *Poly High Optimist* (John H. Francis Polytechnic High School), Los Angeles, n.d.
8. '*It looks terrible*': ibid.
9. '*On 23 April 1942 letters started*': *Los Angeles Times*, 23 April 2006, A-3.
10. '*Oh! I have slipped*': John Gillespie Magee, n.p., 1943. Magee was a 19-year-old fighter pilot during the Second World War, who wrote *High Flight* after having soared into the atmosphere during a high-altitude test flight of a Spitfire V. He died three months later in a mid-air collision.
11. '*As a member*': 2nd A.F. Altitude Indoctrination Unit, *Survival at Altitude for Heavy and Very Heavy Bomber Crews* (Lincoln, NE: LAAF, 1945), v.

12. *'May 2, 1944, Dearest Mom,'*: *Life*, magazine advertisement, 29 May 1944. Polk Miller Products Corp., Richmond, VA, Makers of Sergeant's Dog Medicines.

13. *'Gabriel Heatter, famous with'*: Gabriel Heatter, *There's Good News Tonight* (NY: Doubleday, 1960).

14. *'Any misfits'*: Frank Halm, personal communication, 10 May 2007.

15. *'We almost blew up'*: Wilbur Richardson in discussion with the author, 13 April 2007.

16. *'It is not enough'*: War Department, Bombardiers' Information File (Washington DC [?]: War Department, 1944), 9-1.

17. *'The airplane is your home.'*: Lou Vaughn in discussion with the author, 8 November 2007.

18. *'When you die together'*: Hall discussion, November 22, 2006.

Chapter Eight, Deployment

1. *'Dressing for combat'*: John Steinbeck, *Once There Was a War* (NY: Penguin, 1994).

Chapter Nine, England

1. *'In flying the Vee formation'*: Headquarters, AAF, Office of Assistant Chief of Air Staff, Training, Office of Flying Safety, *Pilot Training Manual for the Flying Fortress B-17* (Washington DC [?]: n.d.), 119.

2. *'LeMay wanted planes'*: Robert (Bob) Brown in discussion with the author, 18 January 2007.

3. *'flying too close'*: ibid.

4. *'I was in a six-plane'*: Vaughn discussion.

5. *'That's the closest'*: ibid.

6. *'Put your wingtip'*: Test discussion.

7. *'You're flying off someone's wing'*: Ibid.

8. *'There is a slight reflected glow'*: Ernie Pyle, *Ernie Pyle in England* (NY: McBride, 1945), 55.

9. *'It is always impolite'*: War Department, *Instructions for American Servicemen in Britain* (Washington DC, 1942), 30.

10. *'The gunners are inveterate writers'*: Bud Hutton and Andy Rooney, *Air Gunner* (NY: Farrar & Rinehart, 1944), 19.

11. *'British slang is something'*: War Department, *Instructions for American Servicemen in Britain* (Washington DC, 1942), 27.

12. *'It became more'*: Carolyn Beaubien, 390th Bomb Group Research Director, e-mail message to author, 14 May 2007.

13. *'The group designation'*: Paul M. Andrews and William H. Adams, *Heavy Bombers of the Mighty Eighth; An Historical Survey of the B-17s and B-24s Assigned to the Eighth United States Air Force, August 1942–June 1945* (Eighth Air Force Memorial Museum Foundation, Project Bits and Pieces, 1995), 229.

14. *'This was a unit'*: Mauer Mauer, ed., *World War II Combat Squadrons of the United States Air Force* (NY: Smithmark, 1992), 408.

15. *'The Men of the Ninety-Fourth'*: Harry Gordon Higel, 'The Men of the Ninety-Fourth' in Harry Slater, *Lingering Contrails of The Big Square A; A History of the 94th Bomb Group (H), 1942–1945* (Privately printed, 1980), 318.

16. *'On the day that Fred'*: ibid.,149.

17. *'This information would have'*: Edward Jablonski, *Flying Fortress; The Illustrated Biography of the B-17s and the Men Who Flew Them* (NY: Doubleday, 1965).

18. *'Notification of parents'*: Dickson discussion, 22 November 2006.

19. *'U.S. fliers were called'*: Dickson discussion, 22 November 2006.

20. *'New crews were told'*: Slater, 186.

21. *'Started in the First World War'*: Ken Zumwalt, *The Stars and Stripes; World War II & The Early Year* (Austin, TX: Eakin, 1989).

22. *'We had more guys'*: Hall discussion, 18 January 2007.

23. *'A more intensive campaign'*: Assistant Chief of Air Staff, Intelligence, *Sunday Punch in Normandy; The Tactical Use of Heavy Bombardment in the Normandy Invasion. An Interim Report*, Washington DC: Headquarters, Army Air Forces. New Imprint by the Center for Air Force History in the *Wings at War Series, No. 2.* (Washington DC: Center for Air Force History, 1992), 6.

24. *'Berlin was being bombed'*: Noble Frankland, *Bomber Offensive; The Devastation of Europe* (NY: Ballantine, 1970).

25. *'The student gets a 16 hour course'*: H.N. Oliphant, 'Prep School for Bomber Crews', *YANK*, 9 July 1943, 8, 9.

26. *'Coal was at a premium'*: Hutton and Rooney, 1944.

27. *'Aircrews stole'*: Frank Halm, personal communication, 25 September 2007.

28. *'A man approached death'*: Ernie Pyle, *Brave Men* (NY: Henry Holt, 1944), 157.

29. *'My name is Sherlock Holmes'*: Arthur Conan Doyle, *The Adventures of Sherlock Holmes* (NY: Barnes & Noble, 1995), 180.

30. *'German pilots and crew'*: Richard Bushong in discussion with author, 22 February 2007.

31. *'Chickenshit is so called'*: Paul Fussell, *Wartime, Understanding and Behavior in the Second World War* (NY: Oxford University Press, 1989), 80.

Chapter Ten, Operational Missions

1. *'Training in the States'*: Hall discussion, 22 November 2007.

2. *'... become a mighty power'*: Gill Robb Wilson, newspaper clipping, n.d.

3. *'Mission data are adapted'*: Kit C. Carter and Robert Mueller, *The Army Air Forces in World War II; Combat Chronology 1941–1945* (NY: Arno Press, 1980); Eric Hammel, *Air War Europa Chronology* (Pacifica, CA: Pacifica Press, 1994); Slater, 1980.

4. *'These losses contributed'*: Jeffrey L. Ethell.

5. *'It must be an inhuman concentration'*: Commanding General, Army Air Forces, *Combat Crew*, 19.

6. *'One airman was "kind of concerned"'*: Donald Nijboer, *GUNNER; An Illustrated History of World War II Aircraft Turrets and Gun Positions*, Donald Nijboer (Erin, Ontario, Canada, Boston Mills Press, 2001).

7. *'I feel like a fugitive'*: Mauldin, 39.

8. *'It was commonly believed'*: Norvel Seeley, *Splendor in the Skies; Echoes From the Past*, March 2007, 5.

9. *'... a combat crew'*: Eaker, 'On the mission before last ...' in *Medical Support of the Army Air Forces in World War II*, Mae Mills Link and Hubert A. Coleman (Washington DC, Department of the Air Force, 1955), 671.

10. *'I sent a copy'*: Bushong discussion.

11. *'Mom would find clippings'*: Brown discussion.

12. *'if it was going to be'*: Leon Schwartz in discussion with the author, 30 November 2007.

13. *'Next, the weather guesser'*: Bushong discussion.

14. *'... gunners went in trucks'*: Richardson discussion.

15. *'... performed a walk-around'*: James (Jim) S. Peters, e-mail message to author, 19 February 2007.

16. *'On the way to our plane'*: Bushong discussion.

17. *'The bomber exists'*: Hall discussion, 22 November 2006.

18. *'The wings had so many holes'*: Dickson discussion, 22 November 2006.

19. *'A truck would come by'*: Test discussion.

20. *'... because the adrenalin rush'*: Bushong discussion.

21. *'Debriefing was held in a room'*: ibid.

22. *'I was always scared'*: Brown discussion.

23. *'... wanted to know'*: Bushong discussion.

24. 'The unknown quantity': C. Ross Greening and J.M. Coppinger, *Not As Briefed* (St Paul, MN, privately printed, n.d.), 12.

25. 'Pink pants': Woodford Agee Heflin, ed., *The United States Air Force Dictionary* (Washington DC: Air University Press, 1956), 388.

26. 'I was sitting enthroned': Michael James, 'The Bombardier'. Magazine clipping from Fred Lull memorabilia/scrapbook. In the author's possession. Magazine name unknown, n.d. Originally printed in the *New York Times Magazine*.

27. 'Coming back from Berlin': Hall discussion, 22 November 2006.

28. 'They were everywhere': Ed Charles, 'BERLIN: 6 March 1944', in *B-17s Over Berlin; Personal Stories from the 95th Bomb Group (H)*, ed. by Ian L. Hawkins, 160.

29. 'Next came the assault': Donald L. Miller, *Masters of the Air; America's Bomber Boys Who Fought the Air War Against Nazi Germany* (NY: Simon & Schuster, 2006), 272.

30. 'Fifteen of the B-17s that were lost': Hammel.

31. 'Three out of seven': Dickson discussion, 22 November 2006.

32. 'If you were on a mission': Hall discussion, 22 November 2006.

33. 'The Perfect Mission': Schwartz discussion, 30 November 2007.

34. 'A milk run is': Schuchardt discussion, 22 November 2006.

35. 'London continued on her way': John Mason Brown, *Many A Watchful Night* (NY: Whittlesey House, 1944), 78.

36. 'Air Medal': Woodford Agee Heflin, ed., *The United State Air Force Dictionary.* (Washington DC, Air University Press, 1956), 31.

37. 'Being victim of the': John Nichol and Tony Rennell, *Tail-End Charlies; The Last Battles of the Bomber War, 1944–45* (NY: Thomas Dunne, 2006).

38. 'So ended the month': Frankland.

39. 'However, on 4 April 1944': David Woodward, *The Tirpitz and the Battle for the North Atlantic* (NY: W.W. Horton, 1954).

40. 'B-24 bombers that were': Carter and Mueller.

41. '… high security punishment camp': Miller, 342.

42. 'I'm sure there were official documents': Bob Dickson, personal communication, 26 March 2007.

43. 'A nice name, Fred': Wallace R. Forman, *Nose Art Name Directory* (North Branch, MN: Phalanx, 1996).

44. 'The Belle of the Brawl': Hammel.

45. 'Me-109s attacked us': Gene Bissell in discussion with the author, 18 January 2007.

46. 'Some of the nose art': Gary M. Valant, *Vintage Aircraft Nose Art* (St. Paul, MN: MBI Publishing, 2001).

47. 'We never painted the name': Ted Hallock in Brendan Gill, 'Profiles; Young Man Behind Plexiglas', *The New Yorker* (12 August 1944), 30.

48. 'One plane's nose art wasn't painted': Test discussion.

49. 'It was not until I went down': Ernie Pyle, *Ernie Pyle in England* (NY: McBride, 1945), 13.

50. 'On the bad nights': Brown, 76.

51. 'Succeeding achievement and meritorious': *The Official World War II Guide to the Army Air Forces, AAF; A Directory, Almanac and Chronicle of Achievement* (NY: Bonanza Books, 1988).

52. 'We never flew Mission #13.': Bushong discussion.

53. 'A second mission': Hammel.

54. 'After the mission on April 27': Hall discussion, 22 November 2006.

55. 'The pilot of the B-17': Charles Alling, *A Mighty Fortress; Lead Bomber Over Europe* (Havertown, PA: Casement, 2002).

56. '… the maintenance men': Slater, 201.

57. 'Air war as such': *YANK*, 12 May 1944, 12.

58. 'With respect to heavy bombardment': Rehm, 1945, 4–12.

59. 'The crew flew 32 missions': Test discussion.

60. *'In fact, none'*: Gerald Astor, *The Mighty Eighth; The Air War in Europe as Told by the Men Who Fought It* (NY: Donald I. Fine, 1997), 255.
61. *'I wish they would either'*: Slater, 202.
62. *'We missed our fighter escort'*: Richardson discussion.
63. *'On the night of May 12th'*: Slater, 186.
64. *'In his post-war memoirs'*: Albert Speer, *Inside the Third Reich; Memoirs by Albert Speer*, translated by Richard and Clara Winston (NY: Macmillan, 1970).
65. *'When the bombardier opened'*: Vaughn discussion.
66. *'… got drunk'*: Hall discussion, 18 January 2007.
67. *'We couldn't go through'*: Al Olivari in discussion with the author, 15 June 2007.
68. *'There were three rings'*: Vaughn discussion.
69. *'We went to Berlin twice'*: Test discussion.
70. *'There was horrendous, horrendous flak'*: Richardson discussion.
71. *'I thought that if we'*: Schwartz discussion.
72. *'An 88mm shell hit'*: Dickson discussion, 22 November 2006.
73. *'Ground gripper'*: Straubel, *Take Our Word For It: The Language of the AAF*, 24.
74. *'In August, 1942'*: www.usaaf.net/ww2/medical.
75. *'About the only qualification'*: Hutton and Rooney, 99.
76. *'And it is valuable'*: David Howarth, *The Shetland Bus* (NY: Lyons Press, 2001), 109.
77. *'So, Roy indeed tempted'*: Andrews and Adams, 141.
78. *'In April and May 1944'*: Historical Division, *Omaha Beachhead; (6 June–13 June 1944)* (Washington DC: War Department, 1945), 3.

Chapter Eleven, D-Day – The Invasion: 'It's on'

1. *'June 6, 1944; Orders of the Day'*: Dwight D. Eisenhower, 'Orders of the Day, June 6, 1944'. Messages to Officers and Men, AEF, Box 148, Principal Series, Dwight D. Eisenhower Pre-Presidential Papers, 1916–52, Eisenhower Library.
2. *'Thirty-nine aircraft'*: Thomas A. Siefring, *U.S. Air Force in World War II* (London: Bison Books, 1982).
3. *'Unfortunately … the strikes on Caen'*: Richard P. Hallion, *D-Day 1944; Air Power Over the Normandy Beaches and Beyond* (Washington DC: Air Force History and Museums Program. US Government Printing Office, 1994), 21.
4. *'American radio audiences'*: Mark Bernstein and Alex Lubertozzi, *World War II On The Air; Edward R. Murrow and the Broadcasts that Riveted a Nation* (Naperville, IL: Sourcebooks, 2003).
5. *'… At the 94th Bomb Group'*: Astor.
6. *'… then a new sound'*: Ernie Pyle, in Normandy (by wireless), newspaper clipping from Fred Lull memorabilia/scrapbook. In the author's possession. Newspaper name unknown, n.d.
7. *'D-Day – the day of'*: Joseph Auslander, *Life*, 22 May 1944, 40.

Chapter Twelve, 6 to Go

1. *'I wrote to my mom every day'*: Bissell discussion.
2. *'Allied and German troops'*: Don Williams, 'Allied Troops Pushing Forward Past Bayeux', *Stars and Stripes*, Mediterranean, Saturday 10 June 1944, 1.
3. *'… the more seasoned doggie'*: Mauldin, 100.
4. *'Giant Blows Are Struck'*: *Stars and Stripes* (Liberation Issue), Monday 12 June 1944, 1.
5. *'The commanding officer'*: Andy Anzanos, *My Combat Diary with Eighth Air Force B-17s; 390th Bomb Group* (privately printed, 2006), 21.
6. *'… had wings and a ramjet'*: Dickson discussion, 18 January 2007.
7. *'You'd hear a put-put-put'*: Hall discussion, 18 January 2007.
8. *'The V-2s were'*: Dickson discussion, 18 January 2007.

9. *'The room was luxurious'*: Leon Schwartz, 'The 205 Days and 35 Missions of one of the 100th Bomb Group's "Luckye Bastardes"', http://www.100thbg.com/mainpages/history/ history5/schwartz/schwartz_main.htm.
10. *'The twenty-ninth mission'*: Hallock, 35.
11. *'Resupply drops'*: Blake Ehrlich, *Resistance: France 1940–1945* (Boston: Little Brown, 1965).
12. *'We flew across all of France'*: Astor, 306.
13. *'I can say that'*: James, 'The Bombardier'.
14. *'Anybody who goes'*: Pyle, *Here Is Your War*, 103.
15. *'You're imbued …'*: Hibbits, 135.
16. *'… a cherished possession'*: Slater, 170.
17. *'Distinguished Flying Cross'*: Woodford Agee Heflin, ed., *The United State Air Force Dictionary* (Washington DC, Air University Press, 1956), 170.

Chapter Thirteen, Homeward Bound

1. *'The New York skyline'*: Anzanos, 79.
2. *'To Fred – good luck'*: Arleen Whelan, photograph inscription. In author's possession.
3. *'Yanks in Germany'*: Stars and Stripes (6 September 1944), 1.
4. *'There was a bus'*: Mack Morriss, 'First Stop Back Home for Air Force GIs', *YANK, Down Under, The Army Weekly*, 21 April 1944, 6–7.
5. *'Pilots and navigators'*: Gill, 'Profiles'.
6. *'in reality a convalescent centre'*: Link and Coleman, 73: 'Convalescent centers were approved for the Air Forces to serve those combat crew members who suffered from operational fatigue …'
7. *'He will try again'*: Ann Kaiser, personal communication.
8. *'Lt. Lull in Europe Battle'*: Poly High Optimist (Los Angeles, n.d.).
9. *'Men who flew'*: Link and Coleman, 672.
10. *'The sight of blood'*: Virgil Jose, in conversation with Fred, the bombardier. Personal communication, 8 February 2008.
11. *'Debilitating too'*: Douglas D. Bond, *The Love and Fear of Flying* (International Universities Press, 1952). *'Debilitating too'*: Miller.
12. *'These factors'*: Rehm, 1945, 4–12.
13. *'I'd wake up after I got home'*: Hall discussion, 22 November 2006.

Chapter Fourteen, Back to Texas – Pilot Training

1. *'This is the army'*: Irving Berlin, *This Is The Army* (NY: This Is The Army, Inc., 1944), 3.
2. *'T'was The Night Before Christmas'*: Author unknown, reprinted from the newsletter of the B-17 Flying Fortress Association, 'Spendor in the Skies; Echoes From the Past', (n.p., n.d.).
3. *'Christmas '44 – that was a difficult time'*: Dickson discussion, 22 November 2006.
4. *'There were as many stars'*: Debs Myers, 'Christmas Time at Home', *YANK, Far East, The Army Weekly*, 22 December 1944, 7.
5. *'Patton Retakes 13 Towns'*: Stars and Stripes (30 December 1944), 1.
6. *'Soviets Smash 20 Miles'*: Stars and Stripes (20 January 1945), 1.
7. *'Employed in'*: The Playbill for the Lyceum Theatre, *The Doughgirls* (NY: 16 April 1944), 18.
8. *'The way that the Theatre'*: Fiorello H. La Guardia, in The Playbill for the Lyceum Theatre, *The Doughgirls* (NY: 16 April 1944), 15.
9. *'Cologne Falls – First Army takes'*: Dan Regan, *Stars and Stripes, Paris Edition* (7 March 1945), 1.
10. *'So Long, Sir'*: YANK (11 May 1945).
11. *'So they've given up'*: Norman Corwin, *On A Note of Triumph* (NY: Simon and Schuster, 1945), 9.

Chapter Fifteen, Texas, Again? – It's Over

1. *'August 8, 1945'*: Daniel F. Smith, *Personal War Diary* (n.p. 8 August 1945), 9. In author's possession.
2. *'With firmness in the right'*: Abraham Lincoln.
3. *'This is the day'*: Daniel F. Smith, 16.

Epilogue

1. *'We were so young'*: Test discussion.
2. *'There was a legend'*: Martin Caidin, *The B-17; The Flying Forts* (NY: ibooks, 2001), 328.
3. *'It was not in his nature'*: John Hersey, *War Lover* (NY: Knopf, 1959).
4. *'Did the war change you?'*: Gene Bissell, Bob Brown,, Richard Bushong, Bob Dickson, Hank Hall, Frank Halm, Wilbur Richardson, Harold Schuchardt, Leon Schwartz, Roy Test, Lou Vaughn in discussion with the author.
5. *'Going Back To Civilian Life'*: War and Navy Departments, 'Going Back To Civilian Life' (Washington DC, 1945), i.
6. *'When you went into the Army'*: James Jones, *WWII; A Chronicle of Soldiering* (NY: Ballantine, 1975), 250.
7. *'dedicated service to the field'*: Los Angeles Unified School District resolution (Los Angeles, 1987), in author's possession.

A Final Word – Bravery in a Plexiglas Nose

1. *'1st Lieutenant Jack'*: US Senate Committee on Veterans' Affairs Report, 'Medal of Honour Recipients: 1863–1978', http://www.army.mil/cmh-pg/.

Glossary

Military Jargon and Era Idioms

There are words and their definitions that are well known, conventional in their use, accepted by most, understood by many, misunderstood by just as many and nearly universal in their meaning, or so some would have us believe. Others are less so. The following list contains both types with apologies to Daniel Webster, professional wordsmiths, lexicographers and *The United States Air Force Dictionary*.

AG: aerial gunner (air gunner): a bomber crewmember who also has other duties in the plane in addition to operating a machine gun, e.g., the radio man.

Airmail: correspondence that was sent via airplane rather than by land transportation, e.g. train or truck. Mail sent by air was more expensive but was most often received faster than by surface mail. During the Second World War, a letter sent by surface mail required a 3-cent stamp, airmail an 8-cent stamp.

Allotment: a specified amount of money from the monthly salary sent to a person of the serviceman's choice, usually a spouse or parent.

American fliers (according to Nazi Germany): 'Air-gangsters.' Sometimes referred to by German civilians as *terrorflieger.*

APO: an address abbreviation for 'Army Post Office'.

CG: career gunner: 'A gunner on a bomber, whose sole duty is to operate a machine gun.' *The United States Air Force Dictionary*, 102.

Chickenshit: 'Chickenshit is so called – instead of horse- or bull- or elephant shit – because it is small-minded and ignoble and takes the trivial seriously. Chickenshit can be recognized instantly because it never has anything to do with winning the war.' From Paul Fussell, *Wartime, Understanding and Behavior in the Second World War.* (See GI below.)

Combat fatigue: the mental and physical exhaustion associated with frequent battle engagements, especially dangerous battle encounters and the expectation of these encounters, all combined with the lack of rest, inclement weather, and the death and maiming of friends and combat comrades. In the air force combat fatigue was used synonymously with 'flak happy' – see below.

Coward/cowardice: see hero/heroism.

Doggie/Dogface: army slang for a soldier.

Feather/feathering (an engine): 'In flight when an engine is no longer putting out power, the airflow causes the propeller to "windmill". It creates a drag almost as though you had put a piece of circular metal the diameter of the propeller on the front of the plane. The pilot shuts down an engine (stopping the electrical and gasoline supply) by actuating a large red button (there is one for each engine) located on the instrument panel. The propeller blades turn so that they are parallel to the line of flight thereby stopping engine rotation.' – Bob Dickson

Flak: an acronym of the German words: *Flieger Abwehr Kanone* (anti-aircraft cannon); deadly explosive belching of metal shards from the bursting of anti-aircraft shells, ack-ack.

Flak happy (aka combat fatigue): the physical fatigue and psychological stress that occurred as a result of aerial combat; so named because of the hazards and horror of flying through the unpredictability of flak.

Flak house: a 'rest home' for airmen where they had '… a chance to forget, relax and gain back some of their expended energies'.

Flak leave: time spent away from assigned duties – usually for R&R (see above, flak house).

Flak shack: often the name given to the 'hut' (see Nissen hut below).

Flak zone: the area over the target where crews could expect the heaviest flak.

Flimsy (flak map): a map given out at pre-mission briefings that showed flak concentration areas for the mission.

GI (GI'd): one of those expressions that can be used either as a noun, verb or adjective. Literally GI means Government Issue but it also can refer to a member of the armed services, usually the army, a 'GI'. As an adjective, it describes the type of article under consideration, e.g., GI soap (a hard yellow bar bigger than a Hershey Bar of chocolate and smaller than a brick, but not much smaller). As a verb, to 'GI a barracks' meant the scrubbing by a GI with GI soap, bleach or other cleanser the inside of the barracks or living area.

To GI a barracks might also include preparing for '… the Saturday morning inspection ordeal where only Government Issue was allowed to be seen, and everything had to be just so – bed properly made, clothes hung just right, shoes shined, etc. I had a small AM radio that I had to hide in the bottom of my footlocker since it wasn't Government Issue. When you were in training to be a pilot, navigator or bombardier – you were also in training to be an officer and a gentleman. You were an Aviation Cadet. In the Aviation Cadet program, you were subjected to strict discipline, which we referred to as "chickenshit".' – Bob Dickson

Ground gripper: 'non-flying individual' often used somewhat derisively by flying personnel – souvenir programme of the Moss Hart play, *Winged Victory*. From the programme section entitled: 'Take Our Word For It; The Language Of The AAF.' 1944.

Hardstand: a paved or compacted surface used to park an airplane.

Hero/heroism: 'The line between heroism and cowardice is pretty hard to define … Some guys go busting into things without figuring the chances. They lack imagination and can't see the possibility of their being blown to hell. Now, my idea of a hero is the guy who is so scared he ought to be in diapers, yet carries on and completes his mission.' – John Hibbits

Initial point (IP): The location at which formation planes turn to head toward the target.

K-ration: a lightweight, packaged, emergency/combat food ration. 'They were better than nothing.'

Lewie: army slang for an officer with the rank of either a second or first lieutenant.

Mae West: a life vest worn in the event of a plane going down while flying over water.

Mess/Mess hall: a military meal or dining hall.

Mess Management (MM/aka KP – Kitchen Police): duty in the mess hall and kitchen including food preparation – better known and often pictured as peeling potatoes (see Bill Mauldin's book, *Up Front*) and the more odious chore of dish washing and pot scrubbing; can also include serving food and cleaning up the mess left in the mess. 'This was what we were assigned to do when it looked like we might have some spare time: "Police the area." That would mean picking up any trash anywhere.' – Roy Test

Milk run: '... milk run, (is) no more difficult (after a fashion, at least, and in comparison) with the task of delivering the morning's milk is to a dairyman.'

Nissen hut (aka, simply, the hut): metal buildings that look like Campbell's soup cans cut length-wise – cold in winter, hot in summer, with a few windows and sometimes two doors. Bunk beds lined each side and there was a coal/coke-burning stove in the middle that did little to heat the interior. Coal was at a premium (it was tightly controlled in Britain through rationing) and scrounging and theft from base supplies was not uncommon (according to Hutton and Rooney).

NCO: non-commissioned officer (aka, non-com) – someone with the rank of Corporal, Staff Sergeant (Staff Sgt or Staff), Technical Sergeant (aka, Tech Sgt or simply as a Tech), or Master Sergeant, the highest ranking NCO.

Not as briefed: 'The unknown quantity, the uncertain element in every aerial combat episode was summed up afterwards, "not as briefed".' From C. Ross Greening and J.M. Coppinger, *Not As Briefed*, 12.

Operation Crossbow: the code-named operation intended to destroy all German rocket launch storage sites in north-western Europe.

Paddlefoot: ground staff, noncombatant, often used with varying degrees of distaste by combat airmen, although the term was not universally applied to all non-flying personnel, especially the ground crew of one's plane who nursed, patched and sometimes swore at and cajoled a plane into the air.

Perfect mission: 'You hit your target; demolished it, and suffered no losses.' – Leon Schwartz.

Prop-wash: 'Air turbulence that could virtually toss a bomber on its back.' – Leon Schwartz.

Sack: cot/bed – the first place a crewman heads for and the last place he wants to leave.

SNAFU: recognised by servicemen worldwide – 'Situation normal; all fucked up.' Elbridge Colby, in his 1942 book, *Army Talk; A Familiar Dictionary of Soldier Speech*, cites SNAFU as a new army term, with the F-word identified as 'foozled'; a word not likely to be used or even known by more than a handful of servicemen and perhaps a few chaplains. The

Mitzi Mayfair, Carole Landis and Martha Raye sing "Snafu."

"SNAFU! WHAT IS THE MEANING OF SNAFU?"

HERE are the lyrics of "Snafu," the new swing number which was inspired by the experiences of Mitzi Mayfair, Carole Landis and Martha Raye when they were in North Africa early this year.

"Snafu" was first sung by the girls in Issue No. 8 of the Army-Navy Screen Magazine, the Special Service news reel formerly called "The War." The words and music of "Snafu" were written by Charles Henderson.

The Army has a new catchword,
The Navy uses it, too;
It seems the Marines
Understand what it means,
I don't, so I'm asking you.

FIRST CHORUS

Snafu! What is the meaning of Snafu?
What's it all about; can't figure it out.
Is it contagious? Or simply outrageous?
Snafu! You hear it ev'rywhere, Snafu!
Is it like a pill, or is it a thrill?

Is it a military secret?
I asked a louey who at first was rather formal,
And then he laughed and shouted: "Situation normal!"
Snafu! The greatest myst'ry in hist'ry.
Fun is fun, but why can't I find anyone
To spill the beans and tell me what Snafu -
means?

SECOND CHORUS

Snafu! What is the meaning of Snafu?
Is it something new that officers do?
Is it a drop kick or only a top kick?
Snafu! You hear ev'rywhere, Snafu!
Is it cold or hot, inspected or not?
Is it a pot of GI coffee?
I wrote my congressman for further informa-
tion;
He said: "You'll have to start your own in-
vestigation!"
Snafu! The greatest myst'ry in hist'ry.
Fun is fun, but why can't I find anyone
To spill the beans and tell me what Snafu
means?

F-word is cited in the official air force dictionary as 'fouled'. SNAFU remained somewhat of a mystery for civilian folks, however (see adjacent clipping from *Yank*).

Square-head: in general, Germany/Germans; more specifically, a German fighter (soldier, airman, sailor); aka, Jerry, Hun, Kraut and, in the prisoner-of-war camps (*Stalag Lufts* for airforce POWs), goons.

Staff sergeant: a noncommissioned officer (NCO) with the lowest rank of sergeant in the air force.

Stuff: et cetera, and so forth, and just about whatever else the user wants it to mean in the context of the communication: 'Last night we really had a swell dinner. Steaks and stuff.' It is very probable that Fred had something in mind like potatoes, vegetables, desserts, milk, coffee, 'and stuff'.

'Sweating me in' (to sweat out): 'wait expectantly.' – *Take Our Word For It; The Language Of The AAF.*

Swell: if some thing, some person or situation was swell, it was considered to be good, maybe even better than good, but probably not great – it was simply, swell, keen, neat or, in some cases, 'the nuts' (see below).

Tail-end Charlie: planes flying in the last position of a flight group were known as Tail-end Charlies and, in this formation position, suffered from the prop-wash of the planes ahead of it. Planes flying in this position also were prime targets for enemy fighters (there was no other aircraft around to support the end plane) and anti-aircraft guns could easily target these planes because they would be able to track them at the end of the formation. Hence the phrase 'Purple Heart position' became synonymous with Tail-end Charlie. Tail-end Charlie was also sometimes given to the position of a bomber tail gunner because of his position at the rear of the plane.

Target of opportunity: an unexpected, unpredicted target. 'Your original target was unavailable because of weather or fog. If you couldn't see your target you bombed whatever reasonable target you could see – usually railroad yards or something else that was a clear legitimate target – like a freight train or what looked like a factory.' – Leon Schwartz

Tech sergeant: a noncommissioned officer (NCO) with the rank in the air force above staff/staff sergeant and below master sergeant.

The nuts: slang dictionaries refer to 'the nuts' as something that has a positive characteristic to it, but Fred uses the phrase in a decidedly negative manner, giving to either its misuse by him or his understanding of the flexibility of its use.

Time hack (hack): the second hand of a 'hack watch' could be synchronised with the minute hand by pulling out the winding knob thus disengaging the watch works. Crews, especially navigators, used these watches so that all time counts could be co-ordinated and accurate across flight crews.

V-weapons: V-1 (buzz bomb): dubbed 'Vengeance Weapon 1' by Joseph Goebbels, this was a pilotless ram jet rocket with stubby wings, a gyro autopilot and a 1-ton payload. 'You'd hear a put-put-put noise like a washing machine, then nothing until it hit with a whomp.' – Hank Hall. **V-2:** 'The V-2s were liquid propulsion missiles that the Germans launched from the continent against England.' – Bob Dickson.

WAC: Women's Army Corps or a member of the Women's Army Corps.

Zoot suit: military uniform issued at the Classification Center; not to be confused with the uniform-like clothing of long suit jackets with wide lapels and baggy pants worn by hep-cats, men-about-town and especially by young Mexican Americans in Los Angeles (pachucos) in the late 1930s and early 1940s. The manufacturing of civilian zoot suits was banned by the War Production Board in the early part of the Second World War as being wasteful of material.

Bibliography

Alexander, Thomas E. *Rattlesnake Bomber Base; Pyote Army Airfield in World War II*. Abilene, TX: State House Press (McMurry University), 2005.

Alling, Charles. *A Mighty Fortress; Lead Bomber Over Europe*. Havertown, PA: Casement, 2002.

Andrews, Paul M. and William H. Adams. *Heavy Bombers of the Mighty Eighth; An Historical Survey of the B-17s and B-24s Assigned to the Eighth United States Air Force, August 1942 – June 1945*. Eighth Air Force Memorial Museum Foundation, Project Bits and Pieces, 1995.

Anzanos, Andy. *My Combat Diary with Eighth Air Force B-17s; 390th Bomb Group*. Privately printed, http://www.lulu.com/, 2006.

Astor, Gerald. The *Mighty Eighth; The Air War in Europe as Told by the Men Who Fought It*. New York: Donald I. Fine, 1997.

Atkinson, Don. 'The day I arrived …' in *GUNNER; An Illustrated History of World War II Aircraft Turrets and Gun Positions*, by Donald Nijboer. Erin, Ontario, Canada: Boston Mills Press, 2001.

Bernstein, Mark and Alex Lubertozzi. *World War II on the Air; Edward R. Murrow and the Broadcasts that Riveted a Nation*. Naperville, IL: Sourcebooks, 2003.

Bond, Douglas, D. *The Love and Fear of Flying*. New York: International Universities Press, 1952.

Bowman, Martin. *Combat Legend; B-17 Flying Fortress*. Shrewsbury, England: Airlife Publishing, 2002.

Brown, John Mason. *Many A Watchful Night*. New York: Whittlesey House, 1944.

Caidin, Martin. *The B-17; The Flying Forts*. New York: ibooks, 2001.

Carter, Kit C. and Robert Mueller. *The Army Air Forces in World War II; Combat Chronology, 1941–1945*. New York: Arno Press, 1980. First published by Albert F. Simpson Historical Research Center, Air University and Office of Air Force History, Headquarters, USAF, 1973. Notes are to the 1980 edition.

Charles, Ed. 'BERLIN: 6 March 1944' in, *B-17s Over Berlin; Personal Stories From The 95th Bomb Group (H)*. Edited by Ian L. Hawkins. New York: Brassey's, 1990. First published as *Courage★Honor★Victory*, 1987, Winston-Salem, NC: Hunter Publishing.

Colby, Elbridge. *Army Talk; A Familiar Dictionary of Soldier Speech*. Princeton: Princeton University Press, 1942.

Commanding General, Army Air Forces, Second Air Force and Training Aids Division. *Combat Crew*. New York: Army Air Forces, n.d. World War Two pamphlet.

Corwin, Norman. *On A Note of Triumph*. New York: Simon and Schuster, 1945.

Crawford, Robert. *The Army Air Corps; Official Song of the United States Army Air Corps*. New York: Carl Fisher, 1939.

Drissey, George D. Chicago, 'Bombsight Does All But Think, Dec. 13 – (UP)'. Newspaper clipping from Fred Lull memorabilia/scrapbook. In the author's possession. Newspaper name, unknown.

Eaker, Ira C. 'On the mission before last …' in *Medical Support of The Army Air Forces in World War II* by Mae Mills Link and Hubert A. Coleman. Washington DC: Office of the Surgeon General, Department of the Air Force, 1955.

Ehrlich, Blake. *Resistance: France 1940–1945*. Boston: Little, Brown, 1965.

Epstein, Daniel Mark. *Sister Aimee; The Life of Aimee Semple McPherson*. New York: Harcourt Brace Jovanovich, 1993.

Ethell, Jeffrey L. *Bomber Command; American Bombers in Original World War II Color*. St Paul, MN: Motorbooks International, 2003.

Forman, Wallace, R. *B-17 Nose Art Name Directory Aircraft; Includes Group, Squadron and Aircraft Serial Numbers and Photo Availability*. North Branch, MN: Phalanx, 1996.

Frankland, Noble. *Bomber Offensive; The Devastation of Europe*. New York: Ballantine Books, 1970.

Fussell, Paul. *Wartime, Understanding and Behavior in the Second World War*. New York: Oxford University Press, 1989.

Greening, C. (Charles) Ross and J.M. Coppinger. *Not As Briefed*. Privately printed, St Paul, MN, n.d. An artist's portfolio of paintings by the author/artist while a POW in Stalag Luft One, Barth, Germany. ('This book is one of a limited edition.')

Hallion, Richard P. *D-Day 1944; Air Power Over the Normandy Beaches and Beyond*. Washington DC: Air Force History and Museums Program. US Government Printing Office, 1994.

Hammel, Eric. *Air War Europa; America's Air War Against Germany in Europe and North Africa, 1942–1945; Chronology*. Pacifica, CA: Pacifica Press, 1994.

Hart, Moss. *Winged Victory; The Army Air Forces Play*. New York: Random House, 1943.

Heatter, Gabriel. *There's Good News Tonight*. Garden City, NY: Doubleday, 1960.

Heflin, Woodford Agee, ed. *The United States Air Force Dictionary*. Washington DC: Air University Press, 1956.

Heide, Robert and John Gilman. *Home Front America; Popular Culture of the World War II Era*. San Francisco: Chronicle Books, 1995.

Hibbits, John. *Take 'er Up Alone, Mister! As told to F.E. Rechnitzer*. New York: Whittlesey House, 1943.

Historical Division. *Omaha Beachhead; (6 June–13 1944)*. Washington DC: War Department, 1945.

Howarth, David. *The Shetland Bus*. New York: Lyons Press, 2001.

Hutton, Bud and Andy Rooney. *Air Gunner*. New York: Farrar & Rinehart, 1944.

Jablonski, Edward. *Flying Fortress; The Illustrated Biography of the B-17s and the Men Who Flew Them*. Garden City, NY: Doubleday, 1965.

James, Michael. 'The Bombardier'. Magazine clipping from Fred Lull memorabilia/scrapbook. In the author's possession. Magazine name unknown, n.d. Originally printed in the *New York Times* magazine.

Jones, James. *WWII; A Chronicle of Soldiering*. New York: Ballantine Books, 1975.

Lent, Henry B. *Bombardier; Tom Dixon Wins His Wings With The Bomber Command*. New York: Macmillan Company, 1943.

Link, Mae Mills and Hubert A. Coleman. *Medical Support of The Army Air Forces in World War II*. Washington DC: Office of the Surgeon General, Department of the Air Force, 1955.

Magee, John Gillespie. *High Flight*. n.p., 1943.

Mauer, Mauer, ed. *World War II Combat Squadrons of the United States Air Force; The Official Military History of Every Active Squadron*. New York: USAF Historical Division, Air University, Department of the Air Force/Smithmark, 1992.

Mauldin, Bill. *Up Front*. New York: Henry Holt, 1945.

Miller, Donald L. *Masters of the Air; America's Bomber Boys Who Fought the Air War Against Nazi Germany*. New York: Simon and Schuster, 2006.

Morgan, Robert with Ron Powers. The *Man Who Flew the Memphis Belle; Memoir of a WWII Bomber Pilot*. New York: Dutton, 2001.

Morrison, Wilbur H. *Fortress Without A Roof; The Allied Bombing of the Third Reich*. New York: St Martin's Press, 1982.

Morriss, Mack. 'First Stop Back Home for Air Force GIs', *YANK, Down Under, The Army Weekly*, 21 April 1944, 6–7.

Myers, Debs. 'Christmas Time at Home', *YANK, Far East, The Army Weekly*, 22 December 1944, 6–7.

Neillands, Robin. *The Bomber War; The Allied Air Offensive Against Nazi Germany*. Woodstock, NY: Overlook Press, 2001.

Nichol, John and Tony Rennell. *Tail-End Charlies; The Last Battles of the Bomber War, 1944–45*. New York: Thomas Dunne, 2006.

Nijboer, Donald. *GUNNER; An Illustrated History of World War II Aircraft Turrets and Gun Positions*. Erin, Ontario, Canada, 2001.

Office of Assistant Chief of Air Staff, Intelligence. *Sunday Punch in Normandy; The Tactical Use of Heavy Bombardment in the Normandy Invasion. An Interim Report*. Washington DC: Headquarters, Army Air Forces. New Imprint by the Center for Air Force History in the *Wings at War Series, No. 2*. Washington DC: Center for Air Force History, 1992. Page references are to the 1992 edition.

Oliphant, H.N. 'Prep School for Bomber Crews', *YANK, The Army Weekly*, 9 July 1943, 8–9.

Panter-Downes, Mollie. 'Letter From London; July 26 (By cable)', *The New Yorker*, 31 July 1943, 34.

Pilot Training Manual for the Flying Fortress, B-17. [Washington DC ?]: Headquarters, AAF, Office of Assistant Chief of Air Staff, Training, Office of Flying Safety, n.d.

Pyle, Ernie. *Ernie Pyle in Normandy (By wireless)*. Newspaper clipping from Fred Lull memorabilia/scrapbook. In the author's possession. Newspaper name unknown, n.d., ca. 6 June 1944.

———. *Brave Men*. New York: Henry Holt, 1944.

———. *Here is Your War*. Chicago: Consolidated, 1944.

———. *Ernie Pyle in England*. New York: Robert M. McBride & Company, 1945.

Rehm, Robert. 'Fifty Missions Over Europe; Psychological Study of An Average Combat Tour' in *Observations of Combat Flying Personnel*, edited by David G. Wright. New York: M.C. Josiah Macy Jr. Foundation, 1945. ('Prepared and Distributed for The Air Surgeon, Army Air Forces by the Josiah Macy, Jr. Foundation, New York 21, N.Y.')

Roosevelt, Franklin Delano. *Fireside Chat, December 24, 1943*. Franklin Delano Roosevelt Presidential Library, Digital Archives.

Schwartz, Leon. 'The 205 Days and 35 Missions of one of the 100th Bomb Group's "Luckye Bastardes"', http://www.100thbg.com/mainpages/history/history5/schwartz/schwartz_main.htm.

Second A.F. Altitude Indoctrination Unit. *Survival at Altitude for Heavy and Very Heavy Bomber Crews*. L.A.A.F. Lincoln, NE: Reproduction Dept., 1/25/45.

Seeley, Norvel R. 'A Front Row Seat'. *Flying Fortress Newsletter*, March 2007: 5–7.

Siefring, Thomas A. *U.S. Air Force in World War II*. London: Bison Books, 1982.

Slater, Harry E. *Lingering Contrails of The Big Square A; A History of the 94th Bomb Group (H), 1942–1945*. Privately printed, 1980

Smith Daniel F. *Personal War Time Diary, August 14, 1944 – November 17, 1945*.

Smith, Kathleen E.R. *God Bless America; Tin Pan Alley Goes to War*. Lexington, KY: University Press of Kentucky, 2003.

Somers, William F. *Fortress Fighters; An Autobiography of a B-17 Aerial Gunner*. Privately printed, 2000.

Speer, Albert. *Inside the Third Reich; Memoirs by Albert Speer*. Translated by Richard and Clara Winston. New York: Macmillan, 1970.

Steinbeck, John. *Once There Was A War.* New York: Penguin Books, 1994. First published 1958 by Viking Press.

———. *Bombs Away; The Story of a Bomber Team.* New York: Paragon House 1990. First published 1942 by Viking Press.

US Centennial of Flight. *Bombardier's Oath.* http://www.centennialofflight.gov/essay/Dictionary/NORDEN_BOMBSIGHT/DI145.htm.

Valant, Gary M. *Vintage Aircraft Nose Art.* St Paul, MN: MBI Publishing, 2001.

War Department. *Instructions for American Servicemen in Britain, 1942.* Cambridge, England: Bodleian Library, University of Oxford, 2004. First published 1942 by the War Department, Washington DC. Citations are to the Bodleian Library edition.

War Department. *Bombardier's Information File (BIF), AAF Form 24B.* [Washington DC?]: War Department, (Approved) 11/23/44. Notes are from reprinted edition.

Wilson, Gill Robb. Newspaper clipping from Fred Lull memorabilia/scrapbook; in the author's possession. Newspaper name, unknown, n.d.

Woodward, David. The *Tirpitz and the Battle for the North Atlantic.* New York: W.W. Norton, 1954.

Yank, Down Under, The Army Weekly, 'SNAFU! What Is The Meaning of SNAFU?' 5 November 1943, 21.

———. 'Pre-Invasion Bombs', 12 May 1944, 4.

Zumwalt, Ken. *The Stars and Stripes; World War II & The Early Years.* Austin, TX: Eakin Press, 1989.

Special Note: Every effort has been made to give credit in the text for quoting copyrighted materials. In some cases publishing firms that hold copyrights to books no longer exist or individual copyright holders are dead and copyright location is lost or untraceable. No slight of authorship is intended in reproducing works cited in this book.

Acknowledgements

If ever:

- an author had a muse, I had mine for *Belle of the Brawl*. M.J. (Jack) Sacia was my constant convivial congenial nudge, supporter, encourager, and gung-ho specialist.
- an author relied on others to bring to light details of a story, I had mine in Kerry Castel de Oro, who gave Fred's letters, scrapbooks and photo albums to me; Ann Kaiser, Mary Braun and Cliff Leviton who were Fred's friends, knew him as an educator and were with him at the end when he needed someone. And, without the introductions provided by George Marrett, the group below would have been largely unknown to me.
- there was a group of who gave of their knowledge and memories willingly, freely and with robust encouragement, it was the guys who allowed me to interview them for personal, technical and historical background for this book and answer my many questions – former B-17 crewmen, heroes all. They are listed alphabetically by name, position, name of the plane in which they flew and their unit designation: Gene Bissell, B-17 Navigator, *Idiot's Delight* and others, Fifteenth Air Force, 97th Bomb Group, 341st Bombardment Squadron (also served as Squadron Lead Navigator, Group Lead Navigator); Bob Brown, B-17 Pilot, *Thunder Mug* and others; Richard Bushong, B-17 Pilot, *Geronimo* and others, Eighth Air Force, 390th Bomb Group, 569th Bomb Squadron; Bob Dickson, B-17 Pilot, *Wheel N' Deal*, Eighth Air Force, 91st Bomb Group, 322nd Bomb Squadron, POW; Hank Hall, B-17 Left Waist Gunner, *Ack Ack Annie*, Eighth Air Force, 91st Bomb Group, 322nd Bomb Squadron; Frank Halm, B-17 Pilot, *Gremlin's Hotel*, Eighth Air Force, 94th Bomb Group, 331st Bomb Squadron and 333rd Bomb Squadron as lead/deputy lead pilot; Albert (Al) Olivari, Togglier/Gunner, *Round Trip Ticket*, Eighth Air Force, 94th Bomb Group, 331st Bomb Squadron; James S. Peters, Sr., Flight Engineer/Top Turret Gunner, *Fuddyhuckle*, Fifteenth Air Force, 99th Bomb Group, 348th Bomb Squadron; Wilbur Richardson, B-17 Ball Turret Gunner, *Kismet*, Eighth Air Force, 94th Bomb Group, 331st Bomb Squadron; Harold Schuchardt, B-17 Pilot (he flew B-17s that did not have a name and rarely flew the same plane twice), Fifteenth Air Force, 97th Bomb Group, 342nd Bomb Squadron, POW; Leon Schwartz, B-17 Navigator, *Fever Beaver*, Eighth Air Force, 100th Bomb Group (The Bloody Hundredth), 351st Bomb Squadron; Roy Test, B-17 Co-pilot, *Bad Penny* (it always turns up), Eighth Air Force, 398th Bomb Group, 602nd Bomb Squadron; Lou Vaughn, B-17 Pilot, *SNAFU Man*, Fifteenth Air Force, 2nd Bombardment Group, 20th Bombardment Squadron. From this group a special thanks to Gene Bissell, Bob Brown, Bob Dickson, Hank Hall, Frank Halm, Harold Schuchardt and Roy Test who read the manuscript for historical and technical accuracy and who made valuable suggestions based on their personal experiences in a war fought so long ago.

- there were those who call it their job to help others, but yet do it in such a way as to make you feel special and that your mission is one of the most important in the world, I had mine at the 390th Memorial Museum, Pima Air and Space Museum, Tucson, Arizona in Carolyn Beaubien, Director of Research and Fred Sachs, Volunteer Researcher, and at the Glendora, California, Public Library reference desk, especially Gaetano Abbondanza who tracked down obscure reference works.
- anyone was lucky enough to have friends who shared private collections of historical materials or their expertise, I have been one of the most lucky to have Robyne Gray who shared her extensive collection of *Yank* magazines; Ed McAleer who shared his collection of *Life* magazines from the war years; Helen Hehr who provided the original *Playbill* for *Winged Victory*; C. Lamar Mayer whose genealogical research expertise brought me to my knees in appreciation; and Linda Trevillian, dubbed my 'Wicked Witch', for her editing skills.
- there was an acquisition editor who kept the faith and the flame glowing longer than anyone ever thought possible, I had mine in Jay Slater and his colleague and content editor Chrissy McMorris at The History Press.
- there were friends and family who endured endless and generally one-way conversations about a topic of only polite interest to them, they would have to be mine – there are too many to list by name but you can easily recognise them by their bent ears.
- and, finally, there was a spouse who endured countless hours alone in a shared home while her partner was moored to a computer keyboard, secluded in his study or was away for days on end conducting interviews and visiting museums and libraries, there is none who has been more supportive or lovingly tolerant than mine – Shirley.

Picture credits: Photographs not credited in the text were taken by Fred or his crewmates or friends and came from his wartime photograph albums. The photographs have not been enhanced or altered except for size to fit page space and are reproduced as they were discovered – worn and faded with time, grainy, perhaps distorted, some with poor focus because they were shot through plane windows during missions, and some victims of the quality of film available during the war. The photograph 'It was supposed to be a rough mission. We went to Germany', provided by Wilbur Richardson, also appears, without attribution, in Harry Slater's history of the 94th Bomb Group, *Lingering Contrails of The Big Square A; A History of The 94th Bomb Group (H), 1942–1945*. The photograph of bomber and fighter contrails, 'Air Portrait', is from *Yank, Down Under, The Army Weekly*, 17 March 1944. The cartoon at the beginning of Chapter 7, provided by Frank Halm, is unsigned but is thought to be the work of Bob Stevens, sometimes described as the air force's Bill Mauldin.

Special thanks are extended to friend and photographer Gary Hammerstrom who established a studio environment in his home to take some of the photographs of war memorabilia.

Copyright Acknowledgements

Grateful acknowledgement is made to the following authors, publishers, agencies, estates, and corporations for use of material cited in *Belle of the Brawl; Letters Home From a B-17 Bombardier:*

Paul Andrews, author of Project Bits and Pieces, *Heavy Bombers of the Mighty Eighth; An Historical Survey of the B-17s and B-24s Assigned to the Eighth Air Force, August 1942–June 1945*. Reprinted with Permission.
Andy Anzanos, author of *My Combat Diary with Eighth Air Force B-17s, 390th Bomb Group*.
The Parker Pen Heritage Collection for permission to reprint the Parker Pen advertisement.
Penguin Group (USA) Inc. for material from: *THE MIGHTY EIGHTH* by Gerald Astor, © 1997 by Gerald Astor. Used by permission of Donald I. Fine, an imprint of Penguin Group (USA) Inc.
The Estate of John Mason Brown for: *Many a Watchful Night*, by John Mason Brown, published by Whittlesey House, 1944. Reprinted with Permission.

Norman Corwin author of *On A Note of Triumph*. Reprinted with Permission.

Oxford University Press for permission to cite from: *Wartime: Understanding and Behavior in the Second Word War* by Paul Fussell. Reprinted by permission of Oxford University Press.

Books International for permission to cite from: *B-17s Over Berlin; Personal Stories From the 95th Bomb Group (H)*, edited by Ian L. Hawkins.

Chronicle Books for material from: *HOME FRONT AMERICA: POPULAR CULTURE OF THE WORLD WAR II ERA* © 1995 by Robert Heide and John Gilman. Used with permission from Chronicle Books LLC, San Francisco.

Globe Piquot Press, reprinted with acknowledgement material cited in *The Shetland Bus* by David Howarth.

Los Angeles Times editorial staff for: 'Women in Pants?! Mayor Draws line', published 23 April 1942; *Los Angeles Times* © 1942. Reprinted with Permission.

Donald Miller for permission to cite lines from: *Masters of the Air*.

Overlook Press for permission to cite lines from: *The Bomber War: The Allied Air Offensive Against Nazi Germany* by Robin Neillands. Copyright 2001 by Robin Neillands, published by the Overlook Press, 2001. All rights reserved.

The Scripps Howard Foundation, especially Patty Cottingham, Vice President for Administration, for permission to cite the works of Ernie Pyle whose work was originally published in various Scripps-Howard newspapers.

Sergeant's Pet Care Products for the use of an advertisement from 1944 for Polk Miller Products Corp., makers of Sergeant's dog medicines. Used with permission.

Norma Slater, wife of the late Harry Slater, for permission to cite lines from: *Lingering Contrails of The Big Square A; A History of the 94th Bomb Group (H), 1942–1945*.

Kathleen E.R. Smith, PhD for permission to cite lines from: *God Bless America: Tin Pan Alley Goes to War*.

Marilyn Somers, wife of the late William F. Somers, for permission to cite lines from: *Fortress Fighters; An Autobiography of a B-17 Aerial Gunner*.

State House Press for permission to cite material from: *Rattlesnake Base; Pyote Army Airfield in WWII* by Thomas E. Alexander.

Studebaker National Museum for the use of an advertisement extolling the qualities of the B-17 engines made by Studebaker Corporation. Used with permission.

Permission has been granted to reprint the following song lyrics:

'I Left My Heart At The Stage Door Canteen' by Irving Berlin
© Copyright 1942 by Irving Berlin
© Copyright Renewed by Irving Berlin
© Copyright Assigned to Winthrop Rutherfurd, Jr., Anne Phipps Sidamon-Eristoff and Theodore R. Jackson as Trustees of the God Bless America Fund
International Copyright Secured. All Rights Reserved. Reprinted by Permission.

'This Is The Army, Mister Jones' by Irving Berlin
© Copyright 1942 by Irving Berlin
© Copyright Renewed
© Copyright Assigned to the Trustees of the God Bless America Fund
International Copyright Secured. All Rights Reserved. Reprinted by Permission.

'White Christmas' by Irving Berlin
© Copyright 1940, 1942 by Irving Berlin
© Copyright Renewed
International Copyright Secured. All Rights Reserved. Reprinted by Permission.

Index

Other titles published by The History Press

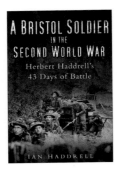

A Bristol Soldier in the Second World War: Herbert Haddrell's 43 Days of Battle

IAN HADDRELL

£14.99

Using primary-source and archive material, this book reveals the tale of a 19-year-old caught up in the midst of one of history's darkest moments. This serves as a poignant reminder of the terrible ordeal that so many brave young men had to face in order to defend king and country, homes and families.

978-0-7524-5169-5

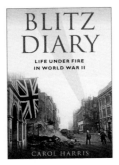

Blitz Diary: Life Under Fire in World War II

CAROL HARRIS

£9.99

In *Blitz Diary* historian Carol Harris has collected together a remarkable series of accounts from the war's darkest days, with heart-warming stories of survival, perseverance, solidarity and bravery, the preservation of which becomes increasingly important as the Blitz fades from living memory.

978-0-7524-5172-5

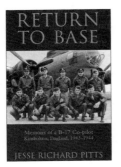

Return to Base: Memoirs of a B-17 Co-pilot, Kimbolton, England, 1943–1944

JESSE RICHARD PITTS

£12.99

Jesse Richard Pitts was a pilot for the B-17 Flying Fortress in the Second World War. In this evocative memoir, Jesse relates his bombing history and personal experiences as a B-17 co-pilot and member of 379th bomb group of the Eighth Air Force.

978-0-7524-4025-5

A Bloody Picnic: Tommy's Humour, 1914–18

ALAN WEEKS

£9.99

A crucial factor that kept Tommy going on the Western Front was his ability to see what was comic in the horror of trench warfare. Providing the same level of amusement now as it did then, *A Bloody Picnic* presents an unusual perspective on how soldiers coped with the grim realities of the First World War.

978-0-7524-5668-3

Visit our website and discover thousands of other History Press books.

www.thehistorypress.co.uk